THE **PRACTICAL PREPPER**

A **COMMON-SENSE GUIDE** TO
PREPARING FOR EMERGENCIES

THE PRACTICAL PREPPER

A **COMMON-SENSE GUIDE** TO PREPARING FOR EMERGENCIES

KYLENE AND JONATHAN JONES

PLAIN SIGHT PUBLISHING
AN IMPRINT OF CEDAR FORT, INC.
SPRINGVILLE, UTAH

The opinions and views expressed herein belong solely to the author and do not necessarily represent the opinions or views of Cedar Fort, Inc. Permission for the use of statistics, sources, graphics, and photos is also solely the responsibility of the author.

ISBN 13: 978-1-4621-1382-8

Published by Plain Sight Publishing, an imprint of Cedar Fort, Inc.
2373 W. 700 S., Springville, UT 84663
Distributed by Cedar Fort, Inc., www.cedarfort.com

LIBRARY OF CONGRESS CATALOGING-IN-PUBLICATION DATA

Jones, Kylene, 1964- author.
  The Practical prepper / Kylene and Jonathan Jones.
     pages cm
  Summary: Written for urban dwellers interested in emergency preparedness.
  ISBN 978-1-4621-1382-8 (alk. paper)
  1. Emergency management--Handbooks, manuals, etc. 2. Survival--Handbooks, manuals, etc.
I. Jones, Jonathan (Jonathan B.), author. II. Title.

  HV551.2.J6625 2014
  613.6'9--dc23

                                    2014012072

Cover design by Angela D. Baxter
Cover design © 2014 by Lyle Mortimer

Printed in Canada

10 9 8 7 6 5 4 3 2 1

We express our sincere gratitude to our family and friends for sharing their talents and supporting us.

Contents

1

Where Do I Begin?

"The journey of a thousand miles begins with a single step."

—Laozi

The very thought of preparing for a possible, undefined future event may seem overwhelming. You may be tempted to simply take your chances and see what happens. But frankly, the odds are not in your favor. Many Americans have already experienced some type of disaster or public emergency. We invite you to join us and become part of the solution: people who take responsibility for themselves and their families. You will enjoy the security and peace that come from knowing you are ready for whatever life may throw your way.

Our journey began as we watched the news and understood the depth of our responsibility to protect our family and community in an increasingly dangerous time. We researched, experimented, and learned great lessons on our road to self-reliance. We learned to value provident living, which allows us to enjoy today while preparing for the future. Teaching has allowed us to gather mountains of input and knowledge, brilliant ideas that work well, and some crazy things we should never attempt. As we look around, we are amazed at the apathy held by those who choose not to prepare. We have tried to understand what thought process would lead them to such a reckless path. We discovered that most people fit into one or more of the following categories:

Oblivious: These people do not believe that anything bad will ever really happen. They are like an ostrich who sticks its head in the sand. If they cannot see it, it obviously does not really exist. The danger to these people is especially great because while their heads are in the sand, they leave their vital parts completely unprotected.

Target Painters: We reserve this name for people who believe that something probably will happen, but they don't want to think about it. They want to paint a target right on their head or their home so the first bomb will drop there and everything will be over quickly. Unfortunately, chances are this is not going to happen. These unprepared souls will be part of the problem, having not developed skills, built up vital stores, or prepared mentally for challenging times.

Rat Racers: Sometimes even we fit into this category. These people understand the need to prepare and have put it on their list, along with a hundred other items demanding attention. They are often so busy with the daily life of work, family, and community that preparing never makes it high enough on the priority list. Though well-intentioned, not much gets done.

Excuse Slayers: These are our favorite students! They actually understand that bad things will happen and are doing their best with the resources they have. They need a little help, education, and motivation. Everyone has a mountain of excuses for not preparing. Remember, excuses are like armpits: everyone has them and they all stink! Excuses prevent the job from getting done. Carefully evaluate the excuses you use. We challenge you to slay them.

Ann Landers summed it up nicely when she said, "If I were asked to give what I consider the most useful bit of advice for all humanity, it would be this: Expect trouble as an inevitable part of life and when it comes, hold your head high, look it squarely in the eye and say, 'I will be bigger than you. You cannot defeat me'" (Landers 2012).

Excuse Slayers refuse to let the lack of time, knowledge, space, or resources defeat them. They make the time to learn, develop critical skills, acquire necessary supplies, and make steady progress toward their goals.

Which category do you fit in? Seeing as you are reading this book, we would venture to guess that you are either a Rat Racer or an Excuse Slayer. You have taken a healthy step by deciding to read *The Practical Prepper*. Stick with it! Join our group of normal, everyday folks who are living our lives the best we can. Practical peppers recognize the dangers that lie ahead. We are not fixated on the dangers that lurk in the future.

We recognize them, take necessary steps to mitigate (reduce, lessen, or decrease) the risk, and then we enjoy the journey, living life to the fullest. The sun will rise in the morning, and we can greet it with confidence and peace. We are ready for whatever life may throw our way.

As you explore the plethora of emergency preparedness information available, you will discover a lot of conflicting information. Some of this is due to personal preference or which product someone is trying to sell. Other information has been poorly researched or never tested in real life. We have spent hundreds of hours researching and many more experimenting at home with our own family. We can tell you what works for us and what the research states. Every home and family situation is unique and will require personal experimentation to discover which options will work best for their situation. We urge you to live the grand adventure as you put the methods to the test and establish a level of comfort before you are in an emergency or disaster.

You are responsible to provide for yourself and your family. Entitlement has invaded our culture, producing an attitude of dependence on others to take care of our needs. This is a dangerous trend, and we encourage you to act with honor and integrity, doing everything in your power to care for your own family and to be a good neighbor. Do the best with what you have, wherever you are. Be part of the solution, not part of the problem.

Prepping is like cooking. A hundred different methods and a thousand various ingredients can result in a delightful meal. Each cook has his or her preferred way of doing things, and sharing a kitchen can be challenging for the accomplished chef. As you prepare for emergencies, you will likely have different ideas and preferences than we do. Diversity is what makes life rich with unique ideas and creative ways to accomplish the same objective.

We have discovered that there is no one right way to accomplish anything. We often have different viewpoints on ways to accomplish various areas of prepping. Much of it relates to our individual frame of reference on life. Jonathan views it through the lenses of an engineer, where everything must be done with absolute perfection or some dam somewhere is bound to burst. Kylene's perspective comes from a life of juggling professional responsibilities while managing a herd of children and a household. According to her, "Good enough is perfect."

We coexist together quite nicely through quality communication and compromise. For instance, Jonathan is highly picky about his water. His profession has educated him on the nasty stuff in tap water. He prefers to drink distilled water. His plan for purifying water is to chlorinate the water and then run it through the filter to remove the residual chlorine. That is, if there is not enough fuel to distill the water. Kylene drinks water from the tap and does not find the slight chlorine taste quite as offensive. Jonathan's water is "perfect," and Kylene's water is "good enough."

You will find your own preferences when it comes to preparing for the challenges that the future might present. Remember there is no one right way. However, there is a wrong way. The wrong way includes not preparing or not making safety a high priority.

Current world events are prompting many individuals to prepare now. While prepping is important, we recommend that you always strive to keep balance in your life. Do not allow fear to motivate your actions. Preparing and making steady progress is critically important, but take time to enjoy the present while preparing for the future.

We begin this journey by exploring some of the possible hazards you may face. We define them and the risks they pose in the next chapter, then make a few recommendations to mitigate their effect. At the end of each chapter we encourage you to create a plan of action. Take time to jot down your ideas immediately. The most difficult task is developing an action plan. The rest is simply checking off each item as it is completed. It is your job to put your plan in place and make steady progress to accomplish your goals.

We invite you to join us on our journey. Work and prepare to face the challenges and emerge stronger for the opportunity to conquer adversity.

2

What Are the Odds?

"These are the times that try men's souls."

—Thomas Paine

Urban emergency preparedness and survival comes with some unique challenges because of the makeup of the urban population. Living in densely populated areas with shared resources such as water, natural gas, and power elevates many risk factors. The highest survival rates tend to be in rural areas. So why not just move to the country? It may not be an option for many people due to employment, schooling, opportunity, or love of the urban lifestyle. Regardless of where you live, steps can be taken to reduce your risk. It is okay to live in a high-risk area if you take proper precautions. It requires understanding the possible risks, designing an appropriate plan, implementing that plan, and steadily taking steps to mitigate the possible damages. It requires risk management.

Risk management is increasing and conserving resources against a time of great need. The hazards and situations discussed in this chapter can clearly create a time of great need. If you have prepared well, your efforts can significantly change the outcome of the incident. Survival demands only basic necessities: shelter, clothing, food, water, and fuel. You will notice many risks require the same steps to prepare. They all tend to involve similar resources, such as a family communication plan, food, water, supplies, skills, and education. You will be amazed how many scenarios you have covered once you have the basics down.

Overall, create a culture of prevention, not reaction. The term "natural disaster" can be a little misleading. We may refer to natural disasters, but in reality there are only natural hazards. For instance, we cannot prevent a tornado from tearing through our town (hazard), but we can prevent it from becoming a disaster by preparing before it happens. We can lessen the impact through risk management and making our families more resilient. We can save lives and money. You decide if you are going to be vulnerable or resilient to the hazards life presents. Preparation has big payoffs.

Some risk factors are specific to densely populated cities. Gang violence is more likely and crime rates are high. Terrorists blend in more easily. International airports are incubators for the spread of communicable diseases and are always located near large metropolitan areas. Most people in cities are removed from their food supplies. Close neighborhood and community relationships are less common as people live busy, isolated lives. Natural hazards easily become disasters when utilities and transportation are interrupted.

There are some hazards where you may have a reasonable amount of control and others that are completely out of your control. Spend your energy and resources where you can make a difference and let go of the things out of your control. We are going to teach you basic risk management skills, which will help you realistically identify the risks your family may face and clearly understand what steps you can take to mitigate those risks.

RISK EVALUATION

The best way to start is by evaluating individual risks. Each person's level of risk for any event depends on a variety of factors including location, community network, resources, knowledge, physical abilities, and more. Risk is traditionally calculated through a basic equation: risk = probability × consequence. We assign numbers to each category and might expect the calculations to be exact because of the perfect nature of math. That is not so with calculating risk in this setting. It is difficult to determine the actual probability of an event. We make an educated guess and assign it a number. The same is true with the consequence—we make an educated guess. Because the numbers going into the equation are subjective, it is impossible for the product to be completely accurate. However, it is a good guess and gives us a place to begin.

Review the following table using the traditional formula for risk evaluation. The larger the number the greater the risk or consequence. Do you see how subjective the numbers assigned can be? Even probabilities assigned from experts will differ. Still, it is a useful tool to decide where to focus your energy.

Formula: Risk = Probability × Consequence

Risk	Probability: Likelihood that event will impact me	Consequence: Significance of possible consequences
This describes the hazard, event, or area of concern, as well as the answer to the equation	1 = No chance/ Impossible 2 = Somewhat likely 3 = Conditions are such that it may occur 4 = Highly likely 5 = Certain event— it will happen, it is just a matter of when	1 = No consequences or inconvenience 2 = Limited damage to property, inconvenience, financial impact, and/or risk of physical injury 3 = Moderate damage to property, inconvenience, financial impact, physical injury, but no loss of life 4 = Significant damage to property and infrastructure, long-term inconvenience, financial impact, personal injury, and/or loss of life 5 = Catastrophic injury; loss of life; destruction of property; tragic economic effects; loss of security, freedom, and/or normal lifestyle

We have completed this table to illustrate possible number assignments based on location and perception of possible consequences. This is not an exact science, so our numbers may be different from the numbers you might assign each category. However, it will still provide a good starting place.

Risk=Probability × Consequence

Risk	Probability: Likelihood that event will impact me	Consequence: Significance of possible consequences
Earthquake Risk = 6	2 = Live in Miami, Florida, with a probability of 28% of a 5.0 earthquake in the next 50 years	3 = Moderate damage to property, inconvenience, financial impact, physical injury, and/or little or no loss of life
Risk = 9	3 = Live in Omaha, Nebraska, with 61% of a 5.0 earthquake in the next 50 years	3 = Moderate damage to property, inconvenience, financial impact, physical injury, and/or little or no loss of life
Risk = 16	4 = Live in San Francisco, California, with a 65% probability of a 5.0 earthquake in the next 50 years or 60% chance of 6.7 in the next 30	4 = Significant damage to property and infrastructure, long-term inconvenience, financial impact, personal injury, and/or loss of life

Risk	Probability: Likelihood that event will impact me	Consequence: Significance of possible consequences
Hurricane Risk = 20	5 = Live in Miami, Florida, with 27% probability in any given year	4 = Personal safety at high risk as well as property
Risk = 2	1 = Live in Omaha, Nebraska, which is too far inland to be affected by hurricane winds	2 = Damage likely to be limited with no personal injury
Risk = 6	2 = Live in San Francisco, California; may experience high tides, storm surge, and intense rain	3 = Possible moderate damage to property, infrastructure, along with economic losses
Tornado Risk = 6	2 = Live in Miami, Florida; largest tornado was an F3 in 1959	3 = Damage likely to be moderate if history repeats itself
Risk = 20	5 = Live in Omaha, Nebraska, with a history of F4 tornado in 1975 and regular watches and warnings	4 = Damage may be high; potential loss of life
Risk = 6	2 = Live in San Francisco, California, where strongest recorded tornado was an F2 in 1958	3 = Moderate damage would be expected

(Statistics gathered from homefacts.com)

Personalize your risk factor for each of the following possible hazards or events. Complete the risk evaluation table at the end of the chapter to help prioritize your efforts. We will help you understand each major hazard, your probability, and ways to lessen the consequences.

A few sites you may want to explore to assist you in scoring your unique risks include:

- Hazards and Vulnerability Research Institute at www.webra.cas .sc.edu/hvri/.

- The Pollution Information Site (www.scorecard.goodguide.com/) will give you a report on toxins, air, and water concerns according to your zip code.

- For current weather and safety information, go to weather.gov or weather.com.

- Probabilities for crime, earthquakes, environmental hazards, tornadoes, and other statistics can be found at homefacts.com. All of the statistics in the above table were gathered from this site.

RISK ASSESSMENT AND MITIGATION

The following items build a foundation for preparing for most of the risks you may face. We will discuss these basics in detail throughout the book. Once you have these items in place, it is easy to prepare for specific threats in your risk assessment.

- Family emergency plan, including communication devices

- Food storage. Three-month supply of everyday foods as well as longer-term basic food storage

- Water storage and purification methods

- Survival kits for each person, in each vehicle and at work or school

- Backup methods to deal with interruptions in public utilities (water, sewer, natural gas, and power)

- Emergency savings account

These are the foundation for battling almost all of the hazards we discuss below. Additional ways to prepare for each specific risk are listed below each hazard. Review each individual risk and calculate your personal risk score in the table provided. You may not need to spend any energy on some of these events while others will require intense preparation.

NATURAL DISASTERS

Drought

Droughts are a period of abnormally low precipitation resulting in a water shortage. It is a common occurrence with at least one region in North America experiencing drought conditions in any given year. Most areas experience some level of drought eventually. Drought conditions are usually accompanied by increased temperatures, elevated fire hazard, insect infestation, plant disease, crop failure, decreased livestock production, and damage to wildlife. The economy is affected by higher food prices, loss of tourism, and increased unemployment rates.

The effects of drought can be reduced by implementing water conservation strategies in everyday life. Consider some of these strategies to reduce the impact a drought could have on your family:

- Learn about droughts. A good source for drought information is www.drought.gov/drought. This site contains regional assessments, maps, and indexes that are helpful in monitoring water shortages.

- Practice water conservation every day. Purchase water-efficient appliances and install low-flow plumbing fixtures in the kitchen and bathrooms. Make it a practice not to waste water.

- Landscape with native or drought-tolerant plants. Use a drip system to water when possible. Mulch around shrubs and garden plants to reduce evaporation and weeds.

- Consider low-water gardening techniques. Check out the film *Back to Eden*, which you can find online for no charge at www.backtoedenfilm.com, to learn how one man successfully gardened with limited water.

Earthquake

An earthquake is an abrupt, powerful shaking of the ground caused by a sudden slip on a fault. We know where earthquakes are likely to occur and the damage they can cause by shaking. Three factors play into the intensity of shaking that a home or structure is likely to experience: the magnitude of the earthquake, the kind of ground the home is built on, and the distance from the epicenter. Earthquake shaking can cause certain soils to behave like liquids and lose their ability to support structures. Soils in low-lying areas with saturated, loose, sandy soils and poorly compacted artificial fill have the highest potential for liquefaction.

Earthquakes can damage vital infrastructure such as roads, bridges, water pipelines, sewer pipelines, and natural gas and electrical distribution systems. Fires often follow earthquakes in urban areas due to gas line breaks and electrical malfunctions. Hazardous materials may be released from refineries, chemical storage and distribution systems, manufacturing plants, railroad cars, and trucks. Dams may fail and cause flooding. Earthquakes can trigger landslides and rock falls.

There is a high probability that emergency services will not be available for a period of time after an earthquake. The 911 emergency system will be overloaded. Firefighters may have limited access due to road damage and little water because of ruptured water lines. Hospitals and medical facilities may be damaged. Emergency rooms, trauma centers, and expedient care facilities may be overwhelmed. After an earthquake, construction equipment, materials, and personnel will be in limited supply. Costs will likely increase. Restoration will take time.

The following are some items you may want to consider to lessen the consequences of an earthquake on your family:

- Go to quakes.globalincidentmap.com to get up-to-date information on earthquake magnitude, depth, and location.

- Visit US Geological Survey (USGS) at www.earthquake.usgs. gov/hazards/qfaults/sitemap.php and click on your state to locate known fault lines in your area.

- Consider purchasing earthquake insurance.

- Identify potential hazards in your home and fix them.

- Keep a gas shutoff wrench near the main gas line in the event you need to turn off your gas.

Extreme Winter Storm

Surviving extreme winter storms is a way of life for many people who live in cold climates. They have successfully managed without electricity for lengthy periods of time and understand how to survive in deathly cold. Extremely cold weather can occur even in areas that enjoy mild winters as climate change occurs. Advanced preparation and knowledge can significantly reduce the chance of serious illness and death from exposure to extreme cold.

Be prepared to hunker down and stay off the roads. Travel is dangerous and not worth risking unless it is an absolute emergency. Consider taking the following steps as a starting point to mitigate the risk of extreme winter storms:

- Plan for alternative ways to heat your home. See chapter 14 to learn more about surviving freezing temperatures without public utilities.

- Purchase a NOAA Weather Radio All Hazards (NWR), which will keep you informed of hazardous conditions in your area. Watch or listen to local weather reports to keep an eye on upcoming storms. A good resource is weather.gov, which will provide information on hazardous weather conditions in your area.

- Prepare your home and make it as energy efficient as possible. Contact your local utility company to request an energy audit. Many have programs that will provide the service free of charge. Visit Database of State Incentives for Renewables & Efficiency (DSIRE) at dsireusa.org to see what incentives and rebates are available in your area for increasing insulation and making your home more energy efficient.

- Stock high-calorie, shelf-stable, easy-to-prepare canned foods and beverages such as soup, chili, stew, beans, ramen, bouillon, tea, and cocoa.

Flooding

Floods are a common, highly destructive hazard. Flooding can go beyond damaged and lost personal property. It can contaminate water supplies and spread waterborne diseases, overwhelm drainage and sewer systems, disrupt power supplies, destroy crops, and close roads. Repairs to infrastructure such as roads, bridges, and public utilities can take a significant time to complete. Local economy may be devastated.

Consider the following to mitigate your risk for flooding:

- Evaluate the risk to your home. Go to msc.fema.gov to find a flood-plain map of your area. Where is your home in relation to surrounding terrain? Are there dams or dykes in your area? Do you live on a hillside where flooding may cause mudslides?

- Study the way water drains around your home. Can you alter the grade to encourage water to flow away from your home?

- If you have a basement, install a sump pump with a battery-operated backup.

- Purchase flood insurance, as necessary. Carefully investigate exactly what the policy covers and make sure it covers your risk adequately.

Heat Wave

The Centers for Disease Control and Prevention (CDC) warns that "climate experts are particularly confident that climate change will bring increasingly frequent and severe heat waves."[1] We are seeing hotter and longer summers, which puts a strain on utilities and causes widespread blackouts. The young, poor, overweight, sick, and elderly are especially vulnerable to extreme heat. An average of 400 deaths are attributed to heat annually in the United States.[2] In 2003, over 70,000 Europeans died as a result of an extreme heat wave because they were used to mild summers and did not understand how to respond to very high temperatures.[3] Crop failure is also common when heat waves occur, as well as wildfires due to dried vegetation.

As demonstrated by the tragedy in Europe, heat waves can be especially dangerous to individuals accustomed to mild climates. Extreme heat can occur almost anywhere. Cities tend to be hotter than rural areas because of the urban heat island (UHI) effect, which can translate into a 5- to 18-degree increase in temperature. This phenomenon is caused, in part, by heat retention of buildings, concrete, and asphalt as well as waste heat created by people, vehicles, and public transportation. Consider some of the following ideas to prepare for extreme heat:

- Plan to beat the heat by preparing your home and understanding what to do. See chapter 17 for more information.

- Stock bottled water, sports drinks, and other nonalcoholic, noncaffeinated beverages to encourage hydration.

Hurricane, Tropical Storm, Typhoon

A tropical cyclone is a low-pressure storm system that produces a spiral arrangement of thunderstorms with heavy rain over large bodies of warm water. It has the ability to generate high waves, storm surges, and tornadoes, which tend to deteriorate rapidly over land. Once the winds reach 39 miles per hour, a tropical cyclone is elevated to a tropical storm and given a name. Once the winds reach 74 miles an hour, a tropical storm is classified as a hurricane. All Atlantic and Gulf of Mexico coastal areas are at risk for hurricanes. In the Northwest Pacific Ocean, they are called typhoons. The Pacific Coast and parts of the Southwest United States receive heavy rains and floods from hurricanes produced off the coast of Mexico. Catastrophic damage can still happen several hundred miles inland from hurricanes.

Fifty-three percent of Americans live near a coast, where hurricanes, floods, and tropical storms are annual rites.[4] It is important to understand your vulnerability and take action to reduce your risk. Storm surge, heavy rainfall, inland flooding, high winds, tornadoes, and rip currents are all possible hazards produced by hurricanes.

If you live in an area where hurricanes are a possibility, consider some of the following mitigation options to decrease your actual risk:

- Go to the National Hurricane Center at NOAA's National Weather Service—www.nhc.noaa.gov—for timely information on hurricane and tropical cyclone activity along with other weather information.

- Learn how your home may be affected by storm surge or flooding. Contact your city planning and zoning department or your insurance agent, or visit floodsmart.gov to learn more about your risk of flooding.

- As mentioned previously, purchase a NOAA Weather Radio All Hazards (NWR), which will keep you informed of hazardous conditions in your area.

- Be prepared to evacuate quickly. Evacuate at first warning to avoid traffic jams and booked hotels. Do not risk being trapped in your car when the storm hits by waiting until the last minute to evacuate. Make sure you have a marked evacuation map in your car with alternate routes. Know how to find higher ground. Always keep your gas tank at least half full.

- Prepare and stock a safe room, or a designated room with a first-aid kit (include prescription medications), battery-powered emergency radio, batteries, flashlight, blankets, water, snacks, and copies of important documents and computer files. The best place to take shelter in a high-rise building is on or below the tenth floor.

- Install permanent hurricane shutters if you can afford them. Storm panels with brackets to hold them in place can also be used. The least expensive option is to board up windows with ⅝-inch plywood, but make sure to prepare them in advance, clearly mark which window they fit, and predrill holes so they can be put in place quickly. Tape will not prevent windows from breaking.

Landslide, Mudslide, Debris Flow

Landslides are mass movements of rock, debris, and soil down a slope. They can be caused by earthquakes, volcanic eruptions, heavy rainfall, deforestation, overdevelopment, and mining. High-risk areas include Washington, Oregon, and other coastal regions; however, they can occur in just about any mountainous area. They move with great speed and force. A mudslide, or a debris flow, is a rapidly-moving landslide that frequently flows in channels. Areas burned by wildfires are highly vulnerable.

When rainfall rapidly saturates the ground, the chance of mudslides increases and can be extremely dangerous, and they can strike without warning. Buildings can be completely swept away with the fast-moving debris. Homes built on steep slopes, on the edges of mountains, in canyon bottoms, near stream channels, or in canyon outlets are at high risk. Areas prone to landslides are beautiful places to live but come with a serious risk factor. Some ways you may be able to lessen some of the risk factors are covered below:

- Visit www.uwec.edu/jolhm/eh2/rogge/hazmap.htm to view a hazard map of landslides in the United States.

- Consider relocating, or consult a geotechnical engineer to learn how you can make your property more resilient.

- Learn what landslides or debris flows have occurred in your area. If they occurred in the past, they are likely to happen again. Consult with local authorities, a county geologist, state geological surveys, or a university department of geology to learn more.

- Learn about emergency response and evacuation plans for your area. Is there more than one route to evacuate your neighborhood? Be prepared to evacuate immediately.

- Watch your property for signs of earth movement: cracked foundation; cracks or bulges in ground or pavement; patch of ground that does not dry out; leaning structure; tilted trees, fences, or walls. Contact a geotechnical expert to evaluate immediately.

Tornado

No place is safe from tornadoes. If the weather conditions are favorable, tornadoes can occur just about anywhere. Tornado Alley, which stretches out across the central plain states, has more tornadoes than anywhere in the world. This area includes Texas, Oklahoma, Kansas, Nebraska, Colorado, North Dakota, South Dakota, Iowa, and Illinois. The warm air from the Gulf of Mexico comes up and collides with the cooler air from the west and creates conditions ripe for tornadoes. A "Super Outbreak" of tornadoes in April 2011 was the deadliest, most expensive, and largest tornado outbreak in the history of the United States.[5] It occurred in Alabama, Arkansas, Georgia, Mississippi, Tennessee, Virginia, and other areas from Texas to New York.

Connective storms producing hail and strong winds that generate tornadoes can also bring heavy rains and cause localized flooding. Tornadoes can range from a few yards wide to over a mile. They can be slow or travel as fast as 60 miles an hour. Size does not predict intensity or strength.

Consider taking these steps as you mitigate your risk of tornadoes:

- Go to the Storm Prediction Center at NOAA's National Weather Service—www.spc.noaa.gov—for timely information on tornadoes along with other weather information.

- Consider installing a tornado safe room in your home. Go to www .fema.gov/safe-room-resources/fema-p-320-taking-shelter-storm -building-safe-room-your-home-or-small-business for instructions on how to build a safe room provided by FEMA.

- Stock a safe room, or designated room, with a first-aid kit (include prescription medications), a battery-powered emergency radio, batteries, a flashlight, blankets, water, snacks, and copies of important documents and computer files.

- Learn what emergency plans your place of employment and schools have in place. Does your daycare provider have an appropriate plan in place?

- Reinforce the connection between the roof and walls with hurricane straps and bracing. Local building codes may have required this depending on where and when your home was built.

Tsunami

Tsunamis are gigantic waves created by an underwater disruption such as an earthquake or volcanic eruption. The seismic sea waves can be over 100 feet high and travel hundreds of miles per hour, slowing as they reach shallow waters. Most of the time they are like a fast-rising flood with very strong currents. The Sumatra Tsunami in 2004 devastated coastal communities and killed nearly 230,000 people.[6] Anyone who lives along a coastline is at risk. The greatest risk is to those within 1 mile of the shoreline and less than 25 feet above sea level.

If you live in or visit a tsunami hazard zone, consider taking the following steps:

- Visit tsunami.gov for tsunami warnings, advisories, or watches. You can receive messages via email, RSS, Internet, radio, NOAA Weather radio, marine radio, and television.

- Many coastal communities are equipped with sirens and warning systems. Know what the tones mean and what to do in the event they are activated.

- Identify danger zones, safe areas, and assembly locations. A family tsunami education video entitled *Tsunami: Know What to Do* is available on YouTube.

Wildfire

Ferocious wildfire seasons grow increasingly more common because of drought, high temperatures, accumulations of fuel, and the continued growth of wildland–urban interface areas. Millions of acres of land are burned and an average of 2,600 homes are lost due to wildfire annually.[7] Wildfires are influenced by topography (physical features of the land), weather (wind, humidity, and temperature), and fuel (vegetation and man-made structures). You are at risk if you live in or near areas with large amounts of vegetation. Fires move upslope; the steeper the slope, the faster it travels. Advanced preparation is critical in reducing the risk of wildfire damage.

A home's ignition risk is determined by the landscape immediately around it (up to 200 feet), along with the materials the home is constructed from. Buildings within 100 feet can ignite one another. Forested areas are beautiful places to live but come with a level of risk that can be lessened to some extent, but not completely. If you choose to live in an area at risk for wildfire, consider taking some of the following steps to mitigate the risk:

- Go to firewise.org for valuable information on preparing your home to survive wildfires.

- Keep your property cleared of leaves, lawn clippings, brush piles, and dead limbs. Prune low-hanging limbs and thin trees and bushes. Do not provide fuel for the fire anywhere near your home. Stack firewood away from your home.

- Consider using noncombustible exterior building materials such as brick, stone, cement tile shingles, or metal roofing if you build or remodel. Fireproof shutters may protect your windows from radiant heat. Wood exterior can be protected by painting with a fire shield barrier, which sinks right into the wood and keeps it from igniting. Plywood decking can be covered with Quikrete cement and painted with a fire-resistant paint.

- Carefully investigate exactly what your homeowners insurance policy covers. Will it cover damages caused by a wildfire? Are there requirements you must meet to be covered?

OUTBREAKS

Pandemic, Epidemic

A pandemic is a widespread epidemic of a contagious disease which affects a high percentage of the population in a large geographic area. Throughout history, pandemics (or sizable epidemics) have included influenza, smallpox, measles, cholera, leprosy, malaria, tuberculosis, HIV (human immunodeficiency virus), typhus, and others. In 165 AD, the Antonine Plague killed over five million people in 15 years. The bubonic plague is thought to have claimed as many as 200 million lives. Over a billion people contracted the Spanish Flu of 1918, which claimed the lives of somewhere between 20 and 100 million people.[8]

Pandemics are no longer contained by geographical boundaries, spreading rapidly due to the global nature of our society. Breeding places include any place with a high concentration of people, such as doctors' offices, emergency rooms, schools, large indoor gatherings, airports, churches, grocery stores, and other crowded locations. Large-scale illness and death could result in overwhelmed hospitals, staffing shortages, and overwhelmed coroner and mortuary services. The infrastructure could be completely devastated, resulting in disruption to transportation, commerce, public utilities (communications, water, gas, electricity, and sewage), emergency response services, and government. We could expect widespread food shortage and civil unrest.

Preparing to deal with the effects of a pandemic involves much more than dealing with flu symptoms. It could drastically alter our way of life for a period of time. Think about reducing the risk of pandemics to your family by implementing the following suggestions.

- Strengthen your immune system. Eat healthy, exercise, and be proactive with your medical care.

- Prepare to self-quarantine for as long as necessary. Secure your home.

- Stock masks, gloves, disinfectants, medications (pain relievers, fever reducers, antidiarrheal medications, and vitamin supplements such as zinc and vitamin C, and so on)—anything you might find helpful to provide comfort and relief to someone who is ill. Purchase a quality medical reference book to help diagnose and treat illnesses. See chapter 20 for more information.

- Consider alternative medicine techniques such as homeopathy, acupressure, essential oils, herbs, and energy therapy.

- Educate yourself on antiviral prescription drugs such as Tamiflu and Relenza and decide if the cost and risks of the medication are worth the potential benefits to you.

TERRORIST- OR WAR-RELATED EVENTS

Biological Weapon

Biological warfare uses infectious agents (viruses, bacteria, and fungi) or biological toxins (poisonous compounds produced by organisms) to kill or harm people. This may result in disruption to the economy and society. Deliberate release of dangerous biological materials has been used throughout history. Water supplies poisoned with infected human or animal carcasses, plague-contaminated bodies thrown over city walls, and contaminated food supplies and arrows infected by dipping them in decomposing bodies are all ancient examples of germ warfare. Modern bioterrorism has made terrifying progress by mutating strains to be significantly more lethal.

Ideal candidates for biological warfare must be easy to obtain, process, and use. These agents are invisible, odorless, and tasteless, making them generally undetectable. They can be delivered through explosives or aerosol sprays, distributed in food or water, or they can even be absorbed through the skin. Once successfully delivered, some forms of infectious diseases are then transmitted from person to person.

Fortunately, effective delivery of biological agents can be problematic. Agents tend to be sensitive to temperature, humidity, elevation changes, wind, or micro weather patterns, or they require large amounts to be effective.

Governments, small organizations, and individuals have all been known to use biological weapons. Cholera, typhus, plague, smallpox, anthrax, tularemia, botulism, viral hemorrhagic fevers, and ricin are a few common biological agents. The effects of biological agents may not appear immediately. Botulinum symptoms will be evident within a day while anthrax or plague symptoms may not appear for two to five days.

Consider the following suggestions to reduce your risk:

- Go to http://outbreaks.globalincidentmap.com to monitor outbreaks, cases, and deaths from viral and bacterial diseases that may indicate biological terrorism.

- Purchase properly fitted military gas masks or high-efficiency particulate air (HEPA) filter masks, which can filter most particles delivered through the air. Inhalation is the most effective means of contamination.

- Prepare a safe room in your home, stocked with supplies, to shelter-in-place. See chapter 16.

- Be prepared to self-quarantine in the event an infectious disease epidemic results from the release of biological weapons.

Chemical Weapon, Hazmat Incident

Chemical weapons are classified as blister, blood, nerve, choking, and riot control agents. Chemical warfare agents (CWA) may come in solid, liquid, or gas form. They tend to have a unique odor or color. Depending on the type of CWA, it may lose effectiveness in a few minutes or hours, but some may persist for several weeks. Symptoms of exposure may appear immediately or within a few hours.

Common methods of dispersion are bombs, munitions, projectiles, spray tanks, and warheads. They are subject to temperature, humidity, and wind and are difficult to deliver. Incidents tend to be confined to a small area of a mile or less. CWA are heavier than air and stay relatively close to the ground.

Hazardous material (hazmat) spills or incidences can cause death, injury, and illness similar to chemical weapons. They can occur during production, storage, transportation, and use of any hazardous material. They are most likely to affect you if you live or work within one mile of a railroad, freeway, hazardous cargo (HC) route, or hazardous material production or storage facility. You can prepare for chemical hazards by taking the following steps:

- Identify the HC routes near your home, school, or workplace. Go to www.fmcsa.dot.gov/documents/safety-security/Routes-for-the-website-9-28-09-508-2.pdf to learn where the routes are in your state.

- Go to http://hazmat.globalincidentmap.com/map.php to see the North American Hazmat Situations and Deployment Map. Click "here" in the lower right-hand corner to see details.

- Be prepared to evacuate immediately. See chapter 4 for more information.

- Prepare a safe room in your home, stocked with supplies, to shelter-in-place. See chapter 16.

- Consider purchasing a properly fitted gas mask or HEPA mask for each member of your family.

Electromagnetic Pulse, Solar Flare

An electromagnetic pulse (EMP) is generated when a nuclear weapon is detonated in the atmosphere. The higher the denotation occurs, the larger the area affected. EMP effects are based on line of sight. Theoretically, one nuclear weapon detonated 200 miles above the earth could cause serious damage to the power grid and electronic equipment across the entire continental United States.

A solar flare, also known as a solar storm, is a series of huge explosions in the sun's atmosphere triggered by magnetic instability. It is a brief eruption of powerful high-energy radiation from the sun's surface. In 1859, a solar tempest caused telegraph wires to short out across the United States and Europe. A minor solar flare in 1989 caused a massive power outage across Quebec, Canada. A 2003 solar storm left parts of South Africa without power for several months.[9] Scientists are cautiously monitoring the rise in solar activity and fear an extended season of solar storms. The more serious storms could produce effects similar to an EMP.

The strong electrical energy pulse is collected by metallic pipes, wires, cables, conduits, or other "antennae," much like a radio signal is collected by a radio antenna or lightning by a lightning rod. High voltages and currents are induced, destroying many types of electrical and electronic devices and systems, including the power grid, communications, computers, and many other systems that run our world. Lightning and surge protectors are generally ineffective.

Though not directly harmful to humans, the indirect effects of an EMP or solar flare would be devastating to society. The United States is the most technologically advanced nation on earth, making it highly vulnerable. Transportation could be severely hampered. Power and communications systems could become disabled. The ability to produce, refrigerate, and distribute food and necessities could be almost obliterated. Hospitals and health care facilities would likely be inoperable. The ability to produce clean drinking water and manage human and other waste could be limited. Our vulnerability to disease and death would increase dramatically. The extent of the damage can only be estimated, but our world as we know it would be dramatically altered.

There are two general scenarios in which an EMP will occur. One is as an act of terrorism. The second is as a precursor to war. Military strategists for decades have assumed that any large-scale military action (particularly a nuclear assault) would be preceded by an EMP to disable communications, create commotion, and diminish the ability of the military to respond effectively.

Consider the following list of ideas to mitigate the effects of an EMP or solar flare:

- Prepare for stores to be closed, public utilities to be disrupted, and civil unrest for at least one year.

- Produce whatever you can on your own property. Incorporate edible plants into your landscape design. If you live in an apartment, plant edibles in pots on your patio. Store garden seeds.

- Invest in quality communication devices and keep them protected in a Faraday cage (a unique storage container designed to shield the contents from static electric fields).

- Keep bicycles and other alternative means of transportation in good repair and have extra parts on hand to make repairs.

- Invest in a variety of good tools. Include a radiation survey meter and dosimeter in this list of tools.

- Consider nuclear blast or fallout shelter options.

Nuclear Hazards

Nuclear energy provides nearly 20 percent of the electricity in the United States from 104 nuclear reactors. These power plants are located throughout the country but are concentrated on the eastern side. According to the Natural Resources Defense Council, five American nuclear power plants experienced emergency shutdowns in 2011 due to natural disasters: Calvert Cliffs due to hurricane, North Anna due to earthquake, Fort Calhoun due to flooding, Browns Ferry due to tornado, and Surry due to tornado. Loss of both primary and backup power for only a few hours could lead to meltdown and release a radioactive airborne plume. The evacuation zone around a nuclear reactor is up to 50 miles, with 120 million Americans living within that distance of a nuclear power plant.[10]

Nuclear weapons produce immediate, as well as delayed, effects. The explosion begins with an intense flash of light and a fireball. At ground zero, almost everything is immediately destroyed. The explosion produces fires from the thermal energy of the blast as well as from ruptured gas and electric lines. The electromagnetic pulse wipes out all electronic equipment within range. Fallout particles are carried high into the atmosphere and travel hundreds of miles. Radioactive particles will affect water supplies, food supplies, and air quality.

Potential targets for nuclear attacks include military bases, strategic missile sites, centers of government, transportation and communication centers, major ports and airfields, petroleum refineries, electrical power plants, chemical plants, manufacturing or industrial centers, and technology and financial centers.

Consider the following suggestions to lessen the effects of a nuclear event on your family:

- Go to the Natural Resources Defense Council's website at www. nrdc.org/nuclear/fallout to see a map of nuclear reactors and learn the risk for your area.

- Alex Wellerstein created an app that will let you see what may happen if a nuclear weapon is denoted at various locations. Visit www.nuclearsecrecy.com/nukemap to select your location and a bomb type to learn how you may be affected.

- Purchase and review *Nuclear War Survival Skills* by Cresson H. Kearny. Learn how to create expedient fallout shelters and survive after a nuclear event.

- Learn how to treat radiation sickness. Purchase a supply of potassium iodide (KI) anti-radiation pills as a thyroid blocking agent in a radiation emergency.

- Consider blast and radiation shelter options. Plan on sheltering for several weeks if necessary.

- Purchase a radiation meter. Learn how to operate it.

Terrorism

The greatest cost of terrorism is our response to it. The heroes on United Airlines Flight 93 refused to allow the hijackers to accomplish their objective. They stood up to evil and prevented the terrorists from accomplishing their mission. This is how we must all respond to terrorism. We need to hold our heads high and live our lives. When we allow ourselves to live in fear, they win.

Terrorist attacks kill relatively few people compared to other hazards. These attacks include the use of biological, chemical, radiological and nuclear materials; hijackings; bombings; suicide operations; kidnappings; shootings; assaults on aircraft or ships; and other acts intended to create fear and panic. Most of the time these attacks are relatively isolated events, but there is the potential for widespread events.

There are steps you can take to reduce your risk. Knowledge is power. Is your home or work located in a high-profile city or tourist attraction thought to be likely terrorist targets? Be cautious in public—look for anything or anyone suspicious and report anything out of the ordinary to local police. Consider the following recommendations for reducing your risk from terrorism:

- Be proactive about security where you work, live, go to school, and travel. Know all emergency procedures.

- Secure your home. Develop self-defense skills. Consider legally carrying a firearm.

- Be prepared to shelter-in-place or evacuate on short notice.

- Prepare for possible deployment of weapons of mass destruction. See chapter 16 for information on radiation shelters.

MAN-MADE EVENTS OR ACCIDENTS

Civil Unrest, Breakdown of Social Order

Major disasters, economic challenges, high levels of unemployment, discontent over corruption, lack of economic opportunities, terrorist attacks, rising fuel and food prices, or scarcity of resources can all result in the breakdown of the normal order of society. Any time emergency responders are overwhelmed, there is an increase in criminal and civilian violence. Civil unrest occurs when people become angry, frustrated, or afraid as a group. An authoritarian crackdown may result in mass unrest on a state or regional level. It can be deadly and destructive. You can expect lawlessness, corrupt police, an absence of emergency personnel, and increased crime, including home invasions, carjackings, burglaries, gang violence, and rioting.

When a breakdown in social order occurs, trucking will likely cease. Mail delivery and medical supply shipments will abruptly halt. Service stations will run out of fuel, store shelves will be empty, food shortages will develop, and manufacturing will cease. In a couple of days, banks will be unable to process transactions and people will begin to panic as food shortages escalate. It may take only a week or so for garbage to begin piling up. Transportation will cease due to fuel unavailability. Medical services will be crippled. Before long, public utilities will be interrupted.

In an effort to control the people, martial law may be declared. Military forces may be deployed to maintain order and to enforce rule over the public. Typically this means suspension of civil rights, civil law, and habeas corpus (the right to be seen by a judge). Curfews may be implemented. Enforced relocations, confiscation of firearms and supplies, and arrests and executions by soldiers are a few examples of how civilians' freedoms may be curtailed.

The events surrounding civil unrest or a breakdown in social order are difficult to accurately predict. Consider the following ideas to limit the risk to your family if you are faced with civil unrest:

- Be prepared to evacuate immediately to a safer, prearranged location or stay indoors for an extended period of time.

- Secure your home. See chapter 18.

- Develop self-defense skills. Learn how to use pepper spray. It may be an effective alternative for personal protection for those unfamiliar with firearms.

- Consider safely storing firearms and ammunition. Train every responsible member of your household to use and care for each weapon. Firearms may be confiscated during martial law.

Economic Collapse

The likelihood of economic collapse (devaluation of the dollar, bank closures, hyperinflation, stock market crash, and so on) is a distinct possibility. The economy is fragile. The Great Depression lasted over a decade. We should not expect a quick recovery. Expect assets to fall in value, money to stop circulating, and credit to be unavailable. Supplies of food, fuel, and necessities will be low, but demand for these items will be high. The collapse could affect local governments and utilities, which may result in loss of water and power. People may panic. Mass riots, looting, and crime will increase. People may freeze or starve to death. Normal commerce may cease for a few years.

An economic collapse will present many difficult challenges. However, to a large extent we have the ability to mitigate some of the consequences. Financial wealth may disappear, but we can work to make sure our families are warm and fed. Recovery may take a while, but it will come eventually. We have to make preparations to endure the difficult times and learn to make the best of it. The old saying holds true: "Use it up, wear it out, make it do, or do without." Life can be good and fulfilling without all the stuff we are accustomed to having. You may want to consider these recommendations for reducing the effect of an economic collapse on your family:

- Develop valuable trade skills such as gardening, seed saving, food preservation, animal husbandry, construction, alternative energy, natural medicine, first aid, auto mechanics, self-defense, handiness, small engine repair, welding, and amateur radio, among others.

- Consider purchasing gold and silver coins after you have built your food stores.

- Practice the art of provident living and self-reliance. Learn to work. Be wise, frugal, and prudent. Get out of debt and live on less than you earn.

- Learn self-defense skills and acquire weapons of choice. Secure your home.

- Work on becoming physically fit and healthy. Access to medical care and medications may be limited. If you have disabilities, explore options and develop a reasonable plan in the event medical care is unavailable.

House Fire

The most common disaster is a house fire. One in every 320 households reports a fire annually, demonstrating great need to take safety measures. Residential fire-related deaths are preventable. Careful planning and safety measures can significantly reduce this risk factor. According to a report published by the National Fire Protection Association, cooking equipment is the number one cause of home fires and nonfatal injuries while smoking materials are the leading cause of deaths from home fires. Heating equipment is the second leading cause. Three out of every five house fire deaths occur in the absence of working smoke alarms.[11]

Consider the following steps to reduce the risk of house fires:

- Develop a family evacuation plan. Test alarms and evacuate the home at least twice a year. Teach family members to close doors behind them to help contain the fire if there is time. Practice using a fire extinguisher.

- Every time you have an evacuation drill, practice stop, drop, and roll: If clothes catch on fire, cover your eyes and mouth with your hands to prevent injury to the face and keep smoke out of your eyes. Roll back and forth over and over until the flames are completely extinguished. Practice will allow the brain to automatically take over, eliminating the delay of trying to remember what to do.

- Ensure each sleeping area has two escape routes (such as a door and window). Install ladders or special equipment to facilitate escape as required by the abilities of the occupant of each room.

- Properly install and maintain smoke alarms (preferably interconnected), carbon monoxide detectors, and fire extinguishers.

Personal Disaster

This risk is unique to each person, so you may have to use your imagination as to what things you might consider a personal disaster. It usually only affects your family. It may include loss of employment, reduction of work hours, chronic illness, personal injury, death of a loved one, mother-in-law moving in, financial loss, separation or divorce, or any event that strains your personal lifestyle.

These suggestions are a starting point of possible steps to mitigate a personal disaster. You can figure out which things are possibilities specifically for you.

- Purchase an appropriate level of life insurance.

- Consider long-term disability insurance.

- Get out of debt and build your savings.

- Embrace opportunities to improve job skills and education.

- Protect your health by exercising, eating well, and reducing stress.

- Spend time with family members. Actively work on building relationships.

- Foster a positive attitude toward life and challenges.

Societal Collapse, Collapse of Civilization

Many die-hard preppers are preparing for the utter and complete collapse of civilization. It has happened before and it can happen again. The history of civilization demonstrates that they are fragile and can be completely destroyed. History also teaches us that humans are resilient. Most of the time when a civilization is left in ruin, it eventually recovers. It doesn't look the same, but some people usually survive and rebuild. Those who prepare will have a significantly better chance of being among those who survive.

Preparations for a complete collapse of civilization would entail preparing to be completely self-sufficient for many years. There would be an ever-present danger from desperate people in a lawless society. You may want to consider the following steps:

- If you live in a densely populated area, arrange a "bug out" location. A well-prepared rural location may increase your chance of survival.

- Secure your home against desperate intruders. Take self-defense courses. Consider storing firearms and ammunition.

- Develop basic skills such as food production and storage, animal husbandry, carpentry, small engine mechanics, first aid, medical skills, and basic cooking. Become a master do-it-yourselfer.

- Have a collection of well-written reference books.

- Cultivate relationships with like-minded people. Diverse talents and resources are vital to establishing a survival network. A community will provide better protection and higher quality of life than a single family.

- Produce everything you can on your own property. Plant fruit trees, berries, and vines. Build a greenhouse to produce year-round. Store garden seeds. Raise chickens or other animals when possible.

- Gather a variety of nonelectric tools and equipment. Learn how to use them.

- Consider building a well-stocked. all-hazards underground shelter to protect against a variety of events that could lead to, or result from, the collapse.

PRIORITIZING YOUR RISK MITIGATION PLAN

Risk planning and mitigation can seem like an overwhelming task. Take a deep breath and review the possible hazards. Calculate your risk scores on the table below.

Personal Risk Scores

Event	Probability 1 = No chance 5 = Will occur	× Consequence 1 = None 5 = Catastrophic	= Risk Score
Drought			
Earthquake			
Extreme winter storms			
Flooding			
Heat wave			
Hurricane, tropical storm, typhoon			
Landslide, mudslide, debris flow			
Tornado			
Tsunami			
Wildfire			
Pandemic, epidemic			
Biological attack			
Chemical attack			
Hazmat incident			
EMP			
Solar flare			
Nuclear accident			
Nuclear attack			

Event	Probability 1 = No chance 5 = Will occur	× Consequence 1 = None 5 = Catastrophic	= Risk Score
Terrorist attack			
Civil unrest, breakdown of social order			
Economic collapse			
House fire			
Personal disaster			
Societal collapse, breakdown of civilization			
Other:			

Which hazards received the highest scores? This information is valuable; it gives you clear direction on where you should focus your efforts. Work on the highest scores first. You may find that many of the mitigation steps taken for one hazard actually work for many of the others as well. Before you know it, you will be the ultimate practical prepper, ready for whatever man or nature has to throw your way.

After a disaster, always assume that you are on your own. Emergency personnel will be spread thin and will go to where the greatest number of people are. Choose to be prepared, take care of your family, and then volunteer to help others. Your best teacher is real-life learning experiences. For example, turn off your power for a few days and see how prepared you really are.

Quite honestly, Jonathan's risk assessment would be a little different from Kylene's. We each see things differently and have different fears. Jonathan is highly concerned with physically protecting the family. Kylene is more worried about putting food on the table and having enough toilet paper for all the bottoms in our house. We are united in working to prepare, so the exact numbers and priorities are not vitally important.

Visit www.theprovidentprepper.org/the-practical-prepper/action-plan-risk to see our family's risk mitigation plan. We have provided a form for you to complete your own personalized risk mitigation plan on that same page. Take a few minutes to thoughtfully complete the form and develop your action plan.

THE POWER IS IN THE PLAN

We recognize it takes a whole lot of brain power to create your risk management plan. Good job! You have a quality foundation on which to build your emergency preparedness and survival plan. The real power is in the plan. Now you know where to start. You will likely tweak and perfect your plan as you move through the process and learn more. We encourage you to adjust as necessary.

Now that you've completed the hard part, we will assist you through each step of preparedness. We will teach you why, what, and how. Our goal is to walk this journey with you. As you become more and more prepared, you will be amazed at what you have accomplished. We hope it will bring you confidence and peace to know that you have taken control of the things that you can. You have done everything you can to protect your family against the dangers that lurk in the future.

John Greenleaf Whittier wrote, "Of all sad words of tongue or pen / The saddest are these, 'It might have been.'"[12] We hope you will never have cause to look back after a disaster with regret and sorrow for a tragedy that may have been avoided through thoughtful preparation. We are confident that through careful, dedicated efforts, lives and property can be saved.

3

Survive or Thrive
Loving Life

"Everything can be taken from a man but one thing: the last of the human freedoms—to choose one's attitude in any given set of circumstances, to choose one's own way."

—Viktor E. Frankl [1]

You have just completed a comprehensive evaluation of the possible hazards you may face in your future. You have a reasonable plan to reduce those risk factors, and we are going to explore exactly how to execute that plan. But first we will discuss the most important aspect of that plan: your personal attitude, resilience, and emotional fortitude.

Quite frankly, we dislike the word *survive*. By definition, to survive is to continue to live or exist in spite of danger or hardship.[2] The word gives little hope of a bright future. Our goal is to *thrive* in the face of adversity. We gain confidence through our preparations and fully expect to embrace the challenges ahead and find joy in the journey. Bad things happen—it is an inevitable part of life. But we are determined to thrive in the face of adversity.

WHO SURVIVES DISASTERS

In the book *The Unthinkable: Who Survives When Disaster Strikes—and Why*, Amanda Ripley discusses historical facts and details of human response to disasters of all kinds. She shows that the response Hollywood portrays of disasters is not how the majority of people respond in the face of danger. The screaming, panic, and survive-at-all-costs mentality is the exception, not the norm. People are generally concerned for the welfare of others and risk their own lives to ensure others are safe.[3]

Why does one person survive an event and another die? Can you do anything to change the odds in your favor? Survivors tend to have some things in common. Amanda Ripley expounds on the following points in her book. They are worth considering.

- A healthy body will increase your odds of surviving. Overweight people have a lower chance of surviving because of physical limitations. They have more health problems, increased sensitivity to heat, and difficulty recovering from injuries. Escaping from a dangerous situation is more difficult for the obese because they move slowly and take up more physical space.

- A good standard of living increases survival rates. Poorer homes are more likely to burn due to space heating, poor construction, or lack of working smoke detectors. The 2010 earthquake in Haiti was only 7.0 magnitude, but it killed 300,000 people. Japan experienced a 9.0 earthquake in 2011 that only claimed 22,000. The difference in the death toll has been attributed to Japan's strict building codes and preparation. The poverty in Haiti did not provide for such preparations.

- Healthy relationships promote survival. We are social creatures who have a deep need to help and to share with one another. As we act upon our charitable nature, happiness and self-esteem increase. A sense of well-being and peace develops. Disasters do not happen to individuals; they happen to groups—strangers, coworkers, family, friends, and neighbors. The healthier the group, the better it can handle the stresses associated with disasters and expedite recovery.

- Resilient people recover more quickly than others from traumatic events. The ability to be resilient can be developed. They believe they can make a difference and influence events. Resilient individuals find meaning or purpose in the craziness that life presents. When bad things happen, they ask what they can learn from the event rather than why it happened. This view cushions the shock of a disaster, makes dangers seem more manageable, and improves performance.

- Survivors have a high sense of self-worth and confidence built through education, training, and experience. Mental rehearsals and playing the "what if" game trains the brain to respond quickly to new situations. Repeatedly developing a plan of action for everyday hazards makes response automatic, eliminating the need for the brain to process new information and increasing response time.

- Your mental state may determine whether or not you survive. The way you perceive your situation in an emergency can magnify it, increasing confusion and irrational behavior, or it can minimize it, allowing for clear thinking. Previously established action plans provide the confidence and ability to perceive a situation as manageable and then act quickly to save lives.

RECOGNIZING FEARS AND LEARNING TO THRIVE

We all have similar—yet different—fears. Take time to look at your fears. What are they? Why do you feel that way? Is there anything that might make you feel safe from that fear? Fear is a highly intense emotion. It cannot be wished away or hidden in a closet. Do not minimize someone else's fear or tell them to "get over it." Exercise patience and work toward understanding. Explore ways of realistically reducing the level of fear.

A common fear of many preppers is that their world may turn upside down and never return to normal. Change can be frightening. How do we help this? Physically prepare for hazards to the best of your ability. Make a decision that even if the world gets turned upside down, you are determined to thrive. You will find joy and peace in whatever life brings to your door. Every time the fear returns, refuse to allow it to dominate your thoughts. Whatever the scenario is that plays in your mind, turn it around. Retell the story with a happy ending. Control your thoughts and choose happy endings.

Thriving in the face of adversity is a choice because you choose your attitude. A positive attitude will improve your health and emotional strength and will benefit everyone around you. The way you look at the challenges presented to you will largely affect your ability to have a positive outcome. Franklin D. Roosevelt said it nicely: "The only thing we have to fear is fear itself—nameless, unreasoning, unjustified terror which paralyzes."[4] Do not fear the future. Plan, prepare, practice, and move forward with faith in a life full of bright tomorrows. We believe the best is yet to come.

THRIVING DURING A DISASTER

How will you respond when a disaster rocks your world? It is important to understand the thought processes you will be faced with in a crisis situation. It is typical for the brain to shut down and life to proceed in slow motion. According to Ripley, most people respond in similar manner by going through three phases:

1. **Denial:** This is the tendency to watch a situation unfold but not believe it is actually happening. This is the deer-in-the-headlights-type response. In order to respond, the threat must be recognized for what it is.

2. **Deliberation:** *What should I do? What are my options?* The most common reaction is actually to freeze and do nothing. The brain slows down, and making the decision takes significantly longer than usual. The brain gathers the information and tries to process options. Prior planning and rehearsing scenarios significantly speeds up this stage. *What do I do if my clothes catch on fire? I do not panic. I know what to do. I drop to the ground, cover my face with my hands, and roll back and forth repeatedly until all the flames are extinguished. Then I slowly stand up and get help. I will be okay.*

3. **Decisive moment:** This is the stage where you act, making the difference between life and death.

These stages are part of human nature. The speed you move through each phase is largely determined by your level of mental preparedness. Practice developing action plans in daily life. *What would I do if . . . ?* These cognitive rehearsals will train the brain and increase your response time in a true emergency.

Numbness, or an inability to remember or make decisions, may affect you when a disaster strikes no matter how well you have prepared. Repetitive physical practice creates muscle memory, which comes in handy when the brain needs to be bypassed.

Make lists. A friend's daughter was given 30 minutes to evacuate due to a wildfire. She called, paralyzed, asking what she should take from her home. Preparing lists in advance can solve this problem. Even a numb brain can check items off a list.

Some disasters last for hours, while others may impact life for months. Taking good care of yourself in spite of a difficult situation is important. Here are a few ideas to help you be your best during an extended crisis:

- Sleep! Recognize sleep as a necessity, a healing practice. Sleep deprivation results in confusion, difficulty thinking, and poor judgment and reasoning. Adequate sleep increases courage and healing and puts life in proper perspective.

- Recognize that life does not go on as usual. Slow down. Do not overdo. There may be much to be done, but pace yourself.

- Remember to drink water and eat. Consume the healthiest diet possible under the circumstances.

- Exercise to decrease stress and maintain physical strength.

- Meditate, pray, and read scriptures.

- Smile, laugh, and play. Find reasons to love life.

- Give yourself permission to mourn loss (of loved ones, comfort, or possessions) and look forward to a bright future.

- Reach out and help others. The best therapy can be forgetting yourself and getting to work helping those around you. This also puts things in perspective. Someone is always worse off than you are.

The goal is to thrive. You will conquer this challenge and emerge stronger for it. It will not defeat you. Get up in the morning, get dressed, and get to work. Put one foot in front of the other and, before you know it, life will start to look up.

THRIVING AFTER A DISASTER

Rebuilding your life and recovering your emotional equilibrium takes time. A disaster or crisis can send you reeling into a world of the unknown. Your sense of security can be shattered, resulting in a range of intense and confusing emotions.

We all view the world through our own frame of reference, which is why emotional responses to traumatic experiences vary so significantly. One person may be emotionally traumatized, another furious, and another might laugh it off and move on. There is no one right way to feel, think, or react. Be patient with yourself and others as you work to recover from a traumatic event.

Intensity, timing, and duration of responses are different for everyone. Responses may not appear until months after the event is over. When a loved one dies, sometimes a person may handle everything quite well and then suddenly after six months have significant challenges. Emotional responses may include irritability, anger, denial, self-blame, blaming others, mood swings, isolation, withdrawal, fear, hyperactivity, nightmares, difficulty concentrating, memory problems, inability to sleep, sadness, depression, grief, and many others. Physical responses can be intense and attributed to other causes. It is possible to experience loss of appetite, headaches, chest pain, diarrhea, stomach pain, nausea, fatigue, and more.[5]

The best way to thrive in the midst of these challenges is through patience and understanding. Recovery is an individual journey that cannot be rushed or avoided. Be understanding, be willing to talk, and just listen. Reestablish structure and routine as soon as possible. Provide regular times for sleeping, eating, and relaxing. Make time to laugh and relax. Share your strength and serve others. Give yourself time to heal and to mourn. Be patient. It will be difficult, but you can do hard things. It will get better.

Our family experienced our own personal disaster when our daughter was killed in a tragic car accident. We have journeyed through a kaleidoscope of emotions. When we gather our family around us, there is still an emptiness where she once was, even years later. Her smile, her infectious laugh, and her deep love for others is greatly missed. For a while, we could only go through the mechanical motions of life, our hearts heavy with sorrow. Faith and time have enabled us to feel joy again and thrive.

PREPARING CHILDREN TO THRIVE IN A DISASTER

Create opportunities for children to have mastery experiences and help them succeed. A mastery experience is an event that requires all of an individual's strength and ability to accomplish, such as climbing a mountain. There comes a point in the journey when you are hungry, cold, and completely exhausted. You look toward the peak and think, *I can't go on. There is no way I will reach that.* However, one step after another you continue, defying physical and emotional limitations until finally you are triumphantly gazing over the valley from the peak.

That becomes a defining event in life to measure all other difficulties against. *If I could reach that peak, surely I can do this.* These events build strength, character, and reserve. Remind children that they are strong and can do hard things. Help them believe in themselves. Never tell them that they are weak or unable to accomplish anything. Children will mirror your emotions as well as your faith in who they are and who they can become.

Parents are blessed with the opportunity to handle small crises every day. Learn from those experiences. When a child shatters an heirloom into pieces, he will immediately look for your reaction. You can choose to yell, belittle, punish, or break down into tears, but what purpose does that serve? The heirloom is gone. What remains is a vital relationship and a critical lesson on what is really important in life. Choose your responses wisely. "Are you okay? That was special, but not as special as you. Will you help me clean it up?" Model reactions to disasters by successfully handling everyday challenges.

Teach children creatively on their own level. A healthy work ethic can be instilled as you work side by side with them and teach them to be self-reliant from an early age. It is empowering for them to know how to do basic tasks like cooking, cleaning, mending, laundry, gardening, caring for animals, or starting a fire. Make sure tasks are age appropriate. Teaching a two-year-old to light a fire is probably not the best idea; however, a curious seven-year-old is perfect. It gives you an opportunity to instill safety rules and prevents a curious mind from exploring a fascinating (and dangerous) activity on his own.

Children are amazing. They can handle more serious information than we give them credit for. Sometimes we have a tendency to try to shelter our children from dangers and difficulties. They are highly observant and hear much more than we may think. Kids process the information within their limited frame of reference. Sometimes this can be devastating. Children fear what they do not understand. It provides great comfort when a family discusses the steps they can take to keep themselves safe.

When frightening events occur in the world, our family openly discusses them together, usually around the dinner table. It might go something like this: "The pictures of the earthquake were really scary. How do you feel about what happened? What would we do if that happened here?" The response from our children of all ages is amazing. They verbalize what they might do to keep themselves safe and convey a sense of security from our preparations. We coach them with a positive, enabling attitude. "What if Daddy and Mommy died? Where would you go? What would you do?" They know exactly what the plan is. They would live with their older sister and be cared for and loved. Life would change, but everything would be okay.

Children generally fear four things will occur in a disaster: they will be separated from their family, someone will get hurt, they will be left alone, or the disaster will happen again. Whatever the fear may be, acknowledge it and come up with a plan. We conquer fear by preparing for our fears. Discuss and plan for each likely scenario as well as other fears your child may verbalize. Write it down. Talk about it and review it frequently.

SURVIVE OR THRIVE ACTION PLAN

As with every other principle taught in this book, preparing to thrive emotionally is an important aspect worthy of time and planning. Take the ideas discussed and expound on them. This is a good time to take the steps necessary to become the person you want to be.

You will find a worksheet at www.theprovidentprepper.org/the -practical-prepper/action-plan-survive-or-thrive, that is designed to help you organize your thoughts into a workable plan. Look at the first action item, "Who survives?" Earlier in the chapter we reviewed traits of people who survive. What do you need to do to increase your chances of survival? Lose a little weight? Develop better relationships? Work to improve your standard of living? Record your plan next to the action item. Create a specific plan for each action item. As you make progress on these action items, you are preparing to thrive.

4

Family Emergency Plan
We Can Make It Together

"Family means no one gets left behind or forgotten."

—David Ogden Stiers

A family plan is critical to surviving any disaster. It provides an opportunity to think ahead, plan for possible hazards, and educate the entire family on agreed-upon procedures. Disasters can be challenging enough without the pain and fear associated with having a missing loved one. This plan is the foundation for your preparedness efforts. Most people spend half of their time away from their homes. Where might you be when disaster strikes? How would you get back together if you were separated?

A family plan applies to everyone, not only those with children at home. Everyone has a network of friends or family who love them and are concerned for their safety. A family may also consist of another individual, roommates, or a group of friends—whoever makes up your personal support system. In this chapter, we will discuss the foundation for a good family emergency plan.

PREDETERMINED MEETING PLACES

We work hard to make our home a safe haven where we can stay through many challenging events. However, some situations may require evacuation no matter how well prepared we are. Entire neighborhoods may be evacuated due to wildfires, floods, hurricanes, tsunamis, military attacks, chemical spills, nuclear events, and a host of other hazards. Personal evacuation may be necessary in the event of a home fire or an event in which your home is no longer a safe place to remain.

The plan should include clearly specified and documented places to meet. Meeting places may vary depending on the circumstances. The following are the meeting places we use in our plan. Yours will likely be a little different.

The **primary meeting place** should be located outside your home. It is used as a meeting place in the event of a sudden emergency, such as a house fire. The ideal location provides shelter, is easily accessible, and is away from fire hydrants. It is critical to regularly hold practice drills. Practice drills ensure that everyone understands what they should do, and drills also help work out bugs in the plan.

We had originally designated our meeting place at the fire hydrant right across the street from our home. It sounded like a good idea at the time, until a fireman warned us that it is actually a dangerous place, because of all the emergency equipment. We changed our primary meeting place to the sidewalk in front of our chicken coop. There is a little overhang that could provide protection in bad weather. During our next fire drill, a few members of the family gathered by the fire hydrant. If it had been a real fire, we might have gone back into the house to search for them and endangered lives unnecessarily. Practice is critical!

The **secondary meeting place** should be outside of your neighborhood in the event that you are unable to return to your home or it becomes unsafe in the area. The meeting place might be at a friend's or relative's home in the same or neighboring city but out of the immediate area. This meeting place might be used in the event of a chemical spill, localized flooding, wildfire, or any event that is local.

The **out-of-area meeting place** should be a pre-determined destination at least 100 miles from your home. This is your safe place or "bug out" location. Having some place prepared ahead of time is important in the event you need to evacuate quickly. Hotels fill up fast in surrounding areas during disasters. The location should be far enough away from your residence that it would not be affected by the same event.

A well-stocked mountain cabin or second home could turn a disaster into a vacation. Most of us need to settle for a trip to Aunt Martha's house. Decide on a location, communicate well, and make sure your safe house, or "bug out" location, has the supplies to accommodate your family. Always have a backup plan in case that location suddenly does not work out.

A **higher-ground meeting place** is a good idea for those who are located in floodplains. If you live within one mile of the coast and less than 25 feet above sea level, you should plan a place to meet that is on higher ground in the event of a tsunami warning.[1] This place need only be far enough away to avoid the high water. Would a dam failure flood your neighborhood? Are you at risk for flooding? Plan a safe place for your family to meet.

The American Red Cross provides free temporary emergency shelters. They try to make them safe, sanitary, and reasonably comfortable. Strict rules and procedures are enforced in order to accommodate large numbers of people. No pets are allowed except service animals.

We do not recommend depending on a public shelter. They offer little privacy and place you in close proximity to strangers. You are bound by the rules of those operating the shelter. Weapons are routinely confiscated. Personal liberties are suspended to maintain order. However, sometimes emergency situations may not leave you with another choice. If you must use a public shelter, the Red Cross has an app that can quickly direct you to open Red Cross shelters.

Now that you have reviewed the above information, document exactly where you are going to meet in the event of an emergency. Complete the worksheet located at www.theprovidentprepper.org/the-practical-prepper /action-plan-family-emergency-plan.

EVACUATION PLAN

Now that you know where you are going, consider an actual evacuation plan. Plan to stay together. It is dangerous to separate for any reason. Once you leave home, you become a refugee and are highly vulnerable.

If you are advised to evacuate, leave as early as possible to avoid being caught in traffic. Do not mess with hurricanes. Make a safe and speedy exit. Many deaths can be avoided by timely evacuation. Follow instructions given by local authorities. A traffic jam caused by thousands of panicked people hitting the roads and freeways at once is a disaster in and of itself.

Always keep gas tanks at least half full. Top off the tank with fuel if possible. Store additional fuel at home. Make sure you have enough to get to your destination. Many evacuees are left stranded after running out of gas because of long hours in bumper-to-bumper traffic. You may want to take an extra can of fuel with you depending on the distance to your shelter.

Money may be difficult to access during a disaster. Keep as much cash as you are comfortable with secured in your home. Banks and ATMs might be out of service. Credit cards might not be accepted due to power or data failure, and commerce may be conducted on a cash-only basis.

Plan for your pets. They are not allowed in food establishments or public shelters. Should they stay or go? If they stay, make sure they are as safe as possible with enough food and water to last for an extended period of time. If they go, choose a destination that allows pets and take all of the necessary supplies to care for them. Keep evacuation supplies up-to-date and easy to grab. See chapter 5 on survival kits.

THE MAP

Obtain a detailed road map of your area and road maps for neighboring states. You will need a marked copy for each vehicle, a copy for each place of employment, one for home, and one to give to a trusted friend or family member. Study the maps and look for possible evacuation routes. Note any areas of danger. Are there places that would be best to avoid? Can your vehicle accommodate rough roads? If not, make sure all roads are paved.

Preplanning all routes is important. Develop contingency plans in the event that one route is blocked. A GPS is a wonderful tool, but it cannot replace a strategically marked map. Do you have at least three ways to enter and exit your city? What if you have to evacuate while you are at work? While your kids are at school? How will you meet up? How can you get home from work?

Identify various routes from your home to your destination and physically mark them on your map. Earthquakes and violent storms can make some roads impassable. Identify at least three routes from your work to your home. Travel each route you have plotted out. Identify possible problem areas such as areas of flooding, factories with hazardous chemicals, or dangerous parts of town. Label each route with a clear identifier. Labeling A, B, C or 1, 2, 3 will facilitate communication.

Make sure everyone knows which route you will be taking so they know where to start looking if you don't show up.

Mark directions to a safe home, or bug out location, and be prepared to brainstorm other possible safe locations in every direction. Plan alternate routes in case roads or bridges in one direction are no longer safe. It may be a good idea to have an alternate location planned in the event that those routes are impassable.

COMMUNICATION PLAN

Your family communication plan should be practiced regularly. Each disaster may provide unique challenges when it comes to communication. Contemplate how you can use a variety of techniques to ensure that effective communication occurs.

Implement a well-practiced system for notifying close friends and family members when you leave. Consider the following ideas to use in your communication plan:

Written communication is a time-honored way to communicate. Practice leaving notes in designated places. Include where, when, and other important information. "Went to Jason Smith's house at 4:30 p.m. on Wednesday, September 14, to plan a Scout activity. Should be back at 6:30 p.m. tonight." The date and time on a note can be invaluable in determining the validity of the information. Was the note left before or after our last communication?

An **out-of-state contact** can be a friend or a relative. Select a dependable, easy-to-contact person with whom you can leave messages in the event of an emergency. Out-of-area calls may go through when local lines are jammed. Educate family members on the out-of-state contact and when it is appropriate to use that person. Hold a drill to see if it works as planned.

Text messages may be delivered even when voice calls are unable to go through. Texting is a great way to communicate with family members throughout the day.

Online communications can be a great tool. Emails may be a good way to leave messages for each other when Internet access is available, even only sporadically. Our children are able to send us regular emails from school-provided iPads. Social media like Facebook is an outstanding tool. Set up your social media to enable you to have access to each family member's friends. When someone is missing, social media can provide you with an army of eyes to search for your loved one and be a valuable source of information.

Corded landline phones may work even when the power is down. Voice over Internet Protocol (VoIP) lines are dependent upon power and Internet service.

Important contact numbers should be written down and posted. We fail to memorize phone numbers because they are programmed into phones and easily accessible. If a cell phone is lost or malfunctions, you will be lost without a written list of contact numbers. These numbers should be posted in the home as well as recorded on the family emergency plan. Update the numbers regularly. List phone numbers for all family members, cell phones, places of employment, schools, day care provider, family physician, pharmacy, emergency services, extended family, and close friends.

Communication devices are of little use if no one understands how to use them correctly. Let young children practice turning them on and off, and dialing every cell phone in the house. Decide on channels and privacy codes for family band radios. Record that information on the family plan for easy reference. Always practice using those settings. Amateur radio is a great family hobby in addition to being a valuable skill. Clearly mark local emergency stations on portable radios so every member will know where to listen for public warnings. NOAA radios are helpful for receiving emergency weather alerts. Refer to chapter 6 for details on communication devices. Decide which communication devices will work best for your family and practice using them regularly.

Now is the time for you to create your family communication plan. Complete the worksheet located at www.theprovidentprepper.org /the-practical-prepper/action-plan-family-emergency-plan.

VITAL DOCUMENTS

Have you ever considered the possibility that you may have to prove your home actually existed in order to file an insurance claim? One of the take-home lessons from Katrina is the importance of keeping a copy of vital documents in a secure location away from your home.

Vital documents and information should be gathered together and stored in a safe location. Make two copies of all documents. Keep one copy at home and one copy in a secure location away from your home in a bank deposit box or with a trusted friend or relative. These documents should be kept together in such a way that makes it easy to grab them and go. See chapter 22 for details on organizing your vital documents.

PREPARE LISTS

An order to evacuate is surrounded by tremendous anxiety and fear. When faced with 20 minutes to decide what to take and what to leave, anyone will find it difficult to make even the simplest of decisions. Having well-planned contingency lists will take away the need to think or decide. The list is right there, and you check off each item one at a time. This also makes it easy for someone else to help with the preparations.

Alleviate the stress by having a written, practiced evacuation plan. In an inconspicuous place, post lists of how to prepare the house and what to grab so nothing will be forgotten.

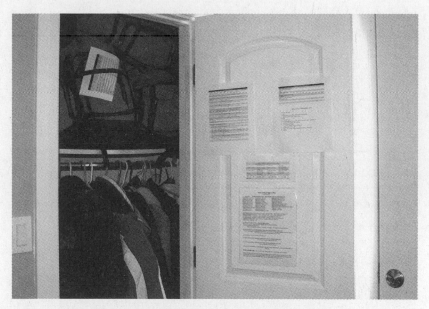

Our personal survival kits are kept inside a coat closet near the front door. A copy of our family emergency plan and other important lists are posted inside the door.

HOUSE PREP LIST

The following is an example of an evacuation house prep list. We keep ours posted on the inside of a closet door so it is readily available yet out of sight. A list like this can help you remember important items as you prepare to leave in a hurry. Items are listed with highest priority first in the event that time is limited. The most important stuff will get done first. We routinely perform similar tasks when we leave on vacation. It is good practice. Create your own list of tasks to prepare your home for speedy evacuation.

Evacuation House Prep

Task	Completed
Place all small valuables in the safe (jewelry, small electronics, computer hard drive, precious heirlooms, and so on). Take out emergency cash, firearms, and other items on a list posted inside the safe.	
Close and lock all windows. Insert security bars or locks. Close blinds and curtains.	
Secure shutters or board up windows, if needed.	
Turn off or unplug all appliances, computers, lamps, and so on, except for the refrigerator and freezer.	
Turn off, or set at minimum, heater or air conditioner.	
Put away all bikes and valuables outside the home.	
Close all interior doors (helps to contain damage if a window breaks during a storm or if a fire starts). Lock and bolt all exterior doors; secure Katy bars or door jammers, except on the door used for final exit.	
Turn on exterior security lights and one interior light.	

Task	Completed
Turn off main water into the home. Drain pipes if weather may be below freezing (to protect pipes).	
Turn off breakers for nonessential power. Turn off power at interior breaker box to everything except refrigerator, freezer, or breaker to equipment that should be kept running (possibly furnace or air conditioner), exterior lighting, and so on.	
Turn off gas—only if situation requires it.	
Leave note on the kitchen counter explaining where you have gone with contact information for reaching you.	
Fill automatic waterers and food dispensers for chickens, cats, and dog.	
Close and lock garage windows and doors, and secure garage. Block view through garage windows.	
Set burglar alarm.	
Close and lock door used for final exit.	
If any danger of flooding, add these tasks:	
Relocate furniture and valuables to a safer location in the home.	
Remove bedspreads, skirts, or comforters and place on top of beds.	
Pile all items in the basement on top of beds, dressers, tables, couches, anything to keep them off the ground.	

Task	Completed
Place furniture legs on top of canned goods (#10 cans of wheat, rice, or beans would be heavy and stable). Cover with a tarp.	
Sandbag bottom of basement door and windows. Create channels to divert water away from home, if possible.	
Place all vital documents in waterproof containers at the highest point in the home.	
Plug drains if there is any danger of sewer backflow entering the home as a result of flooding.	

MASTER LIST OF LAST-MINUTE THINGS TO GRAB

This list is a reminder of things to grab in a hurry. They are usually not kept in an actual evacuation bag but are still vitally important. You may not want to take all these items, depending on where you are going and what you expect when you get back. A good place to keep this list is the top of each survival kit. Individuals should each have their own list. Here is our family list:

- Purse and wallet

- Keys

- Prescription medication, inhaler, ibuprofen, vitamins

- Firearms, ammunition, pepper spray

- Cash

- Fresh produce

- Seasonal clothing: heavy jacket, rain slicker, winter gear, umbrella, etc.

- Important documents

- Vital documents binder

- Contact numbers, maps, etc.

- Portable safe or strongbox

- Backup for all computer files (external hard drive, flash drive)

- Laptop

- Amateur radios

LIST OF PRECIOUS ITEMS WHEN SPACE ALLOWS

Some events may allow for you to take precious items with you. If there is safety elsewhere, but if we expect our home could be destroyed when we return, this is the list of items we would include. Most "things" can be replaced; however, a few cannot. A wildfire would be a good example of a time to use this list. Yours will be different, but this may give you a place to start.

- Photo albums and scrapbooks

- Family photos from the walls

- Memorabilia boxes

- Family videos

- Computer, laptop, and external hard drive

- Business records, tax returns, box of documents

EDUCATION: PRACTICE DRILLS

Nothing will prepare you for an actual event like holding physical drills. Practice runs will help you find the flaws in your plan and increase the chance that everyone will remember what they need to do. A spur-of-the-moment overnight campout could teach a lot about the status of your readiness. Conduct drills when your family least expects it. Expect chaos when you practice. Do not get discouraged. Focus on what went right. Discuss where you might be able to improve. Make a list. The lists you have prepared in advance will be quite helpful.

Education takes place through formal practice drills as well as spontaneous discussion. Precious time used to teach the plan today may make a difference during a disaster. What if an earthquake happened right now? Where are the people you care about? Do they know what to do? Where to go? Do you know?

TRANSPORTATION

How are you going to leave if you are evacuated? Transportation is an important consideration. Do you have enough fuel to get to your destination without refueling? Make a habit of keeping your gas tank at least half full. Anytime our needle creeps below the half line, we tease each other that we are hypocrites if we do not live what we teach. This motivates us to take the time to pull over and fill up.

Keep your vehicle in good repair with regular maintenance (oil changes, filter changes, tire rotation and maintenance, tune-ups, and so on). All fluid levels should be regularly checked and filled. Keep spare parts on hand (wiper blades, oil and air filters, bulbs for headlamps and brake lights), store additional fuel in a safe place and rotate regularly, check the spare tire, keep a flat tire repair kit in the car, and keep marked road maps for your state and surrounding states in your car. Keep a freshly stocked survival kit in your vehicle as well.

This is a sample of a vehicle checklist:

Vehicle Emergency Checklist

	Ready
Gas tank full	
Marked road maps	
Copy of family plan with emergency contact info	
Maintenance up-to-date	
Roadside emergency kit (jumper cables, flashlight, light sticks, flares, gloves, tools, etc.)	
Survival kit	

	Ready
Extra oil and fluids	
Vehicle emergency kit	
Sturdy walking shoes	
Spare tire in good condition	
Jack and tire changing tools	

Alternate forms of transportation include recreational vehicles, bicycles with trailers, motorcycles, all-terrain vehicles, scooters, horses, and your feet.

EMERGENCY SHELTER OPTIONS

Shelter is critical for survival. You must have protection from the elements. Cold, wind, rain, snow, and sun can each be dangerous. Your vehicle may be a primary shelter during an evacuation. If you have to abandon your car, be sure to take something portable for shelter. Tent, tarp, heavy plastic, contractor-grade garbage bags with duct tape, hooded winter coats, and blankets could all prove helpful.

Your prearranged meeting places may provide comfort because you know where you can turn for safety. These friends or family should have supplies and the ability to accommodate your family. In return, you are prepared to accommodate them in the event of an emergency in their area.

Hotel accommodations are great if they are available. Make reservations early and be prepared to travel a long distance to find available rooms. Be careful of the area you choose to stay in. Some hotels may be more dangerous than hunkering down in your car in a safe location.

A quality tent can provide shelter in an evacuation situation. They are handy for camping outdoors as well as creating a microenvironment inside during periods of cold without power. See heating in chapter 14.

Public shelters are breeding grounds for illness. You are in close proximity with alcoholics, smokers, illegal drug users, the mentally ill, and sex offenders along with regular tired, stressed, and hungry people. Public shelters should only be used as a last resort. Your rights are checked in at the door along with your weapons and other items as required by whoever is running the shelter. They are not a safe family environment.

FAMILY EMERGENCY ACTION PLAN

Create a written family plan specifically designed to accommodate the unique needs of your family. We've prepared a simple worksheet to help you complete your plan: visit www.theprovidentprepper.org /the-practical-prepper/action-plan-family-emergency-plan.

The first step is to create a list of contact numbers. Include all contact information as well as the cell phone numbers of close friends and relatives, schools, work, day care providers, physicians, emergency services, and anyone you may need to contact in an emergency. Write them all down! You may find it easier to create an electronic version and print it out. That is fine—just do it now.

Meeting places are next. On your written family plan, record all of your meeting places including names, addresses, and contact numbers. Communication is an important part of your family plan. See chapter 6 to learn more about emergency communication. Add the specific details of your communication plan to your family plan.

The final part of this assignment specifically identifies each family member. Our family plan has contact numbers, meeting places, and communication information on the front and family information and photos on the back. The following sample is similar to what we have on the back of our family plan and might give you an idea of where to start. Protect your identity from thieves by never putting your social security number and date of birth on the same document.

Allergies (NKDA = no known drug allergies), current medications, and dates of birth (DOB), along with any information that may be important for medical personnel to know, should be included on this sheet. Our family plan has changed significantly over the years. It is important to update it annually, which can be simple if you create it in electronic format; simply edit, reprint, and laminate. We like to do it every year when school pictures come out so we have a current photo.

Papa Jones	DOB NKDA	
Mama Jones	DOB NKDA	
Child #1	DOB NKDA Hx: Asthma Albuterol PRN	
Child #2	DOB Allergic: PCN	
Child #3	DOB NKDA Allergic: Bees EPI Pen	
Child #4	DOB NKDA Food allergy: Peanuts	

Congratulations! You have just completed one of the most challenging parts of emergency preparedness. A thoughtfully prepared and practiced family plan is a huge success. You are well on your way to being prepared for the possible events of the future. Remember to make copies of your family plan. We prefer to laminate them. Put one in each survival bag, post one, keep one at work, and keep one in each vehicle along with your marked evacuation maps.

| 5 |

Survival Kits
Living out of a Backpack

"Hope for the best, prepare for the worst."[1]

—Chris Bradford

Emergency evacuation kits come bearing various names: emergency preparedness kit (EPK), disaster bag, what-if bag, GOODie bag (get-out-of-Dodge bag), GO bag (get-out bag), to-go bag, blizzard kits, emergency response kits, scramble pack, get-home bag, survival bag, BOB (bug-out bag), and 72-hour kit. These are all names for a prepared container with critical supplies for use in an emergency.

The names all describe a kit made for a similar purpose—to sustain you in the event you are required to leave your home, get stuck out in the elements, or are unable to leave your place of employment, or so you have the necessary supplies to return home on foot. To simplify life we are going to call them survival kits.

BUILDING YOUR KIT

Basic survival needs include shelter, food, water, and fuel. People have a tendency to try to cover every foreseeable need in one portable bag. That is not going to work. If you evacuate, you will not be living the comfortable life you are accustomed to. It is not like a camping trip complete with s'mores and barbecued hamburgers. This is a temporary state that will likely be highly inconvenient. Our goal with these kits is to provide the basic necessities along with a little comfort.

The length of time a kit should provide for your needs depends on the disaster. Traditionally, authorities have recommended preparing for 72 hours, at which time help should be available. Recent history demonstrates five days might be a more appropriate length of time. Review your risk scores from chapter 2. According to your individual scores, how long do you need the supplies in your survival kit to last?

The perfect survival kit is the one that takes care of you perfectly. There is not a one-size-fits-all for emergency preparedness. We will disappoint you if you are looking for a list of "stuff" to keep in your personal kit. Our hope is to provide ideas to stimulate your thought process and help you on your way to getting the right supplies for the right container in order to create the right kit for you.

The best way to determine if your kit will work well is to evacuate at a moment's notice and live off your supplies for a few days. You will quickly learn what supplies are important and what supplies are not. These questions may help determine if the kit you have created is adequate:

- Is the kit lightweight and easily carried by the owner for long distances?

- Does it meet the unique needs of the individual?

- Does it contain protection for a disaster in any kind of weather?

- Did I pack luxury items?

- Does it contain supplies to collect and disinfect water?

- Does it contain a written meal plan to ration supplies?

- Is the kit properly labeled with name, address, and contact information?

- Does it contain a spare house key and vehicle key?

- Will the container hold up against stress and abuse?

Store your kits where it makes the most sense. A personal survival kit should be near one of the exits to your home such as in the front hall closet, in a mud room, or on hooks in the garage. You might not have time to hunt for it in the basement in a real emergency. Some kits should be stored in the trunk of the car or under your desk at work.

Survival kits contain expensive items, including cash, and are a target for thieves. Take precautions to disguise and protect them.

CONTAINERS

Containers for your evacuation kits are limited only by your need and imagination. They can cost a few dollars or several hundred. If money is tight, explore your local secondhand store and purchase a previously owned container. Use last year's school backpacks for the kids' kits. Worn packs likely look less appealing as targets for would-be thieves. No one would suspect a Barbie backpack to contain valuable firearms or cash.

A high-quality, properly fitted internal frame backpack is a great option for a strong, healthy individual. Buy quality to ensure it will work when you need it. Good packs range in price from $100–$350. These are not a one-size-fits-all bag. Packs must be fitted specifically to the individual in order provide the best comfort over long hikes.

Züca sports bags are an excellent but pricey choice for the average person, an elderly individual, or someone with physical limitations. They are wheeled bags with a light, strong aluminum frame and oversized wheels that have the ability to climb stairs. The frame has a built-in seat, which can be of great benefit for rest as needed. Züca bags range in price from $150–$350. See them at zuca.com. Waterproof covers are available to protect the bag from the elements.

Rolling backpacks with padded shoulder straps are a good option. Look for one with external pockets to allow for greater organization and quick access to supplies. Rolling suitcases or duffel bags made with high-quality materials will also work. A cheap rolling pack would be a big mistake if it fails when you need it most.

Plastic buckets with a gamma seal lid are a convenient waterproof container that can also double as a seat and, if necessary, a toilet. This is a great option if you have transportation—carrying the bucket for long distances would be difficult. We used this method to store our emergency vehicle kit in the back of our van to keep it from getting squished by everything that routinely gets stuffed into the back of a minivan.

Plastic Rubbermaid-type totes can work but significantly limit mobility. These are great for storing supplies in as long as you have transportation. They work fine for storing emergency supplies in a car's trunk, but if you have to start walking, taking it with you would be difficult.

Fanny packs may hold enough supplies to supplement a larger family kit and can be worn by most individuals. These are great for keeping personal supplies close without weighing a lot.

Prepackaged survival kits should be carefully reviewed before purchasing. They can give you a false sense of security. Often quality has been sacrificed to meet consumer demand of a low price. However, there are good ones out there. Thoughtfully tailor the kit to meet your personal needs. Make sure you understand exactly what is in the kit and how to use it.

BASIC SURVIVAL KIT NEEDS

What should you put in your bag or container? Remembering basic survival needs is critical when building an emergency kit: shelter, water, food, and fuel. In evaluating realistic needs, we came up with the nine categories described below. Do not try to pack all of the items listed in each category into a survival kit. They are listed simply to promote your thought process and help with deciding what to pack for each individual and situation.

Hydration

Adequate hydration is at the top of the list. You can only survive for three days without water in the best of situations. Symptoms of dehydration can inhibit brain function, the ability to make decisions, and physical abilities within a very short period of time. Drinking contaminated water can result in illness and death. Water bottles, juice, water filters, and water disinfection supplies (see chapter 8) are important. Remember that alcohol and caffeinated beverages will not hydrate the body.

Maintain Body Temperature, Shelter

You can only survive three hours without adequate shelter in harsh conditions. You must plan to maintain appropriate body temperature. Hypothermia or heat stroke are medical emergencies and can quickly lead to death. Proper clothing is the first line of defense for hot and cold extremes. Pack for local weather conditions. Select fabrics that wick moisture away from your body and dry quickly—wool, wool blends, fleece, nylon, and polyester are ideal. Try to avoid cotton, unless you are packing for hot weather. Select durable, nonrestrictive, loose-fitting clothing.

Consider what you might need to protect yourself from the elements, heat, wet, or cold: coat, jacket, winter hat, gloves, long sleeve light shirt (protection from sun), brimmed hat, Mylar blanket, wool blanket, tent, tarp, fire starting kit, or anything that could protect you from the elements and help maintain appropriate body temperature.

Mobility

Evacuation will require a high level of mobility. Prepare and maintain your vehicle for times when evacuation by car is possible. Consider what items you have that would enable you to be more mobile: bicycles, bicycle trailers, scooter, stroller, wagon, wheelbarrow, hand truck, wheelchair, deer cart, or anything else with wheels. Some items, such as an electric wheelchair, may be great until the battery runs out, leaving you stranded. Comfortable walking shoes and extra socks are critical.

Sanitation

Poor sanitation kills. Plan for a way to prevent the spread of germs and responsibly take care of personal sanitation. Review chapter 9 for expedient toilet ideas. Toilet paper, wet wipes, tissues, disinfecting wipes, hand sanitizer, toothbrushes, toothpaste, feminine supplies, Depends, diapers, soap, shampoo, combs, brushes, hair ties, fingernail clippers, deodorant, washcloths, and towels are just a few ideas. A well-stocked first-aid kit is a must.

Food

Stock nonperishable, high-calorie, high-protein foods that require little or no preparation. A sudden change in diet is sure to cause stomach problems at inconvenient times. Try to stick with foods you are accustomed to, or experiment with the items you pack so you know how your body will react.

Meals ready-to-eat (MREs) can be eaten cold or warmed using an MRE heater. However, they tend to be constipating. Dehydrated or freeze-dried meals are lightweight and require little preparation other than boiling water. Make sure to plan additional water for these meals. Many can be prepared in the original packaging. Granola bars,

Clif bars, energy bars, trail mix, Ramen noodles, dried fruit, instant breakfast mix, oatmeal packets, cold cereal, cocoa packets, jerky, Gatorade mix, peanut butter, tuna packs, and hard candy are examples of lightweight options. Canned soups, beans, pasta, fruit, and stews are heavier but can be eaten out of the can without heating. Remember a can opener.

Carefully plan cooking pans and fuel needs according to the type of foods you have selected. Can you have an open fire at your destination? It is possible to avoid the need to cook altogether.

Communication

You need to be able to receive direction from local authorities and understand what is going on in the outside world, and you need to be able to communicate with loved ones. A written list of contact numbers is critical. See chapter 6 on communication for ideas. Portable battery, solar, or manually powered radio; pen; paper; whistle; signaling mirror; amateur radio equipment; walkie-talkie; alternative energy cell phone chargers; solar-powered battery chargers; or any other form of communication device may be helpful.

Vision

You will never understand how important light is until you are without it. Review chapter 13 for possible light sources. Store batteries separately from flashlights. Light sticks are a great choice for children. Jonathan prefers a headlamp to leave his hands free.

If you wear glasses or contacts, put an extra pair (and contact supplies, if needed) in your kit. You can purchase an inexpensive pair of prescription glasses from an online store. Sunglasses can be helpful if you have to be outside for an extended period of time. Consider a lanyard to keep glasses from getting lost.

Sleep

What do you need to be able to sleep? Quality sleep keeps your brain clear and enables you to make decisions. Blanket, sleeping bag, pillow, ground pad, tent, hammock, mosquito net, pajamas, robe, sleeping pills, or Teddy bear are ideas of things you may want to consider.

Comfort

Luxury items are out, but providing comfort during a time of crisis is important. Kylene gets that through her Snickers bars. A special stuffed animal, blanket, chocolate, Diet Coke, scriptures, pictures, and Nintendo DS are examples of items that provide comfort for different individuals.

Personal "Good Enough" Survival Kit

One of Kylene's favorite sayings is "good enough is perfect." We usually cannot do everything perfectly, and that is reflected in our survival kits. We do the best we can with the resources we have. If we waited to buy the perfect pack and ideal contents, we would not have anything when we needed to get out of Dodge quickly.

Kylene's pack is inexpensive and will not survive any lengthy event. It is much too heavy to transport by foot. Resources are limited and there are many needs. With every rotation, the survival kit gets a little better. The Snickers bars provide her with great incentive to rotate the kits regularly. Our goal is to check our kits every 6 months and replace perishable supplies with fresh ones.

Make a master list of all items in each kit. Attach this list to the top of the kit with an expiration date, or date last rotated, next to each item. The size of clothing is more important for fast-growing children but may also be helpful for adults who eat too many Snickers. This is an example of one of our kits:

Kylene's Survival Kit Master List

Item	Expiration Date, Size, Notes	Rotated, New Date, Size	Rotated, New Date, Size
Long-sleeve cotton shirt, T-shirt	Large		
Jeans, sweat pants	8		
Underclothing, wool socks, regular socks	NA	—	—

Item	Expiration Date, Size, Notes	Rotated, New Date, Size	Rotated, New Date, Size
Hair brush, hair ties, clips	NA	—	—
Washcloth, soap, shampoo, deodorant	NA	—	—
Toothbrush, toothpaste, floss, dental picks	2016		
Toilet paper, tampons, pads	NA	—	—
Portable radio—solar and manual powered	Check		
Flashlight, batteries	2018		
Flashlight—solar and manual powered	Check		
Pepper spray	2016		
Leatherman Multi-Tool	NA	—	—
Reading glasses, case, lanyard	+1.50		
Sunglasses	NA	—	—
Work gloves	Medium		
Keys—vehicles, house, and bug out location	Check	—	—
Cash	NA	—	—
Parachute cord	NA	—	—
Laminated family plan	2014		
Marked maps	2014		
Duct tape wrapped around pens	2018		
Pad of paper	NA	—	—
Scriptures	NA	—	—
6 Snickers bars	2014		

Item	Expiration Date, Size, Notes	Rotated, New Date, Size	Rotated, New Date, Size
6 Clif bars	2014		
Almonds, raw sunflower seeds, dried fruit	2015		
3 cans of ready-to-serve soup (pop top)	2016		
Hard candy	2015		
5 MRE entrées	2018		
2 dehydrated entrées	2018		
3 single-serving juice bottles	2016		
Water bottle filter	NA	—	—
Bottled water	2016		
Pocket stove with fuel tablets	NA	—	—
Fire starters	NA	—	—
Metal cup and utensils	NA	—	—
First-aid kit with medications	2016		
Bandanas	NA	—	—

Last-Minute Items List

Make a list of last-minute items to grab. Some items are needed on a daily basis. Make sure to include them on a list of "things to grab at the last second," and attach the list to each kit. What would you need to grab? What items would you need to take if your home might be destroyed, such as evacuation for wildfires or flooding?

Every scenario is different. Evacuating in a vehicle is different than having to leave on foot. If the vehicle were to be abandoned along the way, is it best to have highly valuable items in it? Take only the items the situation may require.

Kylene's Survival Kit: Last-Minute Items
(Depending on Weather, Transportation, and Destination)

Purse	Firearm and ammo	Winter coat	Fresh foods (bread, fruit, etc.)
Ibuprofen, Benadryl	Cell phone, charger, inverter	Poncho, umbrella	Filled Water-Bricks, cases of bottled water
Prescription meds and vitamins	Amateur radio, equipment bag	Hiking boots, walking shoes, boots	Water filter
Large first-aid kit	Copies of vital documents	Hat, gloves	Canned heat
Books, reading material	Laptop, external hard drive, CPU	Tent, sleeping bags, pillows, solar lanterns	EcoQue portable grill (Pyramid)

Workplace Survival Kit

When you consider how many hours you spend at your place of employment, it makes sense to have important supplies ready. You may need to get creative depending on your personal situation. Having a stash of supplies in your private office is much easier than it is on a construction site or if you are waiting tables at a restaurant. Do the best you can with what you have.

Critically evaluate what you would do in various scenarios. Review your risk scores for areas of focus. How far away do you work from home? Would your employment require you to stay on the job until after the disaster has resolved? Would it be safer to hunker down at work for several days or to try to make it home? How will you communicate with your family?

Jonathan takes public transportation for a 30-mile commute each day. He carries a backpack with him that contains a headlamp, cell phone charger, inverter, work gloves, Leatherman, windbreaker, snacks, water, and other supplies that would be highly useful in the event of an emergency. They are lightweight and take up very little room. He always wears walking shoes or work boots so he does not need to carry an extra pair of shoes.

He has a private office at work, which makes it quite convenient for him to store bottled water, canned foods, snacks, a change of clothing, a personal hygiene kit, a blanket, and a warm coat. Food would be eaten cold out of the container if the power went out. He keeps a bicycle there so he can ride home if other transportation is unavailable.

Take time to carefully look at your place of employment. Does your employer have a plan in place? What are your responsibilities? How can you prepare to survive if you are stranded at work for an extended period of time?

Vehicle Emergency Kit

Most people spend half of their lives away from home. Statistically this means it is highly likely that you might be away from home when disaster strikes. It makes sense to keep an emergency kit in each vehicle. Due to significant temperature fluctuations inside of vehicles, rotating supplies each season is critical.

We have great intentions, which do not always reflect our reality. We had packed a great emergency kit into a bucket with a gamma seal lid and kept it in the back of our van. After two years, we finally got around to changing it. The water bottles had frozen and leaked, ruining the contents of our kit. Flashlights were rusted, flares destroyed, food spoiled, and emergency equipment unusable. Had we needed those supplies, we would have been sorely disappointed.

Consider the ages, number, and physical abilities of all regular passengers in the vehicle. Prepare a kit with items you feel may be valuable. Always carry bottles of water. It might be easier to have 2 kits—one for personal needs and another for the vehicle.

A vehicle kit includes items for the vehicle: sturdy work gloves, road flare, jumper cables, rags, flashlight, folding shovel, tow rope, windshield scraper and brush, basic tool kit, duct tape or electrical tape, Fix-a-Flat, fire extinguisher, and marked maps.

A personal vehicle kit may include sanitation items, hand sanitizer, washcloths, toothbrushes, toothpaste, dental floss, plastic tablecloth, garbage bags, baby wipes, soap, Clorox wipes, tissues, blanket, sturdy walking shoes, socks, rain poncho, winter hats and gloves, first-aid kit, hand and foot warmers, nonperishable foods, and drinks.

We keep this kit in the back of our vehicle.

Emergency Tool Kit

Tools can make a definite difference in survival situations. Some basic tools include a solid knife, a Leatherman Multi-Tool, screwdrivers (flat and Phillips), a claw hammer, lineman's pliers (to cut through wire or nails), utility knife with extra blades, wood saw, hacksaw, crescent wrenches (large and small), axe, and other common tools for vehicle and bicycle repair.

School Survival Kit

Many schools have begun to keep individual class emergency kits. Each student brings a quart ziplock bag of emergency supplies to be kept in the classroom's wheeled tote. The kit is also stocked with water bottles and a first-aid kit.

This kit is only intended to last a few hours until children can be returned home. If your school does not participate in such a program, consider keeping a small kit in your child's backpack.

The purpose of this kit is mostly for emotional support and comfort. In our children's ziplock bags, we include a family picture with all contact information written clearly on the back of the photo. On other family photos we write notes of encouragement and love. Other items include a tiny flashlight, whistle, light stick, dice, playing cards, pen, notebook, small candies, and a granola bar. At the end of each year, the child gets to eat the treats. We add a current family photo, update contact information, change the battery, and use the supplies again next year.

Small comfort items can be packed into a quart ziplock bag for a survival kit at school.

Pet Survival Kit

Determine how to best care for each of your animals. The decision to take or leave a pet should be made well in advance of a crisis. Can they be moved to a safer location? A realistic plan should be made to care for the pet and provide food and water for an extended period of time. Invest in large automatic waterers and feeders if you choose to leave your pet. Practice using them to make sure they work as intended. Remember, pets are not allowed in public shelters.

Pets should be licensed and wear identification tags. Specially designed backpacks or saddle bags are available in sizes to fit most dogs. This will allow the animal to carry some of their own supplies. Consider packing food, water, sanitation supplies, a lightweight water and food dish, leash, muzzle, kitty litter, litter box, copy of immunization records, pet crate or carrier, and a photo for identification purposes.

Young Child Comfort Kit

Under the head of each child's bed we have prepared a small backpack of comfort supplies. This is intended to be used in addition to their survival kit. It is lightweight and can be easily carried by the child. We teach them to grab it if there is a fire or other disaster. It is filled with special fun items and is intended to give them a sense of security, not provide for survival. We let the child include a favorite toy, book, colored pencils and paper, a small game, fruit snacks, juice boxes, comfortable clothes, or whatever they want. They understand that its purpose is to make them feel better when tough times are happening.

We keep a comfort kit under the head of each child's bed. This kit is designed to provide comfort and security, not survival.

Infant Survival Kit

Our daughter and her husband purchased a minivan shortly after the arrival of their first child. We were quite surprised at her choice of vehicles. She had tortured us for years over our "totally uncool" minivan. When we questioned her change of heart, she admitted that babies need so much stuff there was no way to fit it all in a car. Newsflash: babies can survive with a very few basic necessities. All those cool accessories are not necessary for survival, so infants can take up little space. Their needs are similar to ours—food, water, shelter, and sanitation. Do not get carried away with luxury items.

Infants are highly sensitive to the environment and can dehydrate quickly. We recommend a supply of infant formula, even for nursing babies in the event the milk supply is disrupted or the infant gets separated from its mother. Basic needs include water, baby formula, bottle, pacifiers, age-appropriate foods, disposable diapers, baby wipes, comfortable and seasonally appropriate clothing, baby sling or carrier, blankets, and trash bags to dispose of diapers. The list may be expanded to include cloth diapers, waterproof pants, diaper pins, diaper rash ointment, portable baby bed, infant pain relievers, teething gel, thermometer, sunblock, gas relief drops, baby shampoo, hand sanitizer, bucket for dirty diapers, and laundry soap. Stick to the basics and do not overwhelm yourself with "stuff."

Wilderness Survival Kit

You will need a special kit if you drive long distances where you may become stranded or intend to survive in the wilderness. This can be dangerous if you do not have the skills and training to survive in the open. Most city folks who camp just a couple times a year may find real survival quite challenging.

If you think you may need to survive in the wilderness, you will need special tools and supplies. In addition to your personal kit, consider packing rain gear, hiking boots, appropriate clothing, a sturdy lightweight tent, sleeping mats, a survival knife, a compact cook stove with fuel, sturdy cooking pans and utensils, sleeping bags, compact fishing gear, firearms with ammunition, bug netting, bug repellent, tarp, Paracord, small shovel, water filters, an edible plant identification manual, a fire kit, toiletries, heavy-duty trash bags, food, and water.

Family Survival Kit

A family survival kit is designed to contain shared resources for a family. Each family member has their own kit with personal items and snacks while the family kit contains items such as cooking supplies (pots, mixing bowls, cooking utensils), paper towels, tools, sanitation supplies, laundry needs, a clothesline, an expedient toilet, a shower, a large first-aid kit with medications, the majority of the food, a table-cloth, a water filter, and other resources that could be easily shared. This kit will be bulky and heavy. Plan accordingly for transportation.

FIRE KIT

Fire has the power to heat, cook, purify water, provide safety, and provide comfort. Whether or not you have the option of building a fire depends greatly on the situation. Starting a fire in wet conditions can be challenging. Practice your fire-building skills. Start with a sturdy waterproof container and fill it with your favorite fire-starting tools. Here are a few ideas: fire steel and scraper, lighter, butane stick lighter, waterproof matches, storm proof matches, Instafire, cotton balls, petroleum jelly, dryer lint, small candle, gel fuel, Esbit fuel tablets, and a 9-volt battery and very fine steel wool.

First-Aid Kit

First-aid kits vary greatly in size and content. Each individual should have small kits containing assorted bandages and wound cleaners in their personal survival kit. Larger first-aid kits should be designed to accommodate more people and a larger variety of wounds and ailments. We like to keep our first-aid kit in a fishing tackle box. The kit is highly portable and water resistant, and everything is conveniently organized inside. Small kits can be kept in a ziplock bag or small plastic bait organizers with great success.

Every first-aid kit is unique to its owner. You must understand how to appropriately use the items you keep in your kit. Items to consider include a first-aid manual, triangular bandages, roller bandages, sterile gauze dressings, sanitary pads, Band-Aids (variety of sizes, shapes, and children's characters), a suture kit, Steri-Strips, butterfly dressings, moleskin, eye patch bandages, alcohol wipes, iodine wipes, antiseptic cleansing wipes, baking soda, salt, calamine lotion, Benadryl lotion, hydrocortisone ointment or cream, ammonia inhalants, activated charcoal syrup (for poisoning), cotton balls, Q-tips, scissors, sunscreen, a knife, razor blades, antibiotic ointment, tweezers, a thermometer, hydrogen peroxide, alcohol, a flashlight, liquid soap, waterproof matches, needles, petroleum jelly, safety pins, a bulb syringe, eyewash, face masks, super glue, chemical cold packs and heat pads, a constriction band, duct tape, a notebook, a pencil, and lollipops to make little patients feel better.

Medications to consider are pain relievers (liquid and tablet form), antihistamines (liquid and tablet form), diarrhea remedy, antacid tablets, constipation remedy, and, when possible, an EpiPen for severe allergic reactions.

EXAMPLES OF INDIVIDUAL SURVIVAL KITS

We have included a few examples of what some people created for their own survival kits. These are real people, but we changed the names to protect the innocent (or the guilty).

Darla's Bug-Out Bag

Darla is a sixty-year-old single woman with years of military and survival training. The contents of her bags are unique to her. Her plan is to wear sturdy boots, a hat, and old work clothes so that she will not stand out. The outfit makes her gender difficult to distinguish, until you get close, which adds another layer of protection. Her goal is to appear impoverished so she will not be a target for would-be thieves. She plans to load the clip into her Smith & Wesson and tuck it into a concealed holster under her shirt, making sure she has extra ammunition in her pack. A knife and multi-tool is slid into her pocket. Survival items are strategically placed in various pockets for quick access.

Her pack is worn but sturdy, with many pockets. Attached to the outside on a loop is a knife sharpener and flint-and-steel fire starter. Inside the pack she has plastic bags (to place between her socks and shoes to keep her feet dry), fire starters (matches, butane lighter, magnifying glass, cotton balls, and petroleum jelly), fire sticks, parachute rope, military-issue canteen and cookware, slingshot with marbles, poncho, water filter bottle, headlamp with replacement batteries, N95 mask, one-piece knife, bandana, first-aid kit, leather work gloves, toilet paper, and copies of important documents. She refers to her packed clothing as a component system, which can be layered and has multiple uses. The cash she carries is separated and strategically placed, so if she is robbed she will not lose it all. Her food is a variety of lightweight high-calorie items, including instant breakfast drink mixes, ramen noodles, dehydrated foods, trail mix, Fritos (which, she points out, are also an excellent fire starter), and energy bars.

She keeps a "get-home pack" in the trunk of her car, which includes a cheap sleeping bag, sturdy leather work gloves, a wool blanket, a set of old work clothes, a hat, a coat, worn a sturdy boots, a headlamp, a SODIS bottle (see chapter 8), dehydrated foods, and bottled water.

Darla's specialized training enables her to survive on her own for a long period of time with few supplies. She is highly confident in her self-defense skills and exhibits a great deal of expertise with her chosen weapon. Yet with all those skills, her tactical advantage comes from avoiding conflict—carefully choosing to appear to have nothing of value, staying away from dangerous areas, and understanding that any injury could be life threatening during a crisis situation. Darla has a plan with a network of places to go and friends who are prepared to take her in at a moment's notice.

Cranston Snord's Survival Kit Solution

Cranston is a highly prepared, married empty nester who has a little attitude when it comes to his survival kit. He wants to know what it is he is preparing for. In many situations, a 72-hour kit is not going to meet the need. He carries a kit in his wallet, which will take care of 90 percent of his problems. It is a credit card. If he has to leave home quickly, due to a train or truck accident that causes a chemical spill, he would go to a local motel, eat at a restaurant, and send the bill to the negligent company. He also has family and friends who would take him in at a moment's notice.

He admits he might look at things differently if he lived in hurricane country or in a wildfire hazard area. He lives in earthquake country and refuses to leave his home. Even if the home is damaged and unable to be occupied, he plans on living in a tent in his own yard. If he is anywhere else, it is all about getting home.

He does carry a "get-home bag" in the trunk of his car. He has a 30-mile commute through a densely populated area that is subject to extreme weather. His kit includes a change of clothes, hygiene items, food, water, water purification supplies, and cash. He wants to travel light and get home fast. He can deal with hunger but is concerned about water and weather.

Quite frankly, he thinks 72-hour kits are overdone and pushed too much. He plans to shelter-in-place or get home as soon as possible after an event. However, he has a standard 72-hour kit prepared from a list he found in some book just in case.

David's Survival Plan

David is an avid fisherman and hunter. He lives in a metropolitan area in Oregon where he spends much of his free time in the surrounding mountains. If anything happens in the city, he is off to the high country to stay. He is well accustomed to the survival lifestyle and requires very little from the outside world to be happy—except maybe for them to leave him alone and let him fish.

He has a tough old truck, which he keeps stocked for spur-of-the-moment adventures. That truck is his shelter and home away from home. His list includes an extra can of fuel, assortment of firearms, ammunition, knives, fishing gear, camping gear, fly-tying kit, cooking paraphernalia, fire-starter kit, hygiene items, shovel, tools, hatchet, food, sleeping bag, water, and first-aid supplies. He is not concerned about communication.

David thinks a big city disaster would be pretty close to winning the lottery. He would be on vacation while the rest of the world cries and whines about the power being out.

Bob's Not-So-Smart Plan

Bob's plan is typical of his lifestyle. He has no intention of storing a year's supply of food, but he openly admits to having a year's supply of beer. When things get bad, he will just start popping the tops off and pretty soon he won't care. What do you say to that? At least he had a plan? When tough stuff happens, we should expect to see a wide variety of preparedness levels and coping techniques. Bob does not have a survival kit outside of beer. He will be part of the problem.

Molly Mama's Survival Kit

Molly is a young mother with three children under the age of five. Her husband commutes to work and is frequently out of town on business. She is terrified at the thought of having to evacuate with three tiny, energetic children all by herself. Being a dutiful mother, she has planned and executed that plan well.

The two older preschoolers each have a little backpack with a built-in leash attached. They are packed with hand sanitizer, fruit snacks, Goldfish crackers, boxed juices, a change of clothing, Pull-Ups, and coloring items. She keeps an extra diaper bag ready to go at all times for the baby. Molly has a double stroller to push the preschoolers and a front pack to carry the baby if they have to go by foot. She has an emergency kit in her car in the event she gets stranded somewhere as well as 72-hour kits for each family member.

One bonus in Molly's survival kit is an elderly widowed neighbor, Mildred. She has developed a relationship with Mildred, and they serve each other. Together they have come up with a plan that benefits both of them. If anything happens, Molly will pick up Mildred and take her. Mildred can help with the children and has someone to get her to safety. Molly is no longer alone. Both benefit from this relationship.

SURVIVAL KIT ACTION PLAN

We can learn a great deal from these examples. What do you need in a survival kit? What kind of kits do you need? Where is the best place to store it? Your assignment is to create a survival kit for each member of your family (including pets), for each vehicle, and for your place of employment. Personalize each kit with the user's needs in mind. Decide what "stuff" you really need, and do not overpack! Detailed worksheets are available at www.theprovidentprepper.org/the-practical-prepper /action-plan-survival-kits.

| 6 |

Communication
Now We're Talking

"The way we communicate with others and with ourselves ultimately determines the quality of our lives."

—Anthony Robbins

We take fast, reliable communication for granted. A small device carried in a pocket can enable you to communicate with almost anyone anywhere. We expect to be able reach someone instantly. Have you ever been frustrated when coverage was limited? Imagine how frustrating it might be to experience a sudden disruption and be unable to reach a family member to call for emergency assistance. It could be terrifying, but it does not have to be that way. A little advanced planning and practice can help maintain vital communication in many scenarios when convenient cell phone coverage is unavailable.

Review your family communication plan from chapter 4. In this chapter we will discuss the details of communication to increase the chances you will be able to send and receive information in a disaster situation. We will review basic communication devices and explore the benefits and limitations of each one. Keep in mind scenarios in which you need to communicate and which tools or methods might enable you to achieve the desired outcome. Consider your needs, budget, and desired level of expertise as you decide which options to use.

Implement redundancy into your plan. Telecommunications can be amazingly fragile. Plan for systems to fail and have a backup plan for your backup plan. Do not limit your planning to devices alone.

Communication may use words, signs, sounds or behaviors to relay or exchange information, thoughts, ideas, or feelings to someone. Do not underestimate the power of leaving a note.

WRITTEN CONTACT INFORMATION

Have you ever lost a cell phone filled with all your contact numbers? Needed to call a close friend or family member and not known their number because it is stored in your speed dial? Start by composing a list of important phone numbers. Include all of them, even ones you think you would never forget. High anxiety situations can result in slow cognitive functioning and make you unable to recall a frequently used number.

Post this list near your phone. We prefer to post it on the inside of a cupboard door where it is easily accessible but does not add clutter. Make copies for each emergency kit, place of employment, and vehicle. Update this list annually, or more frequently if numbers change. Help children memorize the most important numbers along with vital information, such as your street address. It may be a good idea to have them carry a list in their backpack until they have successfully memorized them.

ONE-WAY COMMUNICATION: INFORMATION GATHERING

Access to emergency information from local authorities is critical. This could include the monitoring of the progress of a storm, a wildfire, or any other hazard that has the potential to cause harm. Timely information can help you take steps to avoid dangerous situations. This information can be found on local television stations, radio stations, and on the Internet.

In an emergency, local, state, or national authorities will communicate important information over the Emergency Alert System (EAS). What stations should you turn to in your area for emergency information? To find out, go to www.nws.noaa.gov/nwr/listcov.htm and search for EAS stations in your area. Include any areas you visit frequently because of commute or travel. Place a label on your emergency radio so everyone knows exactly which channel to tune into during an emergency.

Local EAS Stations

Call Sign	Frequency	Coverage Area

AM/FM Radio

AM/FM radios are a great way to gather information in a crisis and may work even when television and Internet services have been interrupted. Emergency solar-powered, hand-crank, and battery-powered radios work well. Cheap radios are only going to cause frustration. You do not need top of the line, but buy something that works well. Store batteries separately from the radio. A car radio can be used to gather information as well.

NOAA Weather Radio All Hazards (NWR)

NWR broadcasts weather forecasts, warnings, watches, hazard information and other official communications around the clock. It broadcasts post-event information for all types of hazards: natural or man-made disasters, public safety (AMBER) alerts, and environmental catastrophes (chemical releases or oil spills).

Look for NOAA radio models with the Specific Area Message Encoding (SAME) feature, which allows you to program your radio to turn on and wake you up for events only in a specific area (see www.nws.noaa.gov/nwr/nwrsame.htm). This is an incredibly valuable feature to have.

Shortwave Radio

A shortwave radio is a receiver that receives broadcast transmissions from shortwave radio stations. It can monitor transmissions between 3 and 30 megahertz. The radio waves are reflected back from the ionosphere, which provides communication around the curve of the Earth, allowing for worldwide transmissions. Shortwave radios can also monitor some amateur (ham) radio transmissions and keep up on emergency information. Reception is limited by the size and type of antenna.

The benefit of having a shortwave radio is the unique ability to hear communications from areas that might not have been affected by the disaster. Reports from other parts of the world may provide valuable insight on the current situation. It is a good tool for monitoring local emergency channels as well.

Internet

The Internet is a valuable tool for finding emergency information. A satellite service provider may allow you to communicate through many disasters—if your system remains intact. Refer to reputable news and government sites for official instructions. However, do not underestimate the valuable information available on social media. Twitter, Facebook, Google+, and other forms of social media provide some of the best emergency updates with real-time photos and comments posted from phones or mobile devices. Learning what is happening in your neighborhood, connecting with missing family members, or gathering crucial information is possible with these sources. Take time to connect now.

In an emergency situation, you might be able to drive through a residential area and access an unsecured wireless network to send or post valuable information or pictures from a laptop or phone. Driving around a neighborhood to access an unsecured wireless network is called wardriving. If you leave your network unsecured, someone could use your IP address for illegal activities. While an unsecured Wi-Fi network may be helpful in an emergency situation, we recommend securing your own Wi-Fi network with a password.

TWO-WAY COMMUNICATION

Establishing two-way contact with others can be critical in a disaster. These methods of communication allow us to both send and receive information. Let us review the most common forms.

Phones

Landlines, hardlines, plain old telephone service (POTS) are found in many homes and businesses. These phone lines are powered by the phone company and may continue to operate during a power outage. Most cordless phone sets will not work unless they are on a backup power supply, like the commercially available UPS devices used for computers. If your cordless phone has a handset on the base unit, try unplugging the power supply and using the handset—it may or may not work depending on the model. Discovering this before the power goes out is a good idea.

Local calls will tie up two lines. One is taken to send the call and another to receive it. In a large disaster, outbound (out of the disaster area) calls are more likely to go through. Long-distance calls access the fiber optic network and have the ability to handle a much larger volume of calls. It might be possible to call out of state when you are unable to call your next door neighbor. Avoid making nonessential calls during an emergency to free up lines for emergency calls; if service is overloaded, the entire system may shut down automatically.

Cell phones may work during a power outage, as long as towers are operating. An event in another area may disrupt your service by taking out a tower in that area and placing a greater demand on remaining towers. Cell phone availability will depend greatly on the individual event. It is a fantastic tool when you can use it.

As with landlines, cell towers have a limited capacity. A high concentration of cell phone usage may cause one tower to become overloaded and shut down. Text messages may go through when voice calls cannot—they use fewer cellular carrier resources and conserve precious battery power. Do not tie up lines with unimportant chatter during an emergency. Keep conversations short and to the point.

Cell phones only work if the battery is charged. If the power is out, you will need alternate ways to charge your cell phone. A car charger is a great short-term option. Wind-up and solar chargers are another. Power inverters, which can be used in vehicles, are an inexpensive way to charge a phone as well as other devices.

Add an in-case-of-emergency (ICE) contact in each phone. Emergency personnel can use this as an emergency contact if a person is unable to provide information. This simple step may help you reunite with your loved ones.

Satellite phones are ideal for disaster communication, offering voice service, short messaging service, and Internet access. They use orbiting satellites, completely bypassing any damaged equipment and systems resulting from a disaster. They are cost prohibitive for many. An emergency-only calling plan can be $25–$30 a month and $1.50+ per minute, in addition to purchasing a phone. A 200-minute plan can cost around $100 a month.

Voice over Internet Protocol (VoIP) is a technology that allows you to talk over an Internet connection. FaceTime, Skype, magicJack, and Vonage are examples of these services. Some provide video as well as voice services. VoIP allows calls anywhere you have a high-speed Internet connection. Slow connections result in distorted and choppy calls.

Two-Way Radios

Two-way radios allow information to be sent as well as received. They are highly valuable for communicating over short distances as well as relaying information long distance, even across the world with the proper equipment. Information is available for the listening, so talk as if anyone in the world could be monitoring your conversation. Each radio has different capabilities, licensing requirements, price range, and unique range of required skills to operate. These radios can enable communication when phones are not practical or are out of service.

Family Radio Service (FRS) radios are the walkie-talkie-type radios found in most big-box and sporting goods stores. They operate on the UHF band, between 462 and 467 megahertz. Some manufacturers will boast a range of 40 miles. Our experience has only provided for five miles for clear communication in open terrain; in cities or canyons, this range is shorter. Privacy codes are available to allow for more sharing of busy channels, but they do not prevent eavesdropping.

We tried sending these with our children to school but found them ineffective at only five miles due to the terrain. Kylene worked at a hospital seven miles away in direct line of site. They would not work because of a coating on hospital windows designed to prevent radio waves from interfering with medical equipment. However, they work great in Walmart, around the neighborhood, and on camping trips. Practice using them to ensure they work as you intend them to.

The only cost is the initial purchase of $20–40 per radio. No monthly service fee is required. No license is required to operate. Many have rechargeable batteries and may be charged with a wall plug using a charging dock.

General Mobile Radio Service (GMRS) radios are a handheld radio similar to FRS radios. Usually the radios found in big-box and sporting goods stores are combined GMRS/FRS radios. Eight channels in the 462 megahertz range are exclusively for GMRS use. Most transmit only one watt or less, which is not a lot of power; mobile units (if you can find one) often transmit with five watts. GMRS radios are permitted to operate at up to 50 watts and require a license to operate legally. The license is $85, and you must be 18 or older to obtain one at http://wireless.fcc.gov.

Citizen band radio (CB) utilizes a selection of 40 channels near the top of the HF band, near 27 megahertz. As with other two-way radio systems, only one station will transmit at a time. Handheld CB radios are generally less practical due to the need for a long antenna. Typical units include vehicle-mounted or base stations with an external antenna. No license is required for use. Because the frequency of CB shares the characteristics of shortwave, occasionally communications out to 60 miles are possible but should not be counted on.

Amateur radio, popularly known as ham radio, is the most versatile of all two-way radio systems available for general public use. These radios can communicate over great distances using voice, text, image, and data. A license is required to operate amateur radio equipment. The entry-level license, Technician Class, is relatively easy to pass with a little effort. This license gives transmission privileges to all amateur radio frequencies VHF 30 megahertz and above with limited access to frequencies in the HF band above 20 megahertz. This level is perfect for local emergency communication and with proper equipment can cover most of North America. Morse code is no longer required for any amateur radio licenses.

Ham radio operators are the unsung heroes of emergency communications. In our experience, ham radio operators are a wonderful group of people. They have a great desire to help others and donate many hours providing emergency and other communications. Many of them are preppers and might provide a wonderful support network. They are anxious to help beginners succeed.

The total cost for a class (often free), exam, and licensure is usually less than $20. Go to arrl.org for details about licensure and where to find radio clubs and classes in your area. As a licensed operator, you are issued a call sign and are required to abide by strict rules and procedures. A low-end radio will cost less than $100, but serious operators spend significantly more on equipment.

POWER FOR COMMUNICATION DEVICES

None of these devices will work without a power source. However, most of them require little power to actually operate. Carefully consider how you will power your equipment during an outage. There are many solar chargers on the market—just buy quality. Crank generators for manually generating power may be worth looking into. Store backup batteries if needed.

EQUIPMENT PROTECTION

Communication devices are vulnerable to the effects of an EMP and solar flares. We recommend radio equipment be stored in a way that will protect them from such effects. Due to the lower frequency of solar coronal mass ejections, simply keeping equipment unplugged will provide adequate protection. However, to protect equipment from an EMP, a Faraday cage may be necessary. We do not know exactly what will happen, or when it will happen, so take precautions. Keep equipment disconnected from grid energy sources and disconnect antennae or keep them collapsed down. Wind cords tightly. Store radios and equipment in a Faraday cage whenever possible.

A microwave (with the cord cut off) can make an acceptable Faraday cage for vital radio equipment.

A Faraday cage is a sealed enclosure with an electrically conductive external layer. Its purpose is to shield radios and other electronic equipment from EMP damage. Explore ideas online for creating Faraday cages. Anti-static bags are designed to guard electronic components against electrostatic discharge. Some perform better than others. We store our equipment in an old microwave purchased at a secondhand store. The cord is cut off to prevent the power cord from acting as an antenna. It may not be the perfect solution, but it allows for some protection and convenient access. In our busy world, that means the radios may actually get put away.

Test your Faraday cage by placing a cell phone or playing radio inside. Does the cell phone ring or the radio continue to play? If so, the equipment inside is vulnerable to EMP effects. Our secondhand microwave passed the test. The microwave in our kitchen did not. Wrapping the microwave with metal tape may help. The equipment should be protected from the conductive outer layer by wrapping in a nonconductive material (fabric, wood, foam) if necessary.

COMMUNICATION ACTION PLAN

Which communication devices will work best for your personal situation? Complete the action plan at www.theprovidentprepper.org /the-practical-prepper/action-plan-communication. Review your family plan from chapter 4 and make sure you have a good way to communicate with each family member in the event of an emergency. Then practice, practice, practice! Take the radios to Walmart, play around the neighborhood, or go up in the canyon and practice. Develop a network in your neighborhood and practice using radios on a regular basis. Set up a regular time to participate in a radio net where participants check in and listen to a brief class on a communication topic.

Learn the limitations and capabilities of your equipment. Store batteries or backup power sources to ensure you have power when you need it. Protect equipment in a Faraday cage when not in use. Have fun and relax, knowing you are ready to communicate in any emergency situation.

7

Water Storage
Got Water?

"Thousands have lived without love, not one without water."[1]

—W. H. Auden

Water is absolutely critical for survival. The very best way to ensure you have safe water to drink is to store it in your own home. We occasionally hear arguments about why this is unnecessary. True to our excuse slayer nature, we are going to slay this dangerous line of thinking.

Storing water enables you to have access to clean drinking water regardless of the time of day or outside conditions. Water is heavy, making hauling difficult. One gentleman explains that he lives next to a river and does not need to store water. If he needs water, he will just gather some and filter it as needed. Think this through with us. What if the need for water occurs in the dead of winter when the river is frozen over? What if there is a hazmat spill, causing chemical contamination? How about a nuclear event contaminating the water with radioactive particles? What if he needs to shelter in place?

Clean drinking water stored in the protective environment of your home allows you to have safe water accessible at a moment's notice. Considering the vital nature of this resource, we urge you to store as much water as you reasonably can.

BASIC REQUIREMENTS

We need water for hydration, hygiene, medical and first aid, sanitation, and food preparation. We are constantly losing water through respiration, perspiration, and normal elimination processes. That water must be replaced for our bodies to function properly. Our bodies require a minimum of one quart of water per day just to sustain life.

Expert opinions differ on the recommended amount of water people should store. FEMA recommends at least one gallon per person per day for a normally active person. Additional amounts are required for nursing mothers, children, sick people, and extra-active people. The amount doubles during hot weather. This number takes into account two quarts for drinking and two quarts for food preparation and hygiene.

Our personal recommendation is at least two gallons per person per day. We found it quite difficult to survive off two gallon of water per person. Two gallons is much more realistic. One gallon of drinking water per day is a safer estimate, particularly when considering that many disasters create an environment requiring heavy physical labor or exposure to the elements. When the need arises, if you find you can get by with less water, you will be able to stretch your supplies further. In addition to drinking, we need water for personal sanitation, washing dishes, and preparing food. If you have pets, make sure you plan for their needs also.

The next consideration is the length of time you should plan for. Revisit your risk assessment. What hazards are you preparing for? What is the longest period of time you might be without safe drinking water? Store enough water for this length of time, when possible. We recommend at least two weeks' worth of water and much more if you are able to store it practically. One 55-gallon barrel and a few cases of bottled water would meet the basic needs of one person for a month. Water is heavy (8.3 pounds per gallon) and takes up a lot of space, making storing large amounts a bit challenging.

STORING WATER

Have you ever thought about what the shelf life of water really is? Water itself is stable compound of hydrogen and oxygen. If clean treated water is stored appropriately in clean food-grade containers, not much can go wrong. It can store safely for an extended period of time.

Water can be affected by environmental conditions. Factors that play into the shelf life of water include the original quality of the water, light, temperature, and the storage container. Inspect your water supply periodically and check for changes in appearance, odor, and taste, and leakage from the container. The ideal storage environment is a food-grade container in a cool, dark area. Store away from gasoline, kerosene, paint, chemicals, and pesticides. The fumes may penetrate the container and contaminate the water.

Rotating water can be challenging. The official recommendation for water rotation is every six months to a year. This may not be practical or necessary. Think it through: if you start with a clean food-grade container and you put clean water in the container, what could possibly happen to that water? The plastic could leach into the water. Contaminates may have been introduced during the filling process from the environment and have the potential to grow bugs. Algae may grow in transparent containers exposed to light. In the real world, even the best preppers are going to find it a challenge to keep water rotated frequently. Make it a practice to check containers periodically. If the water has changed in appearance or smell, rotate it. If you do not rotate it regularly, be prepared to filter it.

Avoid introducing contaminants when you fill your water containers. We recommend using a potable water hose (generally used for filling recreational vehicles and water tanks), if you are not filling it directly from a household tap. Store with the ends of the hose connected to prevent contamination. Large containers may require a siphon or pump to access the water. Make sure to protect these tools from contamination by storing in the original packaging or wrapping in plastic. The last thing you want to worry about in a water-scarce environment is how to sterilize your water pump. Storing a bung wrench, channel lock pliers, or other appropriate tools needed to open containers is a good idea; the plugs on plastic barrels can be difficult to open without proper tools.

A 55-gallon barrel stores a lot of water in a relatively small space. It weighs over 450 pounds and is difficult to transport, particularly if you need to evacuate. We prefer to store water in a variety of containers. Our personal water storage includes 55-gallon barrels, 15-gallon barrels, 5-gallon containers, reclaimed juice and soda bottles, empty canning jars, and commercial water bottles. The diversity in our water storage makes storing large amounts of water relatively inexpensive and convenient.

If you are concerned about the taste or safety of your stored water, plan to filter it before drinking. Stored water can be easily passed through a quality filter to ensure safety and improve the taste. We will discuss good filter options in detail in the next chapter. The most important thing is to store the water. Properly stored water will always be safer than anything you can get from local water sources after a disaster.

TREATING STORED WATER

Clean food-grade containers and clean drinking water should be used for long-term water storage. You may choose to disinfect the water at the time of storage to ensure there are no microscopic bugs in the water that could multiply during storage. However, if it is a clean container and a clean, chlorinated municipal water supply, disinfecting might not be necessary.

We do not like to add unnecessary chemicals to our water. Sometimes we treat, and other times we do not. It depends on how we feel about the container, water source, and techniques used to fill the container. When our children help, there is a higher likelihood of environmental contamination, so we might choose to treat. If the barrels have never been filled before, we treat. You decide what you are comfortable with. If you have any concern regarding the safety of the container or the water, treat with chlorine when filling. This will kill any microscopic critters who may have been hiding in the container or the water to begin with. It will not remove contaminants such as chemicals, pesticides, and so on.

Chlorine is a common way to treat water for storage. You can use a fresh bottle of non-scented household bleach, a 5 percent stock solution made from powdered chlorine, or powdered chlorine. The following table shows the amount of chlorine we use when we choose to treat water for storage.

Water Storage Treatment

For Long-Term Storage Disinfection		
Container	Treatment	Amount
55-gallon barrel	Calcium hypochlorite, dry powder	⅛ teaspoon
15-gallon barrel	Liquid bleach	1½ teaspoons
5-gallon container	Liquid bleach	½ teaspoon
1-gallon container	Liquid bleach	8 drops
2-liter container	Liquid bleach	4 drops
1-quart canning jar	Process in boiling water bath to sterilize. We just fill clean jars with tap water and do not process the jars.	20 minutes

WATER STORAGE CONTAINER MATERIAL

You can store water in a wide variety of containers made from different materials. Glass is ideal since vapors and gases are unable to permeate it and thereby contaminate the water. The glass will not break down and leach into the water like plastic will. However, glass is heavy and easily broken.

Plastic is lightweight and sturdy. However, plastics leach into the water and can contaminate it. Never use any container that has stored something you would not want to drink. Previous contents may be introduced into your water supply when the plastic leaches. Use only food-grade plastics to store water. Look for the abbreviation *PET* or *PETE* on the bottom of a container, which indicates it is made from polyethylene plastic. Well-cleaned soda or juice bottles work great. Plastic milk jugs are not recommended for water storage. They are engineered to degrade and will leak in a relatively short period of time. Plastic is permeable and should never be stored near gasoline, pesticides, or similar substances. Store out of direct sunlight whenever possible.

Stainless steel can be used to store water. Some types of metal containers will rust. The water may pick up a metallic taste. Do not treat water in a metal can prior to storage. Chlorine is corrosive to most metals.

CONTAINER STYLES AND SIZES

Now we will explore possible options for storing your drinking water. As you review these options, consider the available space and budget you have to work with.

Water storage tanks are available in a variety of sizes in above- and belowground systems. They store a huge amount of water in a relatively small area. Some aboveground tanks are designed to be stored in a garage, take up little floor space compared to water barrels, and may be safe from freezing in a garage. Underground water storage tanks are perfect for operational security. Out of sight, out of mind. The initial investment for a large underground water storage tank can be significant, but it may be worth it if it works with your budget and location.

A 535-gallon outdoor water storage tank.

Water barrels store a large amount of water in a relatively small space. Standard water barrel measurements are 55 gallons (36 inches high by 24 inches wide), 30 gallons (30 inches high by 20 inches wide), and 15 gallons (24 inches high by 15 inches wide). These barrels usually have two bungs (plugs) at the top, which can be difficult to open. A bung wrench or channel lock pliers may be required to open the plugs. Attach one of these tools to the top of a barrel so you will have it when you need it.

A new 55-gallon barrel will cost about $55. It is possible to obtain used food-grade water barrels for a fraction of the cost (free to $20). Clean all barrels well before filling. Water barrels can be stored indoors or outdoors. Barrels stored outside should have plenty of headspace to allow for freezing and be protected from direct sun, which will break down the plastic. Store them off the ground on pallets, if possible.

Our water is stored in a variety of barrels covered with black pond liner to protect from UV damage.

Last fall Kylene decided to fill all of the water barrels. She got greedy and filled one of the barrels to the top. After a lengthy cold winter, we checked our water stores and found one of the barrels was empty and split down the side. It had frozen, ruining the barrel, and our water was lost. The lesson learned: it may be a good idea to listen to an engineer husband who understands that no one is exempt from the laws of physics.

New food-grade containers are best but come with a significantly higher price tag. We clean used food-grade barrels with several gallons of a heavy bleach and water solution. Sometimes we add a few squirts of dishwasher detergent. We leave this solution in the barrels for a few days and let the kids roll them around the yard. We rinse the barrels and repeat the entire process until we feel comfortable with the cleanliness of the barrel. We only use the dish detergent during the initial cleaning because soap tends to leave a residue. Some of our water still has a faint odor of lemon-lime syrup from its original contents, which continues to fade with each rotation. We plan to use this water for hygiene or filter it before drinking. However, if we had to drink it as it is, there is nothing in that water that will harm us.

Commercial water jugs and bottles are convenient and easy to rotate regularly. Some personal-sized water bottles will develop a foul odor and taste when stored in the heat. Store in a cool location to extend the shelf life. Purchase thick plastic bottles instead of the milk carton–type jugs for long-term storage. Several cases of water bottles can be stacked without damaging the bottles.

Glass containers do not retain odors or leach anything into the water. They are at risk in the event of an earthquake. We store water in empty glass canning jars. They take up the same amount of space whether they are full or empty. The official recommendation is to use new lids and process quart jars of water in a water bath canner for 20 minutes. The reality is we would never make the time to do this, so our jars would remain empty. Our empty jars, lids, and rings are sterilized in the dishwasher and then filled with hot tap water. Then they take their place of honor on the shelves with the bottled fruit and vegetables. Our system is not perfect, but we have a lot more water stored because this system works for us.

Reclaimed juice or soda bottles are made of thick food-grade plastic and are ideal for storing water inexpensively. They should be cleaned well to prevent any bacterial growth during storage. Thoroughly rinse bottles and scrub the lids. Disinfect by filling with a chlorine bleach and water solution for an hour or so. We use about one tablespoon of bleach in a 2-quart bottle. Place lids in a container of the bleach solution to soak. Allow to air-dry for a few days, then fill with clean water and store.

Mylar water bags are metallized plastic bags. They are available in 5-gallon bags equipped with a plastic spout and fit into a sturdy cardboard box. The boxes can be stacked up to three high. Care should be used when filling the bags to keep the cardboard dry.

Swimming pool water should not be depended upon for your sole source of water storage. Think of it as bonus backup. It is at risk for all types of environmental contamination. If the municipal water supply has been contaminated, chances are good your pool water will have the same problem. The chemicals used to disinfect the water make it unsafe to drink. We do not recommend using pool water for drinking unless absolutely necessary. It must be run through a high-quality filter with the ability to remove chemical contaminants before consuming.

WaterBricks are a great new item on the market. Check them out at waterbrick.org. These sturdy plastic bricks come in 1.6- and 3.5-gallon containers. An optional spigot allows for convenience when dispensing water. The design is unique and allows the containers to be stacked like bricks. They are heavy duty with a handle for easy transportation. You can fill the bricks with water or dry grains.

WaterBricks are a great way to store and carry water.

Water Storage Option Comparison

Container	Gallons	Advantages	Disadvantages
Underground tanks	Hundreds to thousands	Will not freeze; out of the way; great for operational security; lots of water in small space	Expensive; requires excavation equipment to install
Aboveground tanks	Hundreds to thousands	Some can be stored in garage; lots of water in small space	Expensive; may freeze outdoors or in an uninsulated garage
55-gallon barrel	55	Used barrels available; lots of water in small space	Heavy (450+ pounds)
30-gallon barrel	30	Lots of water in small space	Heavy (250 pounds)
15-gallon barrel	15	Possible to transport	Heavy (125 pounds)
5-gallon container	5	Available in a stackable style; easier to move (42 pounds); can install a spigot for convenience	May take more floor space
WaterBricks	1.6–3.5	Tough, well made; portable; stackable; freeze and thaw well	Expensive

Container	Gallons	Advantages	Disadvantages
Mylar water bags: heavy-duty boxes with metallized 5-gallon bags	5	Portable (40 pounds); can be stacked three high	Caution—do not let boxes get wet; some boxes can be converted to a portable toilet
Reclaimed juice or soda bottles	½–1	Free	Bacteria may grow if not cleaned thoroughly; take up more space
Commercial water bottles	½–1 liter	Convenient; disposable; cases stack nicely	Expensive; concern about plastics; damaged by heat

WATER SOURCES

Identify possible water sources that may be available in the event you exhaust your stored water. Storing water is always the best way to ensure you have safe drinking water. Many other water supplies come with a higher element of risk from chemicals or biobugs ready to make you sick. We will explore water source options you may not have considered.

Beverages such as fruit juices, vegetable juices, sports drinks, and canned milk can provide part of your water requirement. Caffeinated and alcoholic beverages are dehydrating and do not meet drinking water requirements. They have the potential to increase the need for water.

Bottled water is perfect. It is clean, portable, and easy to store. Some bottled water can smell foul if left in the heat. Learn what kind of bottled water you are purchasing. Is it purified or is it simply tap water conveniently packaged? Make sure to rotate it and keep it cool.

Canned fruits and vegetables, broths, and ready-to serve soups can supplement your required amount of water. Fruit liquid tastes great in oatmeal or pancake batter. The liquid from canned vegetables is a great addition to soups or can be used to boil pasta. Be creative and do not waste a drop.

Ice can be a good water source if you can capture it before it melts and drips out of the freezer. When the power goes out, place ice in a container and put it back in the freezer to help other foods remain cool a little longer. If there is space in your freezer, store plastic containers filled with water. This helps your freezer run more efficiently and increases water storage.

Local water sources such as canals, rivers, streams, ponds, and so on are a possibility. Where are the natural water sources near you? How would you transport water back to your home?

Rainwater is usually clean when it falls from the sky. Rainwater can be contaminated with radiation or chemicals, but as a rule it is safe. Gather it in clean containers. Collect it from rain gutters into containers or barrels. Once it has touched any unclean surface, including your roof, you should purify it before drinking.

Rain barrels are designed to capture rainwater from the roof.

Swimming pools and hot tubs are good sources for hygiene water. Chemicals in pool water cannot be boiled out. Stabilizers in pool treatments are dangerous and do not dissipate or evaporate. Pool water must be purified with a filter designed to remove contaminants before drinking (see chapter 8). It might be best to use this water for hygiene purposes.

Toilet flush tank (not the bowl) water can be harvested, if it has not been treated with chemicals. Make sure to purify this water before drinking or using for hygiene.

Water heaters or hot water tanks are a good source of water. Depending on the water heater, there may 20 to 50 gallons of water that can be captured. Be sure to prevent contamination by shutting off the main water valve into the house. Turn off the gas or power supply to the water heater. Start the water flowing by turning off the water intake valve at the tank and turning on the hot water drain valve. Do not turn the gas or electricity back on until the tank has been refilled. Practice this a few times to get the hang of it and remove rust and mineral deposits that build up in the bottom of the tank.

Water remaining in pipes may be collected by gravity flow even after the main supply to the house has been turned off in a multilevel home. To collect the water in your pipes, let air into the plumbing by turning on the faucet in your home at the highest level. A small amount of water will trickle out. Collect the water from your house's lowest faucet.

Well water can be a source of good water, unless it has been polluted. Exercise caution and consider filtering before drinking if other water supplies have been contaminated.

Early warning preparation can provide water, if you take advantage of it. At the first sign of trouble, such as a hurricane warning, fill bathtubs, pitchers, pots, pans, containers, and buckets. Turn off your main water valve to protect the clean water already in your system (pipes, water heater, and so on).

WATER STORAGE ACTION PLAN

You are armed with a mountain of information that you can use to develop your water storage action plan. We have prepared a worksheet to simplify the process. You can find it at http://theprovidentprepper. org/the-practical-prepper/action-plan-water-storage/. Water storage is critically important to your preparedness efforts. It is relatively inexpensive and easy to accomplish with a little creativity.

8

Water Disinfection and Purification
Is It Safe to Drink?

"Water, water, every where, / Nor any drop to drink."[1]

—Samuel Taylor Coleridge

Safe drinking water is absolutely essential for survival. We live in a country where clean drinking water is abundant. In the event of a disaster, that supply may be suddenly disrupted. Surface water will likely become contaminated. Drinking contaminated water can result in serious illnesses such as dengue fever, gastroenteritis, cholera, typhoid, hepatitis, and dysentery to name a few. Diseases resulting from consuming contaminated water frequently costs more lives than the initial disaster.

You can survive less than three days without water depending on the temperature and other environmental factors. One day without water will result in dehydration. Dehydration causes damage to the body and organs: blood thickens, blood pressure increases, risk of heart attack and stroke increase, kidneys begin to fail, muscles lose their elasticity, senses are dulled, and the brain begins to hallucinate. Good hydration is critical to functioning during an emergency situation. Symptoms of dehydration may include headache, extreme thirst, dry mouth, little or no urine output, dark urine, sleepiness, fatigue, feeling dizzy or light-headed, or any combination of these symptoms.

Providing safe drinking water for your family is one of the most important preparedness steps. Fortunately, it is also one of the least expensive.

DANGERS IN WATER

Exactly what could be lurking in the water that has everyone so uptight? We divide them into two categories: biological and chemical.

Biological Dangers

Biological dangers in the water are microscopic organisms that are too small to be seen by the naked eye, namely protozoa, bacteria, and viruses. We call them "biobugs." Protozoa are the largest of the microorganisms and include parasites like giardia and cryptosporidium. These parasites can be resistant to chlorine and iodine disinfection due to the protection of an outer shell. However, they are easy to filter out because of their larger size. Cryptosporidium is one of the most frequent causes of waterborne illness in the United States.

Bacteria are medium-sized microorganisms. E. coli, cholera, campylobacter, and salmonella are examples of bacteria contaminants in our water. Most of these little creatures are large enough to be filtered out using a quality water filter.

Viruses are so tiny (less than one micron) that they float right on through most filtering systems and must be deactivated using other methods. Hepatitis A and E, Norwalk virus, rotavirus, poliovirus, and echovirus are examples of viruses that can cause waterborne illnesses. Drinking contaminated water can be painful and deadly, so it is worth taking the time and effort to kill these invisible threats to our health.

Chemical and Radiation Contaminants

Chemical contaminants cannot be deactivated through any form of disinfection. They are not live organisms. The only way to protect yourself from them is to physically remove them through filtering or distillation. The removal method depends upon the individual chemical. Examples of chemical contaminants could be heavy metals, salts, pesticides, fuels, pollutants, and other chemicals. Municipal drinking supplies are monitored and use methods to control levels of these contaminants to assure water is safe to consume.

In the event of a nuclear incident, water supplies may become contaminated with dissolved radioactive elements or compounds and fallout particles. They cannot be removed from water by boiling, chemical disinfection, or even distillation. Settling and filtering is the safest way to remove radioactive elements from the water. Water may also still need to be disinfected to remove any biological dangers that may be present, depending on the water source.

Water exposed to radioactive fallout is not necessarily radioactive. Most of the radioactive fallout particles may be filtered out and the water safely used. The first few weeks after exposure are the most dangerous. Radioactive iodine particles decay rapidly and contaminated water will become safer over time. Water stored in sealed containers may be covered with radioactive fallout and still be safe. Clean off the dust particles before opening the container to prevent fallout from contaminating the water. Stored water is going to be your safest source of drinking water.

WATER PURIFICATION

Water purification is the process of removing undesirable chemicals and biological contaminates, along with particles (leaves, dirt, and such), to make water safe and pleasant to drink. It involves a series of basic steps: clarification, disinfection, and filtering. Each step is important to achieving safe, clean drinking water. Depending on the water source, one of the steps might not be necessary. For instance, if the source is a contaminated municipal water supply, you may not need to clarify the water. A "boil order" is commonly issued when the water supply is contaminated. The water has already been clarified at the source; you need to disinfect to kill the harmful pathogens in the water.

Let us review each step in detail.

CLARIFICATION

Clarification removes floating or suspended particulate matter before disinfection. Think of it as making the water clear. In this step, water is poured through coffee filters, layers of paper towels, a tightly woven cloth, or anything that will remove the big stuff you can see. Nature clarifies water as it passes through a porous medium such as sand.

You can also clarify water by allowing it to settle for a while. The heavy particles will settle to the bottom, and lighter leaves and twigs float to the top. Skim off the floating particles and gently pour the clear water into another container. Do not allow the sediments on the bottom to flow into the new container.

Clarification is an important step because biobugs can hide in the particles during disinfection. Water must be clarified in order for disinfection to be effective. It is possible to use a commercial filter to accomplish this step, but it will shorten the life of the filter.

DISINFECTION

Disinfection is the second step. This is the process of killing or deactivating microscopic critters that cause illness and death. There are a variety of methods, but not all methods kill all harmful pathogens. We will review some of the most common.

Boiling

The safest method to disinfect water is by boiling. Anytime a municipal water supply is contaminated, a "boil order" is issued to ensure the water is safe to drink. Bacteria, viruses, and parasites cannot survive a temperature of 212 degrees Fahrenheit, which is a rolling boil at sea level. Each 500-foot increase in altitude causes a drop of 1 degree in the boiling point, which means at 5,000 feet, water boils at about 203 degrees. Higher elevations will require longer boiling times to ensure all the biobugs are destroyed.

Boiling is the safest method of water disinfection. This water is boiling indoors on an EcoQue grill using Safe Heat as fuel.

Boiling will not remove contaminants such as heavy metals, salts, and chemicals. Clarify water prior to boiling to ensure that disinfection is successful. The disadvantages to boiling are that it is fuel intensive and water must be cooled before consuming.

Pasteurization

A safe method of disinfection, requiring 50 percent less fuel than boiling, is a technique referred to as *pasteurization*. It can be accomplished using a solar oven or traditional heat sources. According to a study performed by David Ciochetti in 1983, "heating water to 66°C [150.8 degrees Fahrenheit] in a solar cooker will provide enough heat to pasteurize the water and kill all disease causing microbes."[2]

Water pasteurization involves heating water to 149 degrees Fahrenheit (65 degrees Celsius) for several minutes. Milk and other foods require 160 degrees for pasteurization. Boiling disinfection is complete when the temperature reaches 212 degrees. Pasteurization can disinfect at a lower temperature due to a longer exposure time. An effective tool for ensuring water has been pasteurized is a water pasteurization indicator (WAPI). This tiny reusable device is made from a tube filled with soybean fat, which melts and drops to the bottom of the tube when the water has been safely pasteurized. This method will not remove contaminants such as heavy metals, salts, and chemicals.

A WAPI is an effective tool that indicates when water is pasteurized.

Distillation

The distillation process is simple but fuel intensive. The contaminated water is heated to the point of boiling and vaporizes into steam. The other substances (salt, minerals, heavy metals, and so on) remain in a solid state in the boiler. The steam is directed into a cooler, where it condenses back into liquid form. All of the impurities are left behind. Other methods of disinfection kill the microbes in the water. Distillation will remove the biological pathogens along with heavy metals, salts, poisons, and most other chemicals. It will not remove substances that have a lower boiling point than water, such as oil, petroleum, or alcohol.

Water distillers can be purchased in electric or nonelectric models. Plans for DIY solar water distillers (solar still) can be found online.

Chlorine

Chlorine is a popular method of chemical disinfection. Some protozoa such as giardia and cryptosporidium are resistant to chlorine due to a protective outer shell. Therefore, chlorine should be used to disinfect in conjunction with a high-quality filter. The filter will remove the large protozoa while the chlorine kills the viruses that are difficult for many filters to catch due to their small size.

Chlorine dioxide water purification tablets work a little differently than regular chlorine. They work through an oxidation process, not by chlorination. This process requires a longer reaction time of four hours, as compared to 30 minutes for chlorine. Follow instructions listed on the package carefully. They have a shelf life of four years when properly stored. These tablets improve the taste of the water.

Household bleach, such as Clorox, may be used to disinfect water. The chlorine in the bleach has a relatively short shelf life of six months. It loses potency and becomes less effective. Rotate it frequently to ensure adequate strength. The label should read 5.26 to 6 percent sodium hypochlorite. It should not contain any soap, scent, or phosphates.

Add the recommended amount of liquid bleach to clarified water. The American Red Cross recommends adding 16 drops of bleach per gallon of water. Allow the water to stand for 30 minutes. The water should still smell slightly of chlorine. This is called free chlorine. It means that enough chlorine was added to kill all of the bugs with some left over. If you cannot smell chlorine after 30 minutes, repeat and wait an additional 30 minutes.[3]

You can reduce the chlorine taste and smell by pouring water back and forth between two containers several times, or let chlorinated water sit out for a while in an open container. The chlorine will evaporate, and the taste will significantly improve.

Household Bleach Water Disinfection

Amount of Water	Amount of Bleach (Clear Water)	Amount of Bleach (Cloudy or Questionable Water)
1 quart	2 drops	4 drops
2 quarts	4 drops	8 drops
1 gallon	8 drops	16 drops
5 gallons	½ teaspoon	1 teaspoon
15 gallons	1½ teaspoons	1 tablespoon
30 gallons	1 tablespoon	2 tablespoons
55 gallons	5½ teaspoons	11 teaspoons

Dry Calcium Hypochlorite

Powdered or granulated chlorine, such as calcium hypochlorite, has a ten-year shelf life if stored in a cool, dark place. Be careful where you store it. It is a hazardous chemical that can cause chemical burns to the skin, eyes, and mucous membranes. Take precautions by wearing gloves and protective eyewear when handling.[4] The amount of available chlorine is important. Calcium hypochlorite can be purchased in several concentrations. Purchase a brand that has at least 68 percent available chlorine. A 1-pound bag can disinfect thousands of gallons of water.

The goal for water disinfection is one part per million of residual chlorine. That means that after the army of chlorine soldiers has killed all the bugs, there should be one part per million of chlorine soldiers still hanging around. Knowing exactly how much to use is difficult to calculate because the amount of chlorine needed depends on the number of critters that need to be killed. Chlorine is actually used up in the battle. Too much residual chlorine is bad; too little will leave some critters in the water to make you sick. The safer your water source, the less chlorine you need.

The EPA set four parts per million as the maximum residual disinfectant level (MRDL). Drinking water with high concentrations of chlorine may result in stomach discomfort and other negative side effects.[5] Pool test strips can give you an idea of the amount of free chlorine in your water. Do not drink water with over four parts per million without running it through a quality filter to remove the chlorine.

The departments of the Army, Navy, and Air Force released a publication entitled "Sanitary Control and Surveillance of Field Water Supplies" in 2010 in which they set standards for use of calcium hypochlorite for water disinfection in the military. The calculations to create a stock solution from dry calcium hypochlorite on the table below are taken from those military standards.[6]

They recommend, "If your measuring device is not as precise as the number you come up with, it is generally advisable to round the calculated number up to ensure you get at least the dose you intended to provide."[7] To simplify measurements, the calculations on the table have been rounded up from the exact amount in parenthesis to the right. The standard calculation for a 5 percent stock solution is based on dissolving 1 teaspoon of 68 to 70 percent dry calcium hypochlorite in 1½ cups of water.[8]

5% Chlorine Stock Solution Recipe

Homemade Liquid Bleach—Do Not Drink!	
Water	Dry Calcium Hypochlorite
1½ cups	1 teaspoon
1 quart	1 tablespoon (2.7 teaspoons)
2 quarts	2 tablespoons (5.3 teaspoons)
1 gallon	4 tablespoons (10.7 teaspoons)

Liquid chlorine is volatile and will gradually reduce in strength over a short period of time in storage. Dry calcium hypochlorite is stable and can be stored for many years. Making up small, fresh batches of homemade liquid chlorine bleach will ensure its effectiveness in deactivating pathogens in drinking water. The solution can be used to disinfect water following the same directions provided for liquid household bleach (see page 109).

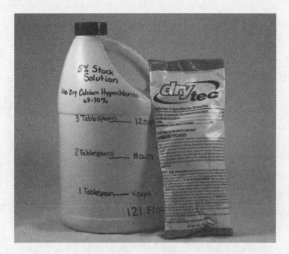

A 5 percent stock solution can be made by mixing 1 teaspoon of dry calcium hypochlorite with 1½ cups water.

When using the stock solution to disinfect drinking water, the military standard recommends mixing and allowing water to stand for a minimum of 30 minutes to ensure adequate disinfection time prior to consuming.[9] Extremely cold water may require additional chlorine or longer contact time to deactivate pathogens in the water.

Dry calcium hypochlorite can be used to disinfect a 55-gallon barrel of water. Fill the barrel with at least 50 gallons of clarified water. Add ⅛ teaspoon of dry bleach powder. Seal the barrel and wait at least 24 hours before consuming. The water should have a slight chlorine odor. If not, repeat the process.

Iodine

Iodine is available in tablet, liquid, and crystalline forms. It will effectively deactivate most pathogens in water, with the exception of some protozoa, such as cryptosporidium. Pregnant women or individuals with thyroid problems should not use iodine. Long-term use of iodine for water purification is not recommended.

Water pH and temperature can affect the amount of iodine required to be effective. Carefully follow instructions on packaging. Shelf life varies for different products from two years for some tablets to indefinite for the crystalline form. Finding the crystalline form is difficult. It has become highly regulated because it is an ingredient in the production of methamphetamine, an illegal drug.

Potable Aqua (tetraglycine hydroperiodide) is a tablet form of iodine used by the military for field water treatment in canteens and by outdoor enthusiasts. It requires at least 30 minutes to deactivate pathogens. The manufacturer recommends a 4-year shelf life for an unopened bottle and one year if opened. "Exposure to heat, humidity, moisture, and air will reduce the effectiveness of the tablets."[10]

Tincture of iodine is the common household form of iodine found in many first-aid kits. The U.S. Army Center for Health Promotion and Preventative Medicine recommends for every one quart of clear water adding five drops of 2 percent United States pharmacopeia tincture of iodine and let stand for at least 30 minutes. Double the amount of iodine for cloudy water.[11]

Solar Water Disinfection (SODIS)

Harmful pathogens in water may be deactivated by placing the water in a transparent container and exposing it to sunlight for five to six hours. Ultraviolet disinfection will even kill the protozoa that are resistant to chlorine and iodine treatment. It may sound too good to be true, but the fact is millions of people use this method every day in developing countries to provide safe drinking water for their families.

Solar water disinfection (SODIS) works as the UV-A light irradiates the microorganisms while the infrared light heats the water. Several factors contribute to the death of microorganisms and pathogens, including light, temperature, nutrition, humidity, and time. SODIS will not remove chemicals, tastes, or smells. It will not treat large volumes of water.

This method is amazingly simple and effective. Follow these simple guidelines to enjoy safe water:

- Start with a clean transparent container no larger than four inches in diameter. Clear food-grade plastic water bottles, plastic soda bottles (1–2 liters), or glass jars with tight-fitting lids work well.

- Use the cleanest water available. Clarify to remove larger particles (see page 105).

- Fill bottle halfway with water and shake vigorously. This will saturate the water with oxygen and increase performance in sunlight. Then finish filling the bottle.

- Place bottle on a dark surface to increase the temperature, which will force the water to circulate inside the container. Light surfaces, such as concrete, will not work as well as dark surfaces. The warmer the water, the faster disinfection occurs.

- Place bottle on its side to allow maximum exposure to the sunlight.

- A clear sunny day, or even a partly cloudy day, will disinfect water in five to six hours. Expose the bottle for two consecutive days if the sky is completely covered with clouds to ensure disinfection. Periods of stormy weather will require alternative forms of disinfection, such as boiling or chemical disinfection.

- Allow water to cool completely before drinking.

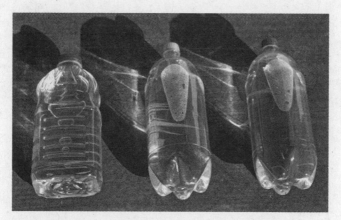

Clear plastic bottles and sunshine are all you need to disinfect water using the SODIS method.

Understanding the basics of solar water disinfection may be one of those tidbits of knowledge that may literally save your life someday. It requires no more than a transparent bottle, time, and sunshine to protect you from acquiring waterborne illness. All you have to do is understand the basics and apply them correctly. Visit www.sodis.ch for more information.

FILTERING

Water filters screen out particles and are effective against pathogens down to a certain size. Many filters are unable to catch the tiny viruses. Water purifiers filter out chemicals and some biobugs as well as using another method to kill the viruses that may get through the filter. When using a water filter, disinfect the water before running it through the filter. The filter may remove the chemical taste and odor, making it more pleasant to drink. The cleaner the water you put into the filter, the longer it will last.

Filter ratings can be a little deceiving. Nominal micron rating refers to the average pore size. Some pores may be larger and some smaller. An absolute micron rating means that is the maximum pore size. Manufacturers may not always disclose the micron rating or specify if it is nominal or absolute.

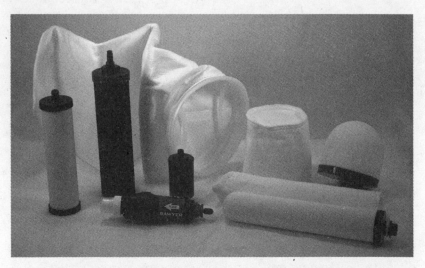

Water filters come in many shapes, sizes, and levels of effectiveness.

All filters are not created equal. Only a few are rated to filter out viruses and do not require disinfecting prior to filtration. Pay close attention to the size of the contaminants the filter is designed to remove. Understand the limitations of your filter and use it correctly to produce safe, clean drinking water. This chart illustrates how the size of the pores in a filter determines the contaminants it has the ability to filter out.

Water Filter Pore Size Effectiveness Guide

Filter Size	Protozoa 1–15 microns (cryptosporidium, giardia, lamblia)	Bacteria 0.2–5 microns (campylobacter, salmonella, shigella, E. coli, cholera)	Viruses -0.02–0.2 micron (hepatitis A, norovirus, rotavirus, poliovirus)	Chemicals
Microfiltration 0.1 micron	Very high	Moderate	Not effective	Not effective
Ultrafiltration 0.01 micron	Very high	Very high	Moderate	Low
Nanofiltration 0.001 micron	Very high	Very high	Very high	Moderate

Even with this knowledge, deciding which filter to purchase can be a little challenging. Consider these questions: What do you want to use the filter for? How much water do you need to filter? How fast do you want to filter the water? Does it need to be portable? Is the filter easy enough for children to use without supervision? What can you afford?

We will review a few water filtration systems in the basic filter categories. This list is not all-inclusive by any means—just some examples to consider. Quality is important. You do not want to find out your filter is a piece of junk by contracting a nasty waterborne illness.

Gravity Filters

Gravity filters use gravity to pull the water through the filter. Water is poured into the top of the container, is filtered, and is accessed through a spigot at the bottom. The cleaner the water when put into the filter, the longer the filter will last. Some gravity filters are not highly portable but are great for use on a countertop in emergencies or for everyday use. They produce large amounts of clean drinking water. Do not allow wet filters to freeze—they may crack and become ineffective. Below are some gravity filters' specifications for you to compare.

Big Berkey

This is a water purifier with four Black Berkey filters.

Filter specs: Black Berkey filter removes nearly all contaminants with a 99.9999% reduction in viruses. Micron rating not published.

Filter life: 3,000 gallons

Flow rate: Up to 192 gallons a day

Cost: System $350, Replacement filter $125 each

Learn more at www.berkeywater.com.

Just Water Bucket Kit System

This is a kit to convert two plastic buckets into a filtration system.

Filter specs: 0.2 micron silver impregnated ceramic filter element

Filter life: One year once in use (gallons not published)

Flow rate: Up to 30 gallons per day

Cost: $38 (buckets sold separately)

Learn more at www.justwater.me.

Sawyer All in One Filter

This is a kit for a bucket or pouch system, or you can attach it directly to your household faucet

Filter specs: Sawyer PointONE uses 0.1 absolute micron hollow filter membrane in-line filter. Point ZeroTWO uses a .02 absolute micron filter with 99.997% reduction in viruses.

Filter life: One million gallons

Flow rate: Up to 540 gallons per day for PointONE and 170 gallons per day for Point ZeroTWO

Cost: PointONE $60, Point ZeroTWO $140

Learn more at www.sawyer.com

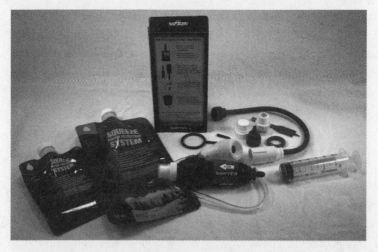

The Sawyer filter is a versatile gravity filter that can be used by filling a pouch with water, attaching it to a faucet, or filtering directly from a bucket.

Pump Filters

Pump filters typically use a hand pump to force the water through the filter in order to clean the water. These come in different sizes, from portable individual pumps to larger pumps designed to service many people. Some examples are included below.

Katadyn Expedition
Filter specs: Cleanable 0.2 micron ceramic depth filter
Filter life: 26,000 gallons
Flow rate: Up to 1,440 gallons per day
Cost: $1500, Replacement filters $200 each
Learn more at www.katadyn.com

Miniworks Ex Microfilter from MSR
Filter specs: Compact 0.2 micron carbon/ceramic element
Filter life: 520 gallons
Flow rate: Up to 374 gallons per day
Cost: $90
Learn more at www.cascadedesigns.com

Pure Water Pump by Seychelle

Filter specs: In-line filter with iodinated resin effective against bacteria and viruses up to a reduction of 99.9999%. Micron rating not published.

Filter life: 100 gallons

Flow rate: Not published

Cost: $40

Learn more at www.seychelle.com

Suction Filters

With these filters, water is sucked through the filter by the individual at the point of consumption. One area of concern with the straw filters is the close proximity of your face to the contaminated water and possibility of accidental contamination. However, they are highly portable. Hydration pack filters can be quite convenient when traveling by foot. Below are some suction filters to consider.

LifeStraw Personal Water Filter

Filter specs: Hollow fiber membrane filter rated to 0.2 microns

Filter life: 264 gallons

Flow rate: Not published

Cost: $25

Learn more at http://www.vestergaard-frandsen.com/lifestraw

Pure Water Straw by Seychelle

Filter specs: Regular filter (removes contaminants and pollutants) and radiological filter (removes radiological contaminants) are both designed to be used with chlorinated water sources. Micron rating not published.

Filter life: Up to 25 gallons

Flow rate: Not published

Cost: $17–23

Learn more at www.seychelle.com

Back Country Hydration Pack by Just Water

Filter specs: 0.2 micron silver impregnated ceramic filter element

Filter life: 75 refills (gallons not published)

Flow rate: Not published

Cost: $45

Learn more at www.justwater.me

Water Filter Bottles

Water filter bottles are a good option for personal water filtration needs. These can be used every day to improve the taste and safety of the water. They are lightweight and perfect for emergency kits or to throw into a suitcase or backpack when traveling. Each bottle is unique in the amount of water it will filter, the price, and the overall effectiveness of the filter.

*Water filter bottles are great
for travel or use in survival kits.*

Sawyer Personal Water Filter Bottle

Filter specs: Uses a 0.1 absolute micron hollow filter membrane in-line filter

Filter life: one million gallons

Flow rate: High—exact rate not published.

Cost: $50

Learn more at www.sawyer.com

Seychelle Water Filtration Bottle

Filter specs: Standard filter uses an ionic absorption micron filtration system; advanced filter includes an iodinated resin that removes 99.9999% of viruses. Micron rating not published.

Filter life: 100 gallons

Flow rate: Not published

Cost: $30 Replacement filters: Standard—$15, Advanced—$21

Learn more at www.seychelle.com

Sport Berkey

Filter specs: Filter removes nearly all contaminants with a 99.9999% reduction in viruses. Micron rating not published.

Filter life: 160 gallons from any source or 640 gallons from municipal water source

Flow rate: Not published

Cost: $31; replacement filter $13

Learn more at www.berkeyfilters.com

WATER DISINFECTION AND PURIFICATION ACTION PLAN

Stored water is your best bet for safe drinking water. Eventually you may run out of your stored supplies, or find yourself without any safe drinking water. We have discussed a variety of options for water disinfection and purification. Remember, you will want to plan for a way to kill the tiny viruses that some filters cannot remove. You also need a way to filter out the protozoa that are not deactivated by some methods of chemical disinfection—and also be able to remove chemical contaminants.

A few filters will do it all. The Sawyer and Black Berkey filters have great virus-removal and contaminate-reduction ratings. All you need to do is clarify the water (remove large particles) and run the water through the filter. We recommend disinfecting water before running it through most other filters. Or, if the water is from a dangerous source, to ensure that viruses are deactivated. Know the limitations of your filter(s) and plan accordingly. Do not risk acquiring a waterborne illness. How much water will your filter clean? What are your water needs?

The worksheet located at www.theprovidentprepper.org/the-practical-prepper/action-plan-water-disinfection-and-purification will help you plan for how you are going to produce clean drinking water for your family. Be sure to consider filtration needs in the event you must evacuate or the water supply becomes disrupted for a long time.

| 9 |

Sanitation
What's That Smell?

"There must be quite a few things that a hot bath won't cure, but I don't know many of them."

—Sylvia Plath

Proper sanitation is critical to survival. The leading cause of illness and death in both natural and man-made disasters is inadequate sanitation, poor hygiene practice, and contaminated and insufficient water supplies. Frequently, more people die after a disaster from poor sanitation than die during the initial event. Outbreaks of cholera, typhoid fever, or dysentery are deadly possibilities resulting from unsanitary conditions. Haiti experienced the worst cholera outbreak in 20 years following the 2010 earthquake. The epidemic claimed over 8,200 Haitians and hospitalized over 370,000.[1]

In this chapter, we will focus on critically important sanitation practices. Due to the nature of this subject, or perhaps because we have become spoiled, we often neglect thinking about and planning for sanitation needs in our preparedness efforts. But, it just might make the difference between life and death.

PERSONAL SANITATION

Maintaining good hygiene during an emergency is vitally important. Use high standards of cleanliness, including brushing your teeth, washing your face, combing your hair, and showering or bathing (or taking a sponge bath if water is scarce). Remember to wash your hands!

Good personal hygiene will help prevent the spread of disease and help maintain personal health and comfort.

SHOWERS AND BATHS

A nice warm shower can make life worth living. Even when power is out and water is scarce, it is possible to be clean and comfortable with a little creativity and planning. Place a large tub or container under the person showering to catch and recycle the water. This water can be used for flushing toilets, in the first stage of washing clothes, or to water plants. Practice different alternative shower or bathing methods to determine which ones will work for you. Here are a few suggestions for makeshift showers and baths:

Keeping clean can reduce body odors, prevent rashes and sores from developing, and reduce the spread of disease.

Gravity solar showers are inexpensive and can provide a much-needed warm shower. Simply expose the black shower bag to the sun for a few hours. The five-gallon-capacity showers may hold enough water for two quick showers. The shower head on ours is fine for cleansing a body but is not the best for washing shampoo out of long hair.

Garden pressure tank sprayers can provide a refreshing shower. The tank may be set in the sun to get warm (black tanks work best), or the water can be heated before filling the tank. Different nozzles are available. Some work better for showering than others. Washing all of the shampoo from thick hair is a little challenging with a tank sprayer, but it makes a great body shower while also conserving water. Sporting goods stores carry nice pressure sprayers that are specially designed for showers for around $100.

Sponge baths are a good option when water is scarce. Simply wipe your entire body using wet washcloths and water. Baby wipes are a great way to take a sponge bath. Wipes are relatively inexpensive and have a long shelf life. They can be discarded after use, preventing additional laundry. Regular bathing, even with baby wipes, can prevent the spread of disease, make others more comfortable around you, and prevent sores from developing.

Tubs or large containers have been used to bathe entire families throughout history. Water was hauled, heated, and dumped into the tub. Traditionally the father would bath first, followed by the mother, and then the children, oldest to youngest. By the time the littlest child had an opportunity to bathe, the water was fairly dirty. Thus the old saying: "Don't throw the baby out with the bathwater."

HUMAN WASTE DISPOSAL

Mother Nature's call cannot be put off for long, regardless of the nature of the emergency or crisis. In fact, these circumstances may actually make the call more frequent and intense. City sewage plants operate on electrical systems and are susceptible to storm damage, power outages, sabotage, and broken pipes from all kinds of disasters. Take time to carefully consider how you will dispose of human waste responsibly if public water and sewer systems fail.

For centuries, people used chamber pots to relieve themselves indoors. Other options include outhouses, or primitive toilets. Feces are a dangerous substance and can spread deadly diseases. Urine, however, is generally safe. When possible, separate urine from feces to reduce the amount of hazardous material. If you are using a bucket toilet, consider having one for urine and another for feces.

Each person generates approximately five gallons of human waste each week. This waste, if not managed properly, becomes a source of odor, illness, disease, and other problems. Never throw human waste on the open ground. If no other alternative is available, bury it in deep trenches and cover with at least two to three feet of soil. Make sure to avoid burying raw human waste where there are high water tables—this can contaminate the water supply and spread disease.

Consider the toilet options listed below, make a plan, and get the supplies needed to ensure you can safely manage the waste your family creates.

A **Luggable Loo,** or bucket toilet, may be a good option for a lightweight portable toilet that you can grab along with your survival kit. Take time to actually sit on a bucket toilet to determine if it is stable enough to support your size and weight. Most are not designed to accommodate large or tall people. The thought of sitting on a bucket toilet full of stinky contents is bad enough. But the image of falling over while sitting on it, splashing the contents all over, makes us cringe.

Keep basic supplies inside so that it is ready to go: toilet paper, baby wipes, garbage bags, disinfecting wipes, feminine products, spray deodorizer, and chlorine bleach or sanitizing chemical. Line the bucket with a plastic garbage bag. Mix one cup liquid bleach, or an appropriate amount of another sanitizing chemical, with two quarts of water. Pour this mixture into the lined bucket. Add a little more disinfectant after each use. Change the bag when it is ⅓ to ½ full. Carefully tie the top and place in a larger lined can. Close the lid after each use to control odors.

This will definitely work for an emergency; however, the smell is offensive, and it is not our favorite option. Possible disinfectants (sanitizing chemicals) include enzyme 300 (nontoxic, formulated for use in treatment plants), Luggable Loo liner with bio-gel, sodium hydroxide (blue liquid in chemical toilets), liquid chlorine bleach, Pine-Sol, ammonia (never mix ammonia with bleach!), baking soda, alcohol, or other disinfectant.

ChemiSan powder, bio-gel waste gelatin, Poo Powder, or WAG BAG are very nice, but pricey, solutions. The powder instantly solidifies to prevent messy spills and controls germs and odors. A WAG BAG fits inside the bucket and is ready to go with Poo Powder. It may be used multiple times. The bag is engineered to break down in six to eight months to make disposal environmentally friendly.

A **permanent port-a-potty** is a great option if you can stay in your home but do not have running water or sewer. Your household toilet can be easily converted to a permanent port-a-potty in an emergency and provide a familiar, inexpensive toilet option.

Turning your familiar household toilet into a no-water toilet option is easy with a supply of garbage bags, duct tape, and disinfectant.

Turn off the water supply to the toilet tank. Then empty the toilet bowl. Lift the lid and seat. Place a garbage bag in the bowl and duct tape the edges around the back and sides of the bowl. Use the toilet as usual. Pour a small amount of disinfectant into the bag after each use to help prevent the spread of germs and disease. Do not use strong disinfectants that might compromise the plastic bag. You may want to add sawdust, kitty litter, soil, or Poo Powder to solidify liquids. The bag may be used several times before changing.

To change the bag, lift the lid and seat. Carefully remove the bag by loosening the taped edges, twist the edges of the bag together, and then seal the bag. Place an empty plastic bucket right next to the toilet and lift the bag into the bucket. Use this bucket for transport to avoid accidental spills. Place the bag in a large bucket with a tight-fitting lid.

Store waste outside if possible. Cover the entire toilet with a 30-gallon trash bag to control odor. Air fresheners or room deodorizers may also be helpful.

Secure contents inside of the garbage bag and place directly into a bucket for safe transport.

Bedside commodes are commonly used for individuals with limited mobility and can be purchased online or anywhere that carries medical supplies. They can be a great alternative toilet. Bedside commodes are well-built. Some can hold up to 350 pounds, and the seat height is adjustable. They easily fold up and require little storage space. The bucket can be emptied as often as desired. Most bucket liners come with a gelling agent, odor neutralizer, and decaying catalyst. Liners can be used three to five times before changing.

Potty chairs are great for small children. Hang on to that chair for emergencies. We actually take ours camping. It is much more convenient for a seven-year-old, who outgrew the chair many years ago, to go outside the tent in a potty chair than to make the long scary trek to the outhouse in the middle of the night. This might come in handy in an emergency.

Chemical toilets are a great option and are regularly used by boaters and campers. They use very little water, and the chemicals keep the smell and spread of disease to a minimum. Chemical toilets have a removable tray at the bottom for easy disposal of waste. They are lightweight and portable when empty. The nice thing about chemical toilets is that they flush so you do not have to smell or view anyone else's waste.

Be sure to store plastic buckets with tight-fitting lids to store waste until you can safely dispose of it. Keep a stock of appropriate chemicals for the toilet. The chemicals have a limited shelf life. Check with the manufacturer for specifics. If the chemicals are unavailable in an emergency, use an alternative disinfectant.

*Chemical toilets are a nicer
solution than bucket toilets.*

A **composting toilet** (sometimes called biological toilet, dry toilet, or waterless toilet) is frequently used in remote locations, such as cabins. A composting toilet system converts human waste into a fertilizer or useable soil through the natural breakdown of organic matter back into its essential minerals. This compost is not safe for use on vegetable gardens. Composting toilets are expensive, but they use little or no water and are practically odorless.

Septic systems are quickly being replaced by sewer systems for a lot of good reasons. If you are fortunate enough to be on a septic system, you may avoid the necessity for backup toilets if your system remains intact. Be sure to perform regular routine maintenance on your septic system. We recommend you still have a contingency plan in the event your system fails or you are required to evacuate.

A **trench latrine** may be a good choice if an outdoor toilet becomes necessary. It can be quickly constructed. Be sure to locate it away from the home and all water sources. Create some type of shelter to provide protection from the weather and for privacy. Dig a trench one foot wide by four feet long by 2½ feet deep. Add a little bit of soil, ash, or lime after each use to help control odor and flies. When the trench is filled within one foot of the surface, sprinkle with lime, fill with soil, and mound with an additional foot of soil. This toilet is used by squatting or straddling the trench.

A **deep pit latrine** is a long-term solution for an extended crisis. A single-seat latrine may be built over a hole that is two feet wide by two to six feet long by six feet deep using available materials to create a shelter and seating area. Make sure the seating area is large enough to prevent it from collapsing into the pit. Consider potential groundwater contamination when locating a site or the depth of the latrine. Be sure to sprinkle with soil, ash, or lime after each use and before closing the pit. Use extreme caution; a hole this size presents a significant cave-in hazard.

Waste storage may be something you need to plan for. In the event you are confined to a shelter, make sure you have buckets with tight-fitting lids for short-term storage of human waste. Plan for five gallons of waste from each person per week. That can add up to a lot of buckets!

Sewage backflow can be a terrible thing to deal with. Sewer systems require electricity to function properly. In some places, raw sewage is pumped uphill to the treatment plant. When the power is out, that sewage can back up in the line and enter homes through drainpipes.

If this occurs, you will most likely need to leave your home due to the potential of disease and the stench associated with raw sewage.

You may be able to prevent that sewage from back-flowing into your home by stuffing a foam ball or bag of rags into the drains. Put the ball or rags into a larger sock or nylon to make removal easier by providing a handle. Inflatable rubber test ball plugs are used to test the pressure in the system and are available at plumbing stores. They may work nicely to plug drainpipes and prevent sewage from backing up into the home. Evaluate your risk and, if necessary, consider installing some type of back-flow prevention device.

SOLID WASTE DISPOSAL

We need only to look at the garbage cans of our neighbors (or perhaps ourselves) to realize most of us generate a significant amount of trash. What would you do if your faithful garbage man didn't come for weeks or possibly even months? Some types of disasters could easily disrupt that service. Garbage is a prime breeding ground for bacteria, insects, and rodents. It also attracts other unwanted pests. Develop a backup plan in the event you have to hold on to your garbage for a while. Your plan may include some or all of the following strategies:

Separate waste to reduce contaminating all of it. Separate cans, glass, and plastic from burnable items and wet garbage. Wet garbage breeds bacteria and draws insects and animals. Mixing garbage contaminates all of it. Reduce bulk by smashing cans, flattening boxes, and compacting whenever possible. Store lots of quality garbage bags. Trash cans or barrels with tight-fitting lids have many uses and might come in handy for storing garbage.

Compost yard waste, kitchen scraps, shredded paper products, and even cardboard to make beautiful garden soil. You can safely compost any manure from animals that do not eat meat. Do not compost human waste, dog or cat waste, meat or grease, poisons, or other chemicals. Establish the composting area away from your home because it will attract insects and flies. Turn your compost pile to facilitate decomposition. Covering the pile with a black tarp will increase the temperature and increase the decomposition rate. The result is rich, dark soil loaded with nutrients for gardening—a much better choice than a stinky pile of garbage.

Burnable trash may be a valuable resource. Burning may not be preferable due to safety and environmental concerns but may become necessary. Cereal boxes, paper plates, cardboard, and so on may be used to fuel small fires for cooking. Cooled ashes can be added to a compost pit or used to control odors and germs in an outhouse. Use great caution when burning anything to ensure the safety of people and property. Burn trash in appropriate conditions and locations. Do not burn plastic, Styrofoam, or other items that release toxins when burned. We store real paper plates instead of Styrofoam because they can be burned, reducing the amount of garbage we may need to deal with.

Burying trash may be required as a result of a prolonged crisis. If this becomes necessary, bury garbage as far away from your home as possible. Dig a hole at least four feet deep. Cover with at least 18 inches of soil to prevent insect and animal infestation. You may want to dig the hole and cover it with a large piece of plywood to allow additional garbage to be added as needed. Weigh the plywood down with large rocks or heavy objects to prevent animals from accessing it. Layering garbage with soil, ashes, lime, or borax may help control odors.

PEST CONTROL

Sharing space and provisions with disease-spreading pests can make bad situations worse. Our precious supplies can be quickly contaminated if these pests are not controlled. Pest control must be an important consideration in sanitation planning.

Insect control is a priority. Prevent breeding grounds by keeping the area clean. Separate garbage and store it away from the living area. Standing water is a breeding ground for mosquitoes, which are known carriers for the spread of diseases. Carefully package all food storage to prevent infestation. Use care to prevent bedding from being contaminated through poor personal sanitation. Do not stop doing laundry! The old saying, "good night, sleep tight, don't let the bedbugs bite" was adopted for a reason. Store insect repellent and insecticides safely and away from food.

Fly control is a must. Not only are flies highly annoying, but they also spread disease rapidly. Keep the area free from animal feces, garbage, and waste products. Keep lids tightly closed on garbage cans. Cover food and clean dishes to prevent contamination by flies. Store fly swatters, fly strips, fly traps, and so on for use as needed.

Rodent control can be challenging. Keep storage areas clean and organized. Store traps and poisons. However, use great caution to prevent accidental poisoning or secondary poisoning. Secondary poisoning can occur when another animal eats a poisoned rodent.

*Keep living and storage areas clean from
disease-spreading rodent droppings.*

*This hole was created by rodents that gained
access to a kitchen pantry from the garage.*

An alternative to poison is a mixture of quick oats with dry plaster of Paris or dry hot mud (from your home improvement store). Add anything the rodents like to eat, such as raisins, fruits, and seeds. Set the dry mixture out where rodents are known to frequent. The creatures eat the oat mixture, and within a few minutes the plaster hardens internally. This concoction can be fatal to any living creature, humans included, so use it with great care. The mixture could be placed in a bait station to reduce the risk of accidental ingestion by pets.

Take time to package food storage to prevent infestation. Rodents can quickly access foods stored in Mylar bags. Consider putting the Mylar bags or packages of food inside plastic buckets for an additional layer of protection. Food stored in boxes, bags, and Mylar bags are at risk of infestation. Even plastic buckets can be compromised by some persistent critters. Storing food in #10 cans is a great way to protect the contents.

BASIC SANITATION SUPPLIES

A supply of basic sanitation items will ensure you never have to run to the store to buy a bar of soap or toilet paper. We recommend maintaining a one-year supply of sanitation items. You can make it through almost any disaster situation with this amount, as well as saving money by stocking up when items are on sale. Track your actual usage of supplies by marking each container with the date it is opened. When the container is empty, record how long it lasted. Individual usage varies greatly. This will give you a fairly accurate rate of consumption and allow you to correctly calculate how much you need for a year's supply. Rotate the items to ensure supplies are kept fresh and nothing goes to waste. This is a list of the basic supplies we stock:

Toilet paper is a high priority on our sanitation supply list. When times get tough, toilet paper may be worth its weight in gold. The average American uses 100 single rolls of toilet paper each year. We have found that 50 double rolls take up less space in storage.

Consider storing 8-inch by 8-inch flannel cotton squares to be used as reusable toilet paper or washable toilet cloths. This sounds rather disgusting, but stay with us for a minute. A long-term disaster may require a little adaptation. The cloth squares are used in place of toilet paper and placed in a bucket of disinfecting solution (chlorine bleach or vinegar mixed with water) after use until you wash them and hang them out to dry. The cloth should be absorbent but should dry quickly. This is a much nicer option than newspaper, leaves, or corn cobs.

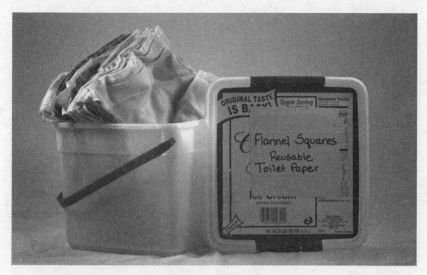

Flannel is a good fabric to create soft squares of toilet paper that can be washed and reused.

A cleansing bottle, such as Peri-Wash or a perineal irrigation bottle, can be used to spray off with, and then pat dry with a cloth. They are available at medical supply stores for around one dollar. Store a bottle for each member of the family so they will not have to share.

Soap can prevent the spread of disease. While it is possible to make wonderful soap at home, it is quite labor intensive. We know how to make soap from scratch, but we prefer to purchase a good supply for storage. Bar soap is relatively inexpensive and has an indefinite shelf life. One bar of soap per person per month is a safe estimate. Liquid soap tends to go a little more quickly, so we store one 13-ounce bottle per person per month. Shower gel amounts vary individually.

Hand sanitizer is an effective way to kill germs without water. If your hands are visibly dirty, hand sanitizer might not work effectively. Most have a high alcohol content and dry out your hands. Remember, hand sanitizer kills the germs but does not clean your hands. Nothing cleans and disinfects like briskly rubbing your hands together with soap and water for 20 seconds.

Shampoo and conditioner are nice to have. Women usually need twice as much conditioner as shampoo. Actual usage depends on the person and the quality of the shampoo. We plan 15 ounces of good shampoo per person per month.

Toothbrushes, toothpaste, and dental floss are important for keeping your teeth clean and healthy. A disaster is a horrible time for a toothache. Thoroughly brushing teeth with just water is highly effective. Baking soda and water can substitute for toothpaste in a pinch, or even dipping a wet toothbrush in kosher salt will work.

Deodorant might not be necessary, but it sure can make it easier to live together in close proximity. A stick of deodorant may last a couple of months depending on the user.

Dishwasher liquid has a long shelf life and many valuable uses. Consumption rate varies significantly. Track usage to get an accurate estimate of what you might need. If you wash dishes by hand, this should be a fairly accurate estimate of your consumption rate. Multiply this number by four if you normally use a dishwasher. This is an important item to stock up on.

Original Dawn dishwasher liquid is our personal favorite. It is mild enough to use as a shampoo substitute and can lubricate squeaky hinges nicely. Mix undiluted Dawn half-and-half with vinegar and you have an amazing bathroom and shower cleaner. Three drops in a gallon of water with a little vinegar makes the perfect window cleaner. Mix a tablespoon of soap in two quarts of water and spray in the garden to kill some varieties of garden pests, including squash bugs and aphids.

Laundry detergent is easy to make, but we still prefer to purchase it. Our family goes through one 146-load container of liquid laundry detergent every six weeks. We multiply this number out to get our par level for one year.

Disinfectants are used to destroy microorganisms before they can make you sick. They do not have to cost a lot of money. Store whatever kind of disinfectants you prefer. Alcohol, vinegar, chlorine bleach, and calcium hypochlorite are excellent options. Alcohol and vinegar have an indefinite shelf life and are good disinfectants. They are not quite as effective as chlorine bleach; however, they are safer to use and will not discolor items. Chlorine bleach has a shelf life of only six months, at which time it begins to lose its disinfecting power. Calcium hypochlorite powder can be made into a stock solution to provide fresh bleach as needed (see chapter 8). It has a shelf life of around 10 years.

Disposable gloves are invaluable when it comes to protecting yourself against disease. They are relatively inexpensive and will store for several years. We stock one-size-fits-all, latex-free vinyl gloves (commercial work gloves) for household cleaning and dirty work. A twin pack with 200 gloves costs under seven dollars. We also keep a supply of medical exam gloves in sizes that fit each individual in our family. They run around ten dollars for 200 gloves. We use these for first-aid and jobs that require gloves that fit well. Additionally, we keep several pairs of thick rubber gloves for the messier tasks.

Garbage bags are another critical basic sanitation item. Buy quality to avoid messy accidents. We keep a supply of contractor-grade black garbage bags, standard black garbage bags, kitchen garbage bags, and plastic grocery bags. Each bag has a different use, and we have found all to be important. Stock a few rolls of duct tape to help hold bags in place when needed.

Feminine products, such as sanitary napkins or tampons, are an important staple. In addition to use for menstruation, disposable sanitary pads are extremely valuable in first-aid kits as dressings for heavy bleeding. **Cloth menstrual pads** are reusable and may come in handy during an extended disaster scenario. These washable pads are made from several absorbent layers and may have a waterproof lining. Patterns are available on the Internet, or go to gladrags.com, lunapads.com, or sckoon.com to see reusable products for sale.

Disposable diapers for infants as well as adults are important to have. It doesn't hurt to stock cloth diapers, cloth wipes, diaper pins, and plastic pants just in case. They may prove quite valuable. These items would be great barter items if you no longer need them.

Each family has different basic sanitation requirements. Carefully consider what your needs are and stock up accordingly.

LAUNDRY

Some days feel like crisis laundry management even without a big emergency. Every time our family experiences the flu or returns from a camping trip, my appreciation for a working washing machine is renewed. What would you do if you did not have enough water to use your washing machine? What if water was available, but no electricity?

Our children would not mind wearing the same clothes 24/7, and we could probably make it through a short-term crisis without worrying about laundry. But what if the crisis outlasts our clean wardrobe? As with any preparedness options, there are inexpensive and expensive options. Choose which works best for your circumstances.

Nonelectric water conservation devices for laundry include the Laundry Pod, the Wonder Washer, and a bucket with a plunger.

Grandma's method has been used successfully for hundreds of years. It is an old-fashioned concept that still works. Use whatever containers are available and adapt her method to your circumstances.

- Sort clothes into lights and darks, similar fabrics, special handling, and level of dirt.

- Start with the dirtiest clothes first. Add one cup of bicarbonate of soda or laundry ammonia to the water. The mixture should feel slippery when you rub your fingers together.

- Use three large tubs—one tub for washing and two for rinsing. (Rinsing can be done with only one tub if needed.) Wash each load one by one and set them aside. Then get fresh water and rinse each load one by one. Then get more fresh water to rinse each load again.

- The initial wash is accomplished by pouring three buckets of warm water into the first tub containing the washboard. Stand behind the board, lean over, and rub with an up-and-down motion, working the dirtiest areas.

- Place the white clothes in a kettle of clean water for boiling. Pour soap over the clothes and fill with additional clean water to cover everything. Boil for 10 to 15 minutes, poking the clothes down in the soapy water from time to time. Fish out the clothes with a stick and put them into the first rinse water tub. Then transfer them into the second rinse tub and wring.

- Scrub colored clothes in the wash water heated by the soapy white load.

- Hang clothes on the line to dry. Remove promptly.

The **Wonder Washer** is a type of pressure washer. It is about the size of a 20-pound propane tank. Maximum capacity is a little less than five pounds of laundry. You add three quarts of water, two tablespoons of soap, and then the laundry. The tank is turned manually by a handle. There is a drain at the bottom. The process is repeated until the clothes are rinsed and ready to dry.

The **bucket-and-plunger method** is a pretty effective way for doing laundry short term. Dirty clothes, water, and detergent are placed in a bucket with a hole cut in the lid to accommodate a plunger. The plunger is used to agitate the clothes. A quality toilet plunger with a few holes drilled in the top will work, but a Rapid Laundry Washer works better. It has internal baffles that send water through the clothes to flush out dirt. Other popular laundry plungers are the Breathing Hand Washer and Washer Plunger.

The **Laundry POD** is a nonelectric washing machine that resembles a salad spinner. The washer sells for a little less than $100. It washes small loads. One gallon of water will wash a load. The water is drained out the bottom and clean water is added through the top to rinse.

The **sailor's method** uses a black garbage bag to wash the clothes. Apparently sailors would fill a black garbage bag with dirty clothes, water, and soap. The black bag took advantage of the sun to heat the water, and the ship's movement agitated the wash. You could adapt this a little by gently pressing on the bag to agitate the clothes. This might be a practical method for washing large items such as comforters, blankets, or sleeping bags that will not fit in five-gallon buckets to be washed.

CLOTHES DRYERS

An old-fashioned clothesline is an effective way to dry laundry. Exposing the clothes to the UV rays of the sun may fade fabric, but it will also help disinfect the laundry. If you are using diapers, reusable toilet paper, or anything that may have retained germs, leave it out a little longer to help disinfect the cloth.

Clothes can also be dried indoors. Ventilate when drying clothes to decrease drying time and prevent moisture from building up. Indoor drying racks come in a variety of shapes and sizes. They make drying more convenient and take up little space. You can also dry clothes by hanging them over chairs or doors.

SANITATION ACTION PLAN

Good sanitation practices always make sense. However, in an emergency situation, implementing good sanitation techniques is critical. It can make the difference between sickness and health, and possibly even life and death. Our challenge to you is to carefully think through the sanitation needs of your family. Educate family members as to the importance of good sanitation practice and how it applies to your family plan.

Use the worksheet located at http://theprovidentprepper.org/the-practical-prepper/action-plan-sanitation/ to create a workable plan, set realistic goals, and get to work to accomplish those goals. Remember that an idea that looks good on paper may not work effectively in reality. Practice to make sure it works for you.

10

Designer Food Storage Plans
What's for Dinner?

"All you need is love. But a little chocolate now and then doesn't hurt."

—Charles M. Schulz

"All is safely gathered in, ere the winter storms begin" are lyrics from the popular Christian hymn, "Come, Ye Thankful People, Come." Throughout history, people have prepared during the plentiful harvests of fall for the upcoming winter when food would be scarce. Great comfort could be found in stores of food that would see families through the cold winter. Lack of stores could lead to hunger, illness, and even death before the next harvest.

While winter storms are still an important consideration, our society has a system in which fresh fruits and vegetables, along with a wide variety of foods, are available all year at local markets. Little consideration is given to preparing for the upcoming winter because of this bountiful year-round harvest. This false sense of security may prove to be disastrous.

Have you ever been to Walmart late in the evening and discovered the shelves empty? Modern inventory systems are operated using *just-in-time inventory*, which means when someone purchases an item, an order is immediately sent to replace that item. There are no longer pallets of inventory kept in back storerooms. Just-in-time inventory dramatically reduces costs, but it has also made the system highly vulnerable. Minor disruptions in the transportation system result in empty shelves.

In addition to winter storms, there are other dangers to consider. Natural disasters—including earthquakes, hurricanes, fires, floods, drought, famine, and epidemics—may strike with little or no warning. Man-made disasters affecting our food supply include war, terrorism, EMP, food contamination, riots, and civil unrest. The list goes on. We need not look far to see evidence of these dangers throughout the world. The best way to protect our families is to take action personally.

In this chapter, we will explore a variety of different strategies for obtaining and designing the right plan for your family food stores. The most versatile food storage plan begins with a 3-month supply of foods you eat every day: canned foods, cereals, crackers, and so on. These supplies are rotated regularly from your pantry. A longer-term supply is made up of grains, legumes, and dehydrated foods packaged appropriately for long-term storage. You can choose to rotate this supply or stash it away for 25 to 30 years as a hunger insurance program.

UNDERSTANDING BASIC FOOD STORAGE NEEDS

Our goal is to provide you with knowledge to help you design a workable food storage plan unique to your family's needs and preferences. Let us review some basic principles.

Why We Eat

We eat for several reasons. The calories in food give us the energy we need to live. Food is our source of vitamins and minerals, providing the nutrition our bodies require for life and health. Memories, traditions, and good times revolve around food and bring us great comfort.

Caloric Requirements

An important reason for eating is energy. Caloric requirements vary from person to person. For example, a man who weighs 150 pounds would have a base requirement of 1,650 calories a day, but then we adjust for activity level. Let us assume an average level of activity, which adds 850 calories to the base. Thermogenesis (calories needed for digestion) would be 247. According to our calculations, this man would need to consume 2,722 calories to maintain 150 pounds. If activity level is increased, because of manual labor surrounding disaster situations, more calories would be required. A healthy food storage plan must take into account realistic caloric requirements.

Nutritional Considerations

Balanced nutrition is vital to health, especially in situations of heightened stress. There are two types of vitamins: water-soluble and fat-soluble. Water-soluble vitamins include B complex (except B12) and C. They can only be stored in the body in small amounts. Deficiency symptoms may appear within a few weeks to several months. Fat-soluble vitamins include D, E, K, and A. They dissolve in fat and are stored in body fat, the liver, and other body parts. Deficiencies take longer to develop due to the storage in fat.

Fifteen minerals are an essential part of our diet: calcium, phosphorus, magnesium, iron, zinc, fluoride, iodine, selenium, copper, manganese, chromium, molybdenum, sodium, potassium, and chloride. Minerals are different than vitamins in that minerals will not break down during the storage process, but vitamin content decreases with storage.

Vitamin and mineral deficiencies may cause a wide variety of ailments, including pain, blindness, confusion, weakness, diarrhea, bleeding, nausea, vomiting, neurological disorders, slow infection and wound recovery, heart irregularity or failure, and so on. Get the picture? Vitamin and mineral deficiencies are serious business.

Where Can I Get Essential Nutrients?

The above is quite a bit to think about, but getting all the right vitamins and minerals is quite easy when you eat the right basic foods. If you store wheat, rice, pasta, oats, dried beans, and dry milk, you have all the important vitamins and minerals covered with the exception of vitamin A (beta-carotene) and vitamin C. Vitamin A is found in deep orange, yellow, and green vegetables. Vitamin C is found in citrus, peppers, broccoli, and so on. Both of these can be found in leafy greens and tomatoes.

Disease-fighting phytochemicals are found most abundantly in fresh fruits and vegetables. Storing the right fruits and vegetables or growing a garden will take care of the vitamins not found in the grains and legumes. Sprouting can also provide many of these nutrients. Storing vitamin supplements might be wise, but remember the body assimilates natural sources better than supplements.

DEVELOP A PLAN

Armed with those basics, let us get to work on developing a plan. You need to know the number of people, their ages, special nutritional requirements, personal preferences, and dietary limitations, along with any special needs. Kylene's big one is chocolate. We promise you would not want to be around her when she's having chocolate withdrawals. Is someone gluten intolerant? Allergic to milk? Does someone hate lima beans? Absolutely love granola? Seriously take these things into consideration. Do not store foods you do not like or will not eat. Tailor the plan for personal needs and preferences.

Next, set a goal for the amount of time you want your storage to last. We recommend a goal of a three-month supply of foods you eat every day and a supply of longer-term storage items. That is enough food to see you through most crises and prevent any from going to waste. It is your plan. How long do you want your food stores to last? Take a minute and complete the first worksheet at www.theprovidentprepper .org/the-practical-prepper/action-plan-food-storage.

There is no one right storage plan when it comes to food storage. We have learned a variety of unique approaches from people. They do not work for everyone, but they are perfect for them. Let us start by learning how to build a three-month supply of everyday foods and then tackle the longer term storage.

Building a 3-Month Supply

A great place to start is by building a three-month supply of food your family eats every day. That can seem like a huge deal if you go to the market and come out with eight carts of groceries, but trust us, it is easier than you think. Chances are your family eats quite differently than ours. You shop differently than we do. There is a plan that is perfect for your unique style. Let us explore some of our friends' various plans for building a short-term food supply.

2-Week Menu Plan

This plan uses a two-week menu to calculate ingredients for three months. Ask each member of your family what their favorite meals are. McDonald's is not an option, so leave that and all other fast food favorites off the menu. Select menus with shelf-stable ingredients. It is okay to include some frozen foods, but wisdom dictates that most ingredients come from shelf-stable, easy-to-store items.

We will use one of our family favorites as an example. Spaghetti with meatballs, green salad, green beans, and garlic bread make a delightful meal, especially when followed with a slice of cheesecake. Shelf-stable ingredients include the pasta, canned spaghetti sauce and green beans, ranch dressing mix, mayonnaise, powdered milk, and no-bake cheesecake. Frozen meatballs and bread dough are in the freezer, which we count in our three-month supply. The fresh green salad is not a good storage item, so it may or may not be available. Dinner will be fine without it.

Gather the recipes from your family survey and make a list of the ingredients for each one of them. You should have 14 breakfast, 14 lunch, and 14 dinner entrées. We have a hard time coming up with 14 different breakfast ideas, so we use seven breakfast entrées and double it. Multiply each ingredient by six and you have a supply of everything you need to make this menu for three months. This plan can save a lot of what's-for-dinner stress.

Plain Old Math

This is the simplest way to plan a three-month supply. For this method, you have 90 breakfast entrées, 90 lunch entrées (optional), 90 dinner entrées, 90 fruit/vegetables/side dishes, and, of course, 90 treats or desserts large enough to feed your family. In addition to this, you need a healthy stock of basics such as flour, sugars, baking powder, baking soda, salt, vegetable oil, shortening, spices, cornstarch, vinegar, bouillon cubes, and so on. The idea is to store what your family eats every day so you never worry about wasting and you always have what you need on hand. This is how it might look for a family of six people.

Breakfast: 30 boxes of cereal, three cans (#10) of powdered milk, 10 pounds of complete pancake mix, three bottles of maple syrup, and 30 packages of muffin mix. Juice mix or hot cocoa are a nice addition. Mix it up anyway you like. You should have a total of 90 basic breakfasts.

Lunch: Many people choose not to include lunch in their planning. That would be fine for adults, but not for children. It can be as simple as 30 cans of SpaghettiOs, 30 cans of mandarin oranges, 30 cans of chili, 6 boxes of crackers, 30 boxes of macaroni and cheese, 30 cans of green beans, and enough drink boxes for each child to have one a day—simple, basic stuff that you will rotate through anyway.

Dinner: Store 15 cans of pasta sauce and packages of pasta, 15 boxes of hamburger helper, 15 cans of soup and 5 boxes of crackers, 15 packages of rice mix, 15 packages of gravy mix and 3 cans (#10) of potato flakes, 15 cans of Chunky Soup and 30 of pounds of rice, 90 cans of meat or 1-pound packages of frozen meat, 90 cans of vegetables, and 90 cans of fruit. Vary the menu any way you like. Shop the sales, but make sure you have basics you eat every day.

Treats: Do not overlook comfort foods. What makes you feel better during times of high stress? It is different for everyone. Ten cake mixes, 10 cans of frosting, 10 brownie mixes, 10 cookie mixes, 5 boxes of graham crackers, 30 packages of Jell-O, and 30 packages of pudding would give you a treat every day for three months. Store a #10 can of powdered eggs, powdered milk, and oil. If you love gum, make sure you have a couple of cases on hand.

Tiffany's Super Simple Plan: Part Math, Part Menu

Tiffany and her husband are busy professionals with a one-year-old daughter. They live in a hot climate with no basement storage. Meals are simple and they eat out weekly. After considering their lifestyle, they settled on a plan that is part plain math and part menu based.

As with most parents, their highest priority is to make sure that their daughter is well fed. The toddler's three-month supply is plain old math: six boxes of multigrain Cheerios, six boxes of assorted crackers, 90 cans of assorted fruits, 90 cans of assorted vegetables, 90 boxes of shelf-stable milk, and 90 juice boxes. Fat is important in a toddler's diet, so the shelf-stable milk is a better option than nonfat powdered milk at this point. Tiffany also stores a three-month supply of baby vitamins.

Breakfast is usually hot or cold cereal. Simple math requires them to store 2 boxes of Cream of Wheat, 6 boxes of instant oatmeal, 24 boxes of cereal, 24 bottles of juice, and 3 cans (#10) of powdered milk. Lunchtime usually consists of leftovers or lunches provided at work. Dave eats 2 packages of oatmeal every day at work, so they store an additional 12 boxes of instant oatmeal for his lunch.

The menu part of the plan comes in with the dinners. Tiffany calculates the ingredients for a dozen of their favorite meals and stores enough for 3 months. Her favorite comfort food is a fruit smoothie. She makes sure she has plenty of frozen fruit. Dave's favorite comfort food is pizza, so they have plenty of frozen shredded cheese, pepperoni, turkey sausage, and other ingredients on hand.

Betty's Box-a-Week Plan

Our dear friend Betty came up with a great plan that works well for her family. She puts shelf-stable ingredients for one week's worth of breakfasts and dinners into one office storage box. Each box is carefully labeled with the contents and dates. She knows exactly how much food she has by simply counting her boxes.

She doesn't worry about missing any ingredients that may have been accidently used for a different meal. The boxes store nicely on top of each other in an out-of-the-way place. Rotation is simple: she takes a box and puts the contents into her pantry. The empty box is filled with a fresh supply and relabeled.

Healthy Harvest

This plan requires a significant investment of time and energy, but it is by far the healthiest, most sustainable, and least expensive way to obtain a food supply. Grow a big garden with all of the fruits and vegetables your family loves. Raise a few chickens for fresh eggs. Bottle, freeze, dehydrate, or store in a root cellar your bountiful harvest. If you do not want to grow everything yourself, share a neighbor's excess produce, purchase seconds at a farmer's market, or watch for great deals at a local market. Barter or trade goods and services.

Take all of those beautiful fruits and vegetables and combine them with rice, beans, pasta, and freshly made bread from your longer-term food supply. Add a freezer full of frozen meats and you have delicious and highly nutritious foods to feed your family. You can produce some of your own and purchase other things that do not make sense to produce yourself.

Fast Food Storage

This is a fun way to get the job done. All of the ingredients for each meal are placed in a reusable gift bag with the recipe attached to the front. When you want to make a meal you just grab a bag, and 30 minutes later, dinner is served. A three-month supply would require 90 breakfast bags, 90 lunch bags (if desired), and 90 dinner bags. It's that easy.

Gather your favorite quick and simple recipes and make copies of them, one copy for each time you would like to eat that meal. Attach the recipe to the front of the gift bag. Place all ingredients in the bag.

Spices should be measured into a snack-sized ziplock bag. Include the appropriate amount of water bottles in the bag for any water the recipe calls for.

After the bag is used, place it with the others to be refilled. Everything is reused, including the ziplock bags that held the spices. The authors of *It's in the Bag*, Michelle and Trent Snow, suggest using regular water, when it is available, and just putting the unopened water bottles back to be used in another bag. Some ingredients may be stored in the freezer, such as hamburger or shredded cheese. The authors also suggest using a CD sleeve for the recipes attached to the bags.

Longer-Term Storage Ideas

Once you have a three-month supply of everyday foods, it is time to get to work on your longer-term storage. This plan is as unique to your family as your three-month supply. Let us look at some real plans together and evaluate them. Remember, our goal is not to convert anyone to our way of eating but to help them design the perfect plan for their diet of choice.

Grandpa Ray's Chunky Soup Plan

Grandpa Ray leads a busy life. His day usually begins with breakfast from McDonald's, lunch from the cafeteria at work, and a simple dinner or out to a restaurant. His cooking skills are limited and he likes it that way. He came up with a plan to store a year's worth of white rice and a variety of Chunky Soups. Not your typical plan, but let us take a closer look at it.

He would need to store 150 pounds of rice and 365 cans of soup to have 2 cups of cooked rice with 1 can of Chunky Soup poured over the top each day. The daily caloric intake would be between 900 and 1,100 calories. A one-year supply would cost less than $600, if he's a really good shopper. The soups would be easy to rotate because he makes this meal a couple of times a week.

Pretty good plan, Grandpa, but let's make it better. It looks like we are missing vitamin C. We could add cans of mandarin oranges and V8 juice. Supplements may also be a good idea. Calcium is missing, and Grandpa hates milk. Maybe some powdered or shelf-stable chocolate milk and Tums could be added to meet that need.

In addition, we would add a variety of dried or canned fruits to increase caloric intake. He really needs over 2,000 calories a day. Grandpa might want to store some pasta to add a little variety. Think about upping the quantities to allow for more than one meal a day.

Developing a realistic plan is important. This is not the best diet, but during a crisis is not a good time to make dietary changes. This plan is high in MSG, preservatives, and sodium, and it could present a problem with diet fatigue even with 30 different types of Chunky soup. However, this is what Grandpa likes and eats, which makes it the perfect plan for him.

I-Hate-Whole-Wheat Plan

The Miller family hates wheat. They live off white bread and avoid whole grains like the plague. Vegetables are usually consumed in the form of French fries. Fast food meals dominate their standard diet. Starving might be a more favorable alternative for this family than eating whole wheat. Instead of refusing to store food entirely, let's explore possible ways to design a storage plan to work with their lifestyle.

White flour has a shorter shelf life than wheat. Enriched white flour has a recommended shelf life of 10 years. It can develop a metal taste and smell after just a few years in a #10 can, but the flour is still good. Remove it from the can and place it in a plastic or glass container. Let it air out for a few days and both the taste and smell will disappear. Flour stores well in Mylar-lined plastic buckets.

White rice, potato flakes, beans, oats, and spaghetti all have a 30-year shelf life and are good choices for long-term storage. These might fit into the Millers' plan. Each one is easy to prepare, and they do not require a grinder or any special equipment. The Millers might consider storing a larger supply of shorter-term storage items. Cases of SpaghettiOs, ravioli, baked beans, macaroni and cheese, or soups can store for several years. Add a few cans of powdered milk and powdered or canned butter, and that macaroni and cheese will be delightful. They probably should store a good supply of gummy bear vitamins.

Grandma's Basement Plan

Grandma is the best. She has been gardening, bottling, and storing food for over 50 years. It is all tucked away in her cool basement, including the very first bottle of peaches she ever bottled. She has stocked up at every case lot sale since 1972. There is a whole lot of food down there, some of it quite dangerous, some of it quite delicious, but who knows what is what?

This kind of plan may provide a false sense of security. If there is ever a good time to get botulism, it is not during a crisis with limited medical care. Those 20-year-old boxes of Cheerios probably contain the powdered remains of a booming insect infestation that has worked its way through even the fresher foods. Thanks for trying so hard, Grandma. Let's make it better.

The shelf life of foods stored in a cool, dry basement can be significantly more than the "best if used by" date on the package. Food decreases in nutritional value as it ages but tends to retain caloric value. It is time to have a cleaning party and go through Grandma's basement. Because she has seen hard times, she has an attitude of "someday you might be really glad you have that." A firm but gentle approach may be necessary.

If the wheat is stored in #10 cans or buckets and does not show signs of infestation, it is probably quite safe to keep and use even after 30 years. That first bottle of peaches from 1960 has got to go. Pour it out in a compost pit and explain that it will help the garden grow even more beautiful next year.

Once all of the questionable food has been disposed of, inventory the rest. Organize the storeroom into categories such as proteins, fruits, vegetables, grains, and so on, which will make locating items much simpler. Keep up the good work, Grandma!

Special Diets

Pay close attention to special diets when storing foods. One example is celiac disease, which is an allergy to gluten. Reactions and intensity vary greatly between people. A basic diet for gluten allergies would not allow for wheat, barley, rye, or oats. However, someone with celiac disease may still eat and store long-term items such as dried beans, white rice, corn, dried potatoes, and powdered milk, along with dehydrated fruits and vegetables.

Do not let anything prevent you from storing the right foods. There is always a way if you look hard enough. You might not be able to store wheat, but very few people have allergies to white rice. We recommend packaging the grains yourself to ensure cross contamination does not occur during the packaging process, if the allergy is severe.

A person with a special diet might consider storing a 6-month supply of everyday foods due to the specialized dietary requirements and consequences of eating foods that cause serious health concerns. This design might require a little more thought and creativity, but it absolutely can be done. No one knows your dietary needs like you do.

Basic Food Security Plan

You can give a child the gift of food security with very little money and space. The space under one twin bed can store 12 cases of #10 cans (72 cans), an average of 360 pounds of grains and legumes, which can have a shelf life of 30-plus years. The cost would be around $200. This amount could provide ¾ of a loaf of bread and one cup cooked beans every day for one year if only wheat and beans were stored—no rotation required.

One year of basic longer-term food storage (72 #10 cans) will fit nicely under a twin bed. No rotation required for foods with a 30-year shelf life.

You could choose to store a variety of grains and legumes that do not require a grinder. Purchase the cans when your child is a toddler and he will be off to college well before the food has passed its prime.

Think about it: A one-year supply of basic lifesaving food and you will never have to clean under the bed. The following table calculates the number of pounds required for survival rations of basic storage grains and legumes.

Basic Long-Term Food Storage Calculations

Storage Item (lbs.) ×	Number of People	= Total (lbs.)
Grains (wheat, rice, oats, corn, rye, barley, pasta, etc.): **300 lbs.**		
Legumes (beans, peas, lentils, etc.): **60 lbs.**		

300 pounds of grain and 60 pounds of legumes stored in buckets.

GENERIC LONGER-TERM STORAGE PLAN

A generic long-term storage plan for one adult might include 300 pounds of grain, 60 pounds of beans/legumes, 40 pounds of sugar, 60 pounds of dry milk, 24 cans of dehydrated or freeze-dried fruits and vegetables, baking soda, and salt. Total cost of a year supply for one person can be less than $450 depending on specific food choices.

These items have a long shelf life (15 to 30-plus years) if packaged and stored appropriately. It would be wise to include some items with a shorter shelf life, such as 25 pounds of fats (like oil), shortening, mayonnaise, salad dressing, peanut butter, baking powder, yeast, and vinegar. Remember to store vitamin supplements. This plan would greatly benefit from storing garden seeds or sprouting grains for increased nutrition.

Many retail stores carry buckets and #10 cans of food storage items, which go on sale periodically. Sugar, white flour, beans, and rice may be purchased in 25- or 50-pound bags at Sam's Club or Costco and put in buckets for longer-term storage. Shop around and get the foods that are right for your storage plan.

300 pounds of grain and 60 pounds of legumes stored in #10 cans.

Commercial Food Storage Plans

Buyers should beware of prepackaged commercial food storage plans. Advertising may be misleading, so be sure you understand exactly what you are getting. Some of these plans have great benefits: a long shelf life, variety of freeze-dried foods, and simple preparation. However, they are quite expensive. Some may be misleading as to the supply of food actually provided and might not meet nutritional requirements. We evaluated a few of these plans. Here is what we found.

- Example A, 1-Year Supply, $1,199.99: Three servings per day for one adult. On the surface this sounds great with menu items such as chicken teriyaki, blueberry pancakes, and maple and brown sugar oatmeal. A closer look reveals a daily caloric intake of only 500 to 700 calories. In order to achieve the caloric intake required for our 150-pound man, we would have to purchase five of these supplies for a grand total of $10,000 for a one-year supply of food for one person.

- Example B, 1-Year Supply, $8,999.99: Three entrées per day for two adults and three children—only $2.37 per serving. This plan provides between 600 and 800 calories per day per person. When did you last pay $2.37 for a packet of instant oatmeal or tomato soup? In order to achieve an adequate caloric intake, you would need to purchase at least four of these packages for a total of $36,000. That is significantly more than our annual food budget.

That being said, a commercial food storage plan may be the perfect plan for you. They have a long shelf life, are easy to prepare, and can be stored away waiting for an emergency. They may be a great way to supplement a basic food storage plan. Just know what you're getting.

Jones Family Storage Plan

Our storage plan is unique to our family. We eat lots of whole grains and beans. Most of our food is made from scratch. We have a supply of everyday foods, as well as longer-term storage, and we rotate through most of it. We have fruit trees, berry bushes, a vegetable garden, and chickens. We spend time bottling, freezing, and dehydrating during the harvest. It is a lifestyle that is not possible, or even desirable, for some, but we love it.

Our food is stored in a cool basement on sturdy shelves that make rotation easy, organization possible, and quick assessment of needs simple. It is our own little store. When there is an incredible sale on an item, such as peanut butter or canned soup, we purchase a few cases. We have a kitchen pantry that we take supplies from to cook every day. When the pantry gets low, we replenish from our basement stores. Newly purchased foods are always taken to the basement storage and placed behind the older food. Our grocery budget is smaller than many. Yet our plan allows us to eat well and have a healthy supply of food stored.

Our storage plan is based on a three-week menu plan of our favorite meals. Jonathan lists all of the ingredients for those recipes on a spreadsheet. Ingredients for one batch of bread every other day and treats four times a week are included in the calculations. Instead of planning each side dish, we plan to serve a fruit and vegetable with each meal. Those numbers are easily calculated per container.

Some items, such as ketchup, we estimate weekly usage and simply add them in. This spreadsheet allows us to accurately assess exactly how much we need of each item to reach our goal. It can be calculated for a three-month, six-month, or one-year supply of food.

When canned green beans go on sale, we know exactly how many cans to purchase to meet our goal. Those will be consumed within the year, so theoretically we never waste expired foods. We used to stock up randomly at case lot sales, but we found that some foods just sat on the shelves. Canned salmon is a good example. We do not usually eat it, but it sounded like a good idea to add protein to our storage. The cases sat in our storage room for a few years until they were fed to the cats one can at a time. Now we only purchase foods that we normally eat.

HOME PRODUCTION

Home gardens are a sustainable way to ensure you have nutritious foods to eat. As a society, we have become distanced from our food. We purchase it in boxes, bags, and containers, not realizing where it really comes from. The ability to produce at least some of your own food is a critical survival skill. Producing your own food in an urban setting can be challenging, but it is possible. Even if you only have a patio or balcony, you can grow something. Community gardens are gaining popularity in large cities.

Urban Homestead is located in Pasadena, California, on a 0.2-acre lot. They grow over 6,000 pounds of fruits, vegetables, and herbs annually in a 0.1-acre garden. View their amazing success story at www.urbanhomestead.org and glean some great ideas on how to produce lots of food in a small amount of space.

One four-foot by four-foot raised garden bed can produce 30 to 60 pounds of vegetables annually. Edible plants can be interspersed with traditional landscape, providing food along with beauty. One mature dwarf apple tree (eight to ten feet tall) will produce between three and five bushels of apples each year. That's 126 to 210 pounds of apples that can be eaten, stored, dried, bottled, juiced, or shared. It would be easy to plant dwarf fruit trees along a back fence that would ripen throughout the summer and fall.

Carefully consider using whatever space you have available to grow at least some food. The fresh produce you contribute to your long-term food supplies will greatly benefit your diet as well as your mental health.

Children learn to enjoy fresh fruits and vegetables
when they grow the plants themselves.

FOOD STORAGE ACTION PLAN

We have reviewed a variety of food storage strategies. The best plan is a combination of everyday foods complemented by a supply of longer-term storage. Remember, the purpose of longer-term food storage is to sustain life during an extended crisis. Three months of everyday food storage will get you safely through the majority of disasters without compromising your current diet.

Now it is time for you to thoughtfully consider what form you want your food storage plan to take. The ultimate goal is to have a supply of food to help you make it through tough times. The Bible tells the story of Joseph in Egypt. In response to a dream of Pharaoh's, Joseph stored grain during years of plenty for a time of famine. Egypt flourished while surrounding nations starved. Similarly, your storage plan should be designed to see you safely through the really tough times.

Complete your action plan using the worksheet located at www.theprovidentprepper.org/the-practical-prepper/action-plan-food-storage. It will help organize your thoughts and begin designing your perfect plan.

11

Food Storage
How and Where

A full pantry is an indication of true wealth and wisdom.

In chapter 10 we explored the strategies for an effective food storage plan. Now it's time to explore the best storage methods and how to find space to store your precious supplies. Food storage is a financial investment, and, as with any investment, it must be protected.

These beans were purchased at the same time but stored differently. The beans stored in a garage and then outside in a plastic bucket were hard, dark, and slightly greasy. An identical bucket was stored in a basement and were in great shape after 14 years of storage. The beans stored in a #10 can in a basement did not appear to have changed at all in 14 years. Storage conditions matter.

ENEMIES TO YOUR FOOD STORAGE

Ready or not, it happens—you are in a crisis and suddenly need the valuable food you have faithfully stored. Terror strikes as you realize your grain is infested with insects or disease-ridden rodents, making it no longer fit for human consumption. Storing your food properly is critical to ensure safe, nutritious food when you need it most.

Enemies to food include air, chemical contamination, insects, light, moisture, rodents, temperature, and time. When stored in optimal conditions, some foods will maintain quality and nutrient contents for over 30 years. Improper storage may result in a waste of resources, serious illness, or death from foodborne illnesses such as botulism. We will review each of these bad boys and help develop strategies to combat them.

Air: Room air contains about 21 percent oxygen, which oxidizes many of the compounds found in foods. Oxygen allows for the growth of insects and bacteria. Removing or displacing the oxygen from the packaging helps increase the shelf life of low moisture foods.

Chemical contamination: Use only food-grade containers to store food. Never store food in any container that has been used for non-food items—it is not worth the risk. Do not store food next to any volatile chemical compounds because they may be transferred to the food and affect odor, flavor, and safety. In other words, do not store your wheat next to gasoline.

Insects: Buy fresh, quality food products to begin with. Weevils, small flour beetles, dermestid beetles, larder beetles, moths, and other pests will infest, destroy, contaminate, and consume food. Insects come in various life stages and require special handling to destroy each stage. Storing food in a container with an oxygen-free environment will destroy insects in all stages.

Light: Irradiation by sunlight produces physical and chemical changes in food. Light speeds deterioration of both food and packaging. Direct sunlight is especially damaging. Foods are best stored in a dark environment or in containers that keep light out.

Moisture: Low-moisture foods have the longest shelf life. Good candidates for long-term storage should have a moisture content of 10 percent or less. Mold growth and chemical degradation of all grains is supported if the moisture level is over 12 percent.[1] High levels of moisture allow bacteria to grow. This results in spoiled grain, which is unfit for use. Caution: Botulism poisoning may occur when moist products are stored in reduced oxygen packaging.

Make sure to package food storage in a dry place with low humidity, such as an air-conditioned home. Store containers off the floor, especially concrete. Storing food on pallets or wooden boards lined up a few inches apart on the floor can prevent moisture from wicking up from the concrete into storage containers. Good airflow under and around storage items reduces moisture problems. Moisture can destroy some food packaging. If you are storing foods in a humid area, it may be wise to invest in a dehumidifier.

Rodents: Secure your storage area to prevent access by rodents. These critters deposit waste products in stored grains. Mice can chew through a Mylar bag or foil pouch quickly. They can also chew through plastic buckets. Rats have been known to chew through metal garbage cans. If you have a rodent problem, take care of it immediately. Traps and poison bait can be quite effective, but keep them out of the reach of children and pets! Keep your storage area free from spilled grain or food. Do not underestimate how effective a good cat can be at keeping the mice population under control.

A rodent nibbled a hole in corner of this Mylar bag.

Temperature: Storage temperature and temperature fluctuation have a significant effect on the shelf life of stored foods. According to the USDA, every 10-degree drop in temperature doubles the storage life of seeds. This also applies to food storage. It is possible to double, triple, or even quadruple a product's shelf life by storing at lower temperatures.

Optimal storage temperature for shelf-stable food storage is between 40 and 60 degrees Fahrenheit. The cooler the storage area, the longer the retention of quality and nutrients. The average room temperature is between 64 and 73 degrees. The average basement temperature is between 55 and 65 degrees. Root cellars are designed to be very high in humidity. Metal will quickly rust in a root cellar.

Freezing temperatures do not damage stored grains. However, never allow canned foods (e.g. canned fruits, vegetables, beans, meats, and so on) or glass jars to freeze. Freezing changes food textures and leads to rust, bursting cans, and broken seals that may let in harmful bacteria. Notice the significant difference in potential storage life of grains stored in a basement at 60 degrees verses in a hot garage at 80 degrees.

Potential Storage Life Stored at Constant Temperature

Storage Temperature	Storage Life (Years) for Grain, #10 Can	Storage Life (Years) for Canned Goods
40°F (root cellar)	45	16
50°F	35	12
60°F (basement)	25	8
70°F (room temp.)	12½	4
80°F	6	2
90°F	3	1
100°F	1½	6 months

Time: As food ages, color, flavor, aroma, texture, and appearance deteriorate and nutritional value diminishes. Some foods may become unsafe to consume over time. White rice, pinto beans, corn, wheat, rolled oats, pasta, potato flakes, dehydrated apple slices, and sugar are examples of low-moisture foods that can be stored for 30-plus years if stored appropriately. However, foods high in fats or oil—such as brown rice, shortening, and vegetable oils—will go rancid in a much shorter period of time.

The best way to combat this enemy is to regularly rotate your food stores so it never gets old. This may be challenging if you store foods you do not eat on a regular basis. Consider rotating by donating items to local food banks while they are still good and replacing with a fresh supply. It is best to "eat what you store and store what you eat." This assures you are not adjusting to a new diet while trying to cope with a big crisis at the same time.

ACTUAL SHELF LIFE

The actual shelf life is not determined by the date on a can but by storage conditions as discussed above. We were given a unique opportunity to personally test some food storage purchased in 1960. It had been stored under the stairs in a basement for 45 years. To our surprise, it was still edible. The wheat made great bread. The dehydrated applesauce and other foods looked and smelled fine. Everything we tasted was of acceptable quality. We did not consume all of it due to the decreased nutrient content, but it would have been safe if we were desperate.

We also had the opportunity to evaluate wheat that had been stored in sacks and square metal cans since the early 1970s. To our surprise, even the sacks of wheat showed no evidence of infestation. The cans were rusted on the exterior, but the wheat was fine. We chose not to consume this wheat because we were not confident where it had been. Our chickens enjoyed it.

The steamboat *Bertrand* sunk to the bottom of the Missouri River in 1865. In 1968, canned food items were recovered from the wreckage:

> Among the canned food items retrieved from the *Bertrand* . . . were brandied peaches, oysters, plum tomatoes, honey, and mixed vegetables. In 1974, chemists at the National Food Processors Association (NFPA) analyzed the products for bacterial contamination and nutrient value. Although the food had lost its fresh smell and appearance, the NFPA chemists detected no microbial growth and determined that the foods were as safe to eat as they had been when canned more than 100 years earlier.
>
> The nutrient values varied depending upon the product and nutrient. NFPA chemists Janet Dudek and Edgar Elkins report that significant amounts of vitamins C and A were lost. But protein levels remained high, and all calcium values "were comparable to today's products."
>
> NFPA chemists also analyzed a 40-year-old can of corn

found in the basement of a home in California. Again, the canning process had kept the corn safe from contaminants and from much nutrient loss. In addition, Dudek says, the kernels looked and smelled like recently canned corn.[2]

We are not advocating storing foods for long periods of time. The point we are trying to make is that most food is edible long past the date printed on the can. As a rule, rotating food storage is the best way to receive optimal quality and nutrients from the products. We purchased a few too many cans of peaches during a case lot sale one year. The first year the peaches were firm and delightful. As the years past, the peaches became softer and mushier, but maintained the flavor.

The "best if used by" date is the length of time food maintains most of its original nutrients and quality. "Life sustaining" shelf-life is the length of time food will sustain life and is still edible. Minerals and carbohydrates do not change significantly during storage. Proteins can deteriorate and denature. Fats can go rancid, developing bad odors and flavors. Vitamins may be destroyed by light, heat, and oxidation. Calories are not destroyed during extended storage.

Do not let the date on shelf-stable food products discourage you from stocking up on a good supply of commercially canned products. They are perfect for maintaining a supply of foods that are easy to prepare, require no fuel to consume, and add great diversity to a diet. Rotate these supplies in your everyday cooking.

FINDING ROOM TO STORE IT ALL

Finding room to properly store your food can be quite challenging. Many apartments and homes are not storage friendly. Ideal storage conditions are in a cool, dry basement on sturdy shelves designed to facilitate effective rotation. Quite frankly, most of us do not have an ideal place to store our food. You will have to use a little creativity to get the job done.

A college student living in a dorm room really does not have many options for much food storage. Maybe a few cans of stuff in the bottom of the closet or under the bed, but that is about it. In this case it might be best to store some food with a good friend or family member who has more space. Students are highly vulnerable. They live in densely populated areas and depend on public food establishments that are not prepared to serve during a disaster. Brainstorm a strategy that might at least provide basic needs for a week or two.

Closet space can be altered to accommodate additional storage. Line the floor with boxes of #10 cans. Is there any wasted space at the very top of the closet? Could you add another high shelf? What about installing a narrow shelf right above the inside of the closet door? Would a row of canned goods fit behind the clothing on the shelves?

This 12-inch shelf is strategically placed over a door just inside a small toilet room. It holds a year's supply of toilet paper for four people, along with feminine products for two. It is not visible outside the toilet closet. It's a perfect use of previously unused space to store bulky items.

Where do you have dead space in your home? The space above kitchen cupboards is often unutilized. Can you modify it to provide additional storage space? Do you have small, rarely used kitchen appliances you could part with to make space for a few more cans of food? Do you have space above the refrigerator, washer, or dryer? Under beds, dressers, or chests? Behind furniture? How about under the stairs? Behind the couch, bookcase, or piano? Inside suitcases?

Can you add shelves anywhere? Is there unused space in your existing pantry? Would additional shelves allow for a higher concentration of storage items? Can you install sturdy shelves that go clear up to the ceiling in the laundry room? How about shallow shelves in between exposed studs in a garage or basement? Can you put shelves along an entire wall and disguise it with curtains? Always construct sturdy shelves. Food storage is heavy. Anchor prefabbed shelves securely. Install bars or bungee cords to prevent food from tumbling off the shelves during an earthquake.

This storage room utilizes a rotation rack for canned goods, floor space for buckets, and sturdy shelves to hold heavy food items.

Campers, trailers, and boats might provide storage space. We store our extra propane tanks inside of a tent trailer away from the house. Build a small shed in a sheltered area outside your home. What about in your garage and up in the rafters? Store only items that are not sensitive to fluctuation in temperature in these areas. Canning supplies take up a lot of space but would store nicely on garage shelving.

Root cellars and crawl spaces can be a lifesaver. High moisture levels can damage some items. Store items in moisture- and pest-resistant containers, such as plastic buckets or sealable totes. You could even use an old chest freezer or barrel and bury it in the ground if needed.

Organize your home. Are you taking up valuable storage space by saving high school wrestling tights, 8-track tapes, or 20-year-old tax returns? Go through everything you have stored. If you have not used it in a few years, do you really need to keep it? Maybe those wrestling tights have sentimental value, but how about getting rid of some of the other junk.

Our bottled and dehydrated foods are stored on these sturdy shelves. Storing the bottles up on shelves, instead of in boxes, encourages rotation and easy visualization of inventory. Some of the bottles are tucked into old socks to cushion and help with easy cleanup of glass in the event of an earthquake.

Preppers are an interesting breed of gatherers and savers. The mentality of "someday I might be glad to have that" may need to be replaced with "is this vital to my survival, comfort, or emotional security?" Stuff owns you. As you learn to part with unnecessary things, you will find a renewed sense of freedom. Jonathan teases Kylene about storing so many boxes of old kindergarten drawings and pictures. Kylene harasses Jonathan about savings spare parts for vehicles sold years ago. Everyone has their sacred cow—best to leave those alone and find space somewhere else.

Do not store old, needs-to-be-fixed stuff to be used during an emergency. If it does not work now, why would it be helpful in an emergency?

Organize everything you own so you know where it is when you need it. Seriously evaluate your possessions. What purpose do they serve? Would a garage sale help finance a supply of basic foods? The peace a full pantry brings is worth the effort.

This basement storage room takes advantage of unused space.

LONGER-TERM FOOD STORAGE CONTAINERS

Most grains and legumes come in bags that are not effective for long-term storage. If you intend to store foods for a long time, take great care to package foods into appropriate containers using methods to prevent insect infestation. We will review a variety of options available for long-term storage.

#10 cans are perfect for long-term storage of dry (10 percent moisture or less), shelf-stable, and low-oil-content foods. Foods do not react with the metal can due to a food-grade enamel coating. All dry foods, except sugar, should be packed with an oxygen absorber to prevent insect infestation and preserve quality of food. These cans provide a true oxygen barrier, which makes them a great choice. Protect cans from moisture to prevent rust. Do not store in direct contact with concrete floors or walls.

Foil pouches/Mylar bags: Pouches are made from several layers of laminated plastic and aluminum. Food-grade plastic separates the food from the aluminum. The bags effectively protect against moisture and insects, but they allow a very small amount of oxygen transfer over time. Pouches are not rodent proof. Consider storing pouches in rodent-resistant containers. Do not allow pouches to come in contact with concrete floors or walls. Store only low-moisture (10 percent or less), shelf-stable, and low-oil-content foods in foil pouches.

Mylar pouches for longer term storage.

PETE (polyethylene terephthalate) plastic bottles: Use only PETE bottles since other bottles might not provide a suitable moisture or oxygen barrier. PETE bottles will have *PETE* or *PET* under the recyclable symbol on the bottom of the bottles. Examples may be some 2-liter soda bottles, juice bottles, and so on. Never use containers which have previously stored nonfood items.

Make sure to clean bottles well and allow to air-dry for several days. These bottles will work to store grains but will not maintain the same high quality over time as #10 cans. For dry foods, use one oxygen absorber packet in each gallon-sized or smaller bottle. Protect from light and rodents. PETE bottles may also be used for water storage.

PETE bottles are an inexpensive way to store food and water.

Plastic buckets: Food-grade plastic buckets with gaskets seals are good candidates for grain storage. Dry ice (CO_2) should be used to prevent insect infestation. Oxygen absorbers are not effective in plastic buckets because they depend on the absence of oxygen to kill insects. Plastic buckets are not a true oxygen barrier. There is a slow transmission of oxygen through the polyethylene walls of the container over time. Store buckets at least ½ inch off the floor to allow for air circulation. Avoid stacking buckets over three high to prevent damage to the lids.

Dry foods (less than 10 percent moisture) are candidates for bucket storage. Some leaching of the plastic into the food may occur. This is not harmful. You may consider lining the bucket with food-grade plastic or a Mylar bag if this is a concern. The five-gallon buckets, as well as polyethylene (plastic) bags, do not maintain an oxygen-free environment.

We store packaged items like bags of pasta, salt, baking powder, powdered sugar, and a variety of other items in their original packaging inside of plastic buckets. The bucket provides an extra layer of protection from critters as well as maintaining freshness. Problems with high levels of moisture can also be solved by keeping food in original packaging inside of plastic buckets. This method does not prevent insects already inside the packages from multiplying.

Storing foods inside plastic buckets in original packaging protects against moisture as well as rodents.

TREATMENT METHODS

Desiccant/silica gel: Desiccant removes the moisture from the surrounding air. When placed in an airtight container, it will produce a low-humidity environment. It prevents rust, corrosion, oxidation, mildew, fungus, mold, and so on. It is frequently used in manufactured products as well as food storage. Silica gel packaged in Tyvek meets FDA requirements to be used in dry food packaging.

Layer small packets throughout the storage container and seal immediately. Discard after opening. Some forms of bulk desiccant may be "rechargeable" by exposing to heat for an extended period to release absorbed moisture. Place in shallow baking pan at 250 degrees for several hours. Desiccant is not edible, so be sure you do not spill it in your food.

Desiccant should be placed on the bottom of the container or buried deep in the grain. It should not be placed next to an oxygen absorber. Desiccant negatively affects the performance of the oxygen absorber if in close proximity.

Diatomaceous earth is a natural substance in the form of a white powder from the fossilized remains of marine diatoms. They are microscopic with "sharp spines that make them dangerous to exoskeletal insects, but not to animals with internal skeletons."[2] The spines create multiple microscopic wounds in the insects, resulting in death.

There are different forms of diatomaceous earth, some of which are dangerous to humans. Do not use the kind intended for pool filters. Safe forms may be purchased at your local feed store, garden center, or hardware store. Read the label before purchasing. Mix one cup of diatomaceous earth thoroughly with 40 pounds of grain, grain products, or legumes. It is a dust, so avoid breathing it in while mixing, but has no taste and is not harmful to humans. Note: Diatomaceous earth does not kill insect eggs or pupae—only adult insects.

Dry ice is frozen carbon dioxide (CO_2). It displaces oxygen and is the recommended treatment for grains and legumes stored in plastic buckets. It will control most adult and larval-stage insects, but will not destroy eggs or pupae. Multiple applications are not necessary unless there is an infestation. If you decide to treat again, wait 2–3 weeks for insects to mature from the surviving eggs and pupae.

Use one ounce of dry ice per gallon or three to four ounces in a five-gallon bucket. The dry ice will slowly sublimate, and the CO_2 will displace the lighter air, pushing it out the top of the bucket. It may be a good idea to use a desiccant package along with the dry ice for moisture control.

Wipe ice crystals from the dry ice with a clean towel. Wrap dry ice in paper towel to prevent it from burning the food it comes in contact with. Place wrapped dry ice in the bottom of the container. Pour grains on top of the ice, leaving one inch at the top of the container. Snap the lid down only halfway on the container to allow carbon dioxide to escape as the dry ice sublimates (changes from solid to a gas). This can take a few hours depending on the amount of dry ice. Seal only after the dry ice has completely sublimated. Monitor bucket for a few moments to ensure the lid does not bulge. If it does, open and release the pressure. The lid being pulled down slightly is an indication of the partial vacuum created by the carbon dioxide being absorbed into the product.

Freezing will kill live pests, but might not kill insect eggs. Multiple freezing and warming cycles may be required to kill all insects and hatching eggs. Freeze 1- to 15-pound bags of grain for two to three days, then allow to gradually warm for 24 hours.

Oxygen absorbers remove the oxygen from the container and will kill adult insects and prevent larval insects from surviving. Oxygen absorbers are small packets that contain iron powder. They are made of a material that allows oxygen and moisture to enter but does not let the iron powder leak out. The moisture in the food causes the iron to rust. As it oxidizes, the iron absorbs oxygen.

Oxygen absorbers are more effective at removing oxygen than vacuum packaging. Air is roughly 21 percent oxygen and 79 percent nitrogen. The oxygen absorber packets remove only the oxygen. The remaining air is mostly nitrogen, which does not allow for the growth of insects. Use only with products that are low in moisture (10 percent or less) and low in oil content. Remember, botulism poisoning may result from storing products high in moisture in a low-oxygen environment.

Oxygen absorbers are an effective way to prevent insects from surviving in stored dry foods.

Use oxygen absorbers in containers that provide a sufficient moisture and oxygen barrier, such as #10 cans with seamed lids, foil pouches, PETE bottles with airtight screw-on lids, and glass canning jars with metal lids that have gaskets.

BOTULISM

One significant consideration is botulism, a rare, deadly poisoning caused by toxins produced by the bacteria *Clostridium botulinum*. This bacteria is found in soil and water throughout the world. High-moisture, low-salt, low-acid environments without oxygen or refrigeration favor its growth. Clostridium botulinum produces toxic spores that may be found in incorrectly canned or preserved food. Botulism may potentially cause death and is considered a medical emergency. There are three common types of botulism:

Infant botulism usually occurs in babies between two and six months when bacterial spores grow inside the intestinal tract. Bacteria may be introduced by eating honey but more likely from exposure to contaminated soil.

Wound botulism can enter the site of a wound so small you might not notice you have it, such as a scratch. The bacteria can multiply, resulting in a dangerous infection as it produces the toxin.

Foodborne botulism thrives in low-oxygen environments and produces dangerous toxins. When food containing the toxin is eaten, it disrupts nerve function, resulting in paralysis. The source is often home-canned foods that are low in acid, such as beets, corn, or green beans. It has also occurred from a variety of other sources, like fermented seafood, smoked or raw fish, cured pork and ham, sausage, honey, corn syrup, chili peppers, olives, soups, spinach, asparagus, potatoes, and oil infused with garlic.

Symptoms of foodborne botulism usually begin within 8–36 hours of exposure. Diagnosis may be challenging since botulism poisoning may resemble a variety of other illnesses at the onset. Early medical intervention increases the chance of survival. No fever is present with botulism poisoning. Symptoms may include difficulty speaking or swallowing, blurred or double vision, facial weakness on both sides of face, drooping eyelids, dry mouth, trouble breathing, nausea, vomiting, abdominal cramps, and paralysis.

The most immediate danger is the inability to breathe. Clinical diagnosis is the usual form of diagnosis. Lab tests can confirm the diagnosis, but they may take a few days to get the results. Immediate treatment is essential to save life. Some doctors may try to clear the digestive system by inducing vomiting and bowel movements. An anti-toxin injection is available. It can attach itself to the toxins, preventing further damage, but it will not repair nerve damage that has already occurred. Patients may need to be on a ventilator for several weeks as the effects of the toxins gradually diminish.

The saying "an ounce of prevention is better than a pound of cure" is applicable here. The serious consequences of exposure to botulism make prevention critical. It might just be a sure death sentence to be exposed to this toxin when good medical care is scarce. The following is a list of suggestions to keep your food supply free from botulism toxins:

- Clean foods well before cooking or processing.

- Use proper techniques when canning foods at home to ensure all bacteria is destroyed. Follow up-to-date local USDA extension agency guidelines, making sure to adjust cooking times for high-altitude areas.

- Never eat preserved foods if the container is bulging, leaking, or moldy, or if the food smells bad.

- Consider boiling all home-canned vegetables and meats, without tasting, for ten minutes. Boil spinach and corn for at least 20 minutes before consuming. Add one minute of boiling time for each 1,000 feet above sea level. If it looks spoiled, smells funny, or foams during heating, do not risk it. Throw it away.

- Store oils infused with herbs or garlic in the refrigerator.

- Long-term storage items such as wheat, white rice, rolled oats, dry beans, and so on should have a moisture content of 10 percent or less. Storing moist items in a low-oxygen environment encourages microbial growth and may result in botulism poisoning.

- Dried fruits and vegetables (unless they are dry enough to snap inside and out) should not be stored in reduced oxygen packaging (such as #10 cans or pouches with an oxygen absorber).

- Vacuum packaging will not prevent botulism in moist products. It is appropriate to use a vacuum sealer to prolong shelf life of dry items (less than 10 percent moisture such as wheat, dry beans, and so on) intended to be stored at room temperature or moist items kept in refrigerator or freezer only.

Botulism is rare in our society because of strict commercial food processing guidelines along with a good supply of clean water. However, *rare* does not mean it can't happen to you or your loved ones. Take some time to evaluate your longer-term storage items. Have you improperly stored any moist items in a reduced-oxygen environment? If you have, dispose of them now.

Home-processed foods are great if you are following established up-to-date safety guidelines. Your local extension agency is a good resource and can answer specific questions for you. Do not take chances with the health you are preparing so hard to protect. We encourage safety first in all of your efforts.

STATUS CHECK

Now that you know how to store the food correctly, take inventory and evaluate your food storage. Are there any enemies that need to be attacked? If in doubt, throw it out! Food storage is a wise investment that is worth protecting. This is a learning process. We learn by making a few mistakes and then correcting those mistakes now, while we can.

LIVING WITHOUT REFRIGERATION

Refrigeration is so much a part of our everyday life that imagining how we would function without it is difficult. Perishable items can make us terribly ill if they are not stored at the appropriate temperature. Great-grandma did just fine without a refrigerator. With some serious effort, we can survive without one too. A generator will work for a little while, but there is a more sustainable solution. Each of our personal situations varies greatly. You may live in an apartment, condominium, tract home, or on a large piece of land. Take the principles you learn and work to apply them in your personal circumstances.

Let us begin by reviewing some basic principles of "root cellaring." A root cellar will not maintain a constant temperature like a refrigerator, so it is unsafe to store foods like fresh meat in one. You need a place that is cool, ventilated, humid, and dark.

Cool temperature (optimal is 32 to 40 degrees) is the goal, which makes location selection critical. Select a site with good drainage and minimal sunshine. A north-sloping hill or shaded area is ideal. The earth is a natural insulator. Constructing a cellar below the frost line or piling insulation on top helps maintain a cool temperature while avoiding freezing.

Dirt or gravel floors allow the earth to naturally humidify the air, prolonging the life of produce. Good drainage ensures the area will not become waterlogged. Increase humidity by dumping water on the gravel floor.

Ventilation assists in control of both temperature and humidity. It moves ethylene gas produced by ripening produce, increasing storage life and quality. Air movement reduces mold and mildew.

Darkness prevents light from deteriorating foods and encouraging sprouting.

An accessible location increases overall functionality and usefulness.

ROOT CELLAR IDEAS

Garden row: We enjoyed amazingly sweet carrots in mid-February, dug just before dinner from Grandpa Paul's garden. He simply covered his row of carrots before the hard frost with a very thick layer of straw (to prevent the ground from freezing) and a black tarp held down by bricks (to keep the moisture out). This is a great way to store some root crops through the winter.

Basement bathroom: We have friends who store winter squash in an unused bathroom in their basement. They close off the ventilation to the room and leave the window slightly open all winter long. They have put a portable shelving unit in the bathroom to store the squash on. We have personally tasted delicious sweet meat squash from their makeshift root cellar that was over nine months old. They get an A+ for successful creativity.

Buried barrel: An underground barrel is a reliable old favorite. Once again select a shady spot. Dig a hole large enough to place the barrel in at a 45-degree angle with the bottom of the barrel top at soil level. Place rocks or gravel in the bottom of the hole under the barrel. Put the barrel in the hole and cover with at least two feet of dirt by mounding it up. Layer the vegetables between hay, straw, leaves, and so on inside the barrel, making sure to have a good layer of insulation on top. Cover the barrel with a thick layer of insulation and a board or something to keep the insulation in place.

Uncle George uses a variation of this method. He buried a metal garbage can upright, with holes drilled in the bottom for drainage. The lid fits snugly in place to keep rodents out. He built a simple wooden cover to place over the top. The top is insulated by covering it with a thick pile of leaves.

He placed leaves in the bottom and then layered vegetables and leaves alternately in the can. The vegetables never freeze, and they stay nice and fresh through the winter months.

A metal garbage can with holes drilled in the bottom for drainage.

The can lid fits snugly and is covered with a wooden box lid.

The lid is covered with leaves to insulate vegetables from the cold.

Plastic storage container: Potatoes will store well all winter long in a plastic storage container with a tight-fitting lid. Start with a layer of sawdust, wood shavings, or even straw on the bottom of the container. Add layers of potatoes, alternating with more layers of insulation. Do not allow potatoes to touch one another. Place the container in the garage or basement and remove potatoes as needed through the winter.

Potatoes, and other root vegetables, can be stored by layering them in a plastic storage container with leaves, straw, or sawdust.

Buried refrigerator: Select a shady spot or one on the north side of the home. Take an old refrigerator and remove the motor, shelves, and drawers. Disable the latch to ensure no children accidently get trapped inside. One foot of drainage on all sides and on the bottom is necessary. Dig the hole one foot larger than the refrigerator. The refrigerator should sit just below ground level. Line the hole with gravel or rocks for drainage. Place the refrigerator on its back so it opens like a chest. Pour gravel in the space around the sides of the refrigerator. Run a small vent pipe into the refrigerator for fresh air.

Cover the top of the refrigerator with a large mat, board, or some material to protect from water. Cover with bales of hay or straw to insulate. Apples, Asian pears, beets, carrots, celeriac, kohlrabi, potatoes, rutabagas, and turnips store well in a buried refrigerator.

Window well: We experimented storing potatoes and winter squash in milk crates inside of a window well on the north side of our home. We covered the top of the window well with a piece of plywood and stacked bales of straw on top for insulation. The crates stacked nicely and allowed air to circulate around the vegetables.

We placed a darkening curtain in front of the window, but small amounts of light were apparent through the top. The warmth of the house prevented the window well from being as cool as we might have liked it to be. However, it still performed fairly well. We were able to access the food by opening the window and taking out a crate at a time. It was quite convenient.

Woodbox cellar: Dig a hole about two by two by four feet (or larger) and construct a wooden box to put in it. Line the box with mesh hardware wire to keep out rodents. Place a layer of leaves, straw, or moss on the bottom then add your vegetables. Place three to four inches of additional insulation material on top of the vegetables and set a hardware cloth-lined lid on top. Place bales of straw or hay on top to insulate it.

Traditional root cellars will perform better than the alternative methods we described above, but they can be much more costly to build. Do the best you can with what you have.

OPERATIONAL SECURITY: PROTECTING YOUR PANTRY

Occasionally, we hear the comment, "I don't need to store food. I have a year's supply of guns and ammo. I will take whatever I want." This mentality never ceases to amaze us. There are people who are actually planning on forcibly taking food at gunpoint instead of storing their own.

First of all, this plan relies on others around them actually storing food, not to mention the kind of food they actually like to eat. Hope they like lima beans and lentils. Second, most people who store food also store guns and ammunition. Do they really think people will just stand there while their supplies are hauled off? Finally, this mentality will get you killed quickly and still leave your family hungry.

In addition to those less-than-brilliant souls, there are good people who will be struggling during hard times. Normally honorable people can resort to unthinkable acts when they are desperate. If your neighbors have labeled you as a prepper, your family will be a target, even if you have exhausted your supplies.

We suggest you practice a little operational security and fly under the radar. Share details of your plan on a need-to-know basis. It is best not to store all of your supplies in one place. When neighbors visit and see your pantry is as empty as theirs, the word will spread. Kylene usually has a stash of chocolate hidden away for rough days. If she stored it on the pantry shelf, the children would eat every bit of it and she would be left without any. The same idea can be applied to your family food stores. Consider building a cache of supplies. A cache is a place where you hide items or make them inaccessible.

Be creative as you develop your cache. You may want to store supplies at a trusted friend or family member's home, perhaps in the storage room in a box labeled something uninteresting, like *Grandma's Knitting Projects*, *Jon's Day Timers 1984–2000*, or *Boy's Clothes Size 10–12*. If you label it *Kylene's Chocolate Stash*, you have totally missed the point. Keep it realistic but uninviting. Keep notes so you do not forget where you have supplies stashed. Kids love to share information with their friends. It may be best not to disclose details of your cache to them.

Cache ideas are limited only by your imagination. Even in an apartment you can find places in tops of closets, under beds or furniture, in a laundry closet, or behind a couch. If you own your home, many more options are available to you. Bury an open-top barrel, old freezer, old refrigerator, or other watertight container to store longer-term food storage in. Put this container in a shaded area that can be easily dug up when needed. Store only waterproof and rodent-proof items in these. Splitting up your provisions may ensure you have something left to get you through the tough times.

How much do you need to store? The goal is to have enough to survive until you have a reliable source and resources to purchase what you need. Return to your risk assessment. What are you preparing for? How long until you will once again have the ability to purchase the items you need? That is how long your supplies should last.

FOOD STORAGE: HOW AND WHERE ACTION PLAN

Take a few minutes to evaluate your current supplies. Note the items that need to be addressed and make a to-do list. Remember, good enough is perfect. It is better to have a less-than-perfect storage system than to have nothing while you wait to build your dream storage room. Do what you can now, make steady progress, and enjoy the peace that comes with knowing you have prepared for a rainy day. Complete the work-sheet located at www.theprovidentprepper.org/the-practical-prepper/action-plan-food-storage-how-and-where to help organize your action plan.

12

Fuel Safety and Storage
Come on, Baby, Light My Fire

Be wise—don't do stupid things!

Fuel is one of the four basic necessities for survival. It is an important consideration in your quest to prepare. You need to be able to heat your homes, cook your food, and power vital equipment. Fuel gives you the ability to maintain the standard of living you enjoy. This chapter will provide you with the education required to understand plausible options, how to safely use them, and how to store them appropriately.

Fuels can be extremely dangerous. We cannot stress enough the importance of using wisdom in your use and storage of fuels. Be wise—don't do stupid things! Place the safety of your loved ones before any other objective. Never store a flammable or combustible fuel in any building that you can't afford to have burn down. Always judiciously follow manufacturer guidelines when storing or using any fuel.

As part of our research, we reviewed the material safety data sheet (MSDS) on each fuel. These sheets are available online and explain how each fuel should be handled and stored, and what toxins each produce as a result of burning (hazardous combustion products). Note that the amount of chemicals released will vary depending on the temperature and amount of oxygen present. Always provide adequate ventilation when burning anything. Install working smoke and carbon monoxide detectors. Keep fire extinguishers handy.

Carbon monoxide poisoning is a real concern. According to the CDC, carbon monoxide poisoning is responsible for over 15,000 emergency room visits and 500 deaths annually.[1] Most incidences occur in the winter months. Alternative heating and power sources during power outages—such as portable generators, charcoal briquettes, propane stoves and grills—are listed among the likely causes. Carbon monoxide poisoning is often misdiagnosed because it exhibits flu-like symptoms in the early stages. Do not risk exposing your family to this dangerous toxin. Be wise!

FUEL STORAGE GUIDELINES

Most flammable or combustible fuels should be stored in a similar way. Ideal storage conditions include

- Approved, tightly closed container

- Cool and dry

- Out of direct sunlight

- Well-ventilated area

- Away from sources of ignition (sparks or flame, including pilot lights)

- Away from oxidizing agents (e.g. hypochlorite, oxygen, hydrogen peroxide, and so on)

- Preferably not in garage or home

- Stored in a detached building

Explore the possibility of purchasing fuel cabinets to store some of your fuel in. Fuel storage cabinets are a bit pricey but are a safer option for some fuel storage. These cabinets help contain fumes and protect fuel from ignition sources. In some places, the law requires 25 gallons or more to be stored inside fuel storage cabinets. An online search will quickly reveal your fuel storage cabinet options. Your local fire department can explain legal guidelines in your area.

The very components of flammable and combustible fuels that make them useful and perform well also make extreme caution necessary in both storing and handling the fuels. Noncombustible fuels—such as coal, wood, Instafire, or charcoal—are much safer to store, even in very large quantities.

Burning the fuel can be dangerous. We recommend the following precautions be taken:

- Read and diligently follow manufacturer guidelines both for devices and fuel.

- Keep out of reach of children.

- Attend to spills or leaks immediately.

- Install working carbon monoxide and smoke detectors.

- Use caution with open flames.

- Never burn anything that indoors produces carbon monoxide.

- Always provide adequate ventilation when burning anything.

- Store fuel in accordance with local guidelines and ordinances.

LIQUID FUELS

Liquid fuels are combustible or energy-producing molecules from which you can harness the energy to power a variety of equipment. The fumes are flammable, but usually not the actual liquid. Ease of use and transportation makes these fuels quite valuable for home use, while their highly flammable nature makes them especially dangerous.

Alcohol

Alcohol is a good storage fuel with a long shelf life. It will lose potency quickly if left open since the alcohol will evaporate. While alcohol burns only half as hot as some other fuels, it works well for cooking and heating. Pure forms of alcohol burn clean enough for indoor use, but alcohol can still produce small amounts of carbon monoxide and carbon dioxide when burned. Always provide ventilation when burning any flame. Use caution when storing since alcohol has a low flash point (ignition temperature) and is highly flammable. Store away from chemicals.

Denatured alcohol is an excellent alcohol fuel and is available in hardware stores in the paint section. Most manufacturers of alcohol devices recommend denatured alcohol for fuel. Store it in a tightly sealed container. Shelf life depends on the container and can range from two years to indefinite.[2]

Ethanol or ethyl alcohol (Everclear) is a grain alcohol that can be purchased at a liquor store and is about 95 percent alcohol. Container sizes vary from state to state. It produces a nearly invisible blue or clear flame, so be careful not to burn yourself.

Methanol (wood alcohol) burns well but is toxic and is easily absorbed through the skin and mucous membranes. Long-term exposure can be quite dangerous. We recommend using a safer alcohol for fuel.

Rubbing alcohol (isopropyl) is another good alcohol fuel. It may be purchased in different strengths. The higher the percentage of alcohol, the better it will burn. Two types of rubbing alcohol are readily available: 70 percent strength and 91 percent strength. The 91 percent strength will burn better due to the higher alcohol content,[3] whereas the 70 percent strength contains 30 percent water (water does not burn).[4] Isopropyl alcohol produces a yellow sooty flame.

Notice the difference in alcohol as it burns. Denatured burns so clean the flame is nearly invisible. Caution: It is very hot! The 91 percent isopropyl produces a much larger, hotter flame compared to the 70 percent isopropyl alcohol.

Canned heat comes in a small metal can filled with alcohol or a flammable gel that does not burn quickly. It is made to be used as a chafing dish fuel or in a portable Sterno camping stove. Canned heat is available under a variety of brand names (Sterno, Safe Heat, and so on) and will burn for two to six hours depending on the variety purchased. It creates a visible flame that goes straight up with little spread. Canned heat may be purchased in cases of 12 cans that stack and store nicely. Shelf life of unopened cans is ten years if stored in a cool, dry place.[5]

Safe Heat stores nicely. Each flat package of cans will provide up to 72 hours of burn time.

Coleman Fuel/White Gas

This clear fuel is a camping favorite and will burn hot even at sub-zero temperatures. The liquid and vapor are highly flammable. Do not use Coleman fuel indoors because it produces vast amounts of "carbon monoxide and other asphyxiants during combustion."[6] The fuel should be stored in the original container in a cool, well-ventilated area away from ignition sources, heat, pilot lights, static electricity, and open flame. An unopened container, with no rapid temperature changes, has a shelf life of five to seven years. An opened container will remain viable for up to two years.

Diesel

Diesel fuel is easily obtained and can be used to power a generator. Conventional diesel has properties similar to gasoline but is less flammable. It may gel in cold temperatures, which will inhibit the ability to pump it with a regular fuel pump. Special low-temperature diesel contains additives that may help (but not prevent) this problem. Diesel produces carbon dioxide and monoxide, as well as noncombusted hydrocarbons, or smoke. Never use indoors or near doors or windows, as this may allow leaks to enter the home and create a carbon monoxide poisoning risk.

Diesel should be stored in approved yellow fuel cans in a cool, well-ventilated place or in aboveground tanks. The smaller containers can be purchased at sporting goods stores or retailers, such as Walmart. Diesel has an 18- to 24-month shelf life, which can be extended almost indefinitely by annually adding a quality fuel stabilizer, such as PRI-D.[7]

Gasoline (Unleaded)

This fuel can be found in most households in a variety of common equipment, including automobiles. Gasoline does not actually burn. The flames ignite, causing the liquid to evaporate and burn. It combusts easily and is highly volatile. The utmost care should be exercised in both use and storage because any leakage has the potential of being extremely dangerous. The safest place to store gasoline is the tank of your car. If you keep your tank half full, you will always have fresh gasoline to power a generator or enough to evacuate an area.

Gasoline has a short shelf life. Within a year, the fuel will begin to degrade and can damage equipment. A good quality fuel stabilizer, such as PRI-G, can be added annually to extend the shelf life indefinitely. Gasoline should only be stored in approved red containers in quantities within the local ordinance levels. In our area, gasoline storage is limited to ten gallons in an attached garage. Citizens may store up to 25 gallons total in an unattached garage or shed. Storing large quantities is hazardous.

Kerosene

Kerosene (also known as kerosine, paraffin, or kero) is an oily fuel used for heating and cooking. It is available in different grades. Klean

Heat is an example of a premium grade of kerosene that burns cleaner than standard. Standard kerosene is available in two grades: K-1 and K-2, the main difference being the level of sulfur. K-1 has a sulfur level below 0.05 percent, which makes it an acceptable fuel for unvented kerosene heaters and cooking devices.

We personally do not burn kerosene indoors. Care should be taken since kerosene vapors have the ability to travel long distances into other rooms. Keep away from ignition sources such as open flame, pilot lights, electrical outlets and switches, and static electricity. The manufacturer of Klean Heat recommends refueling outdoors in an open air area. If refueling must occur indoors, open all windows and doors to maintain cross ventilation of moving fresh air. Klean Heat still produces dangerous by-products of combustion such as carbon monoxide.[8] Kerosene produces carbon monoxide, carbon dioxide, nitrogen dioxide, and sulfur dioxide when burned.[9] Use great caution if burning indoors to maintain adequate cross ventilation. Kerosene has a shelf life of two to five years and should be stored in original packaging or in approved blue containers. A high-quality fuel stabilizer, such as PRI-D, added annually can extend the life of kerosene indefinitely.

Lamp Oil

Lamp oil is a liquid petroleum product in the same family as kerosene, designed to burn cleanly in lanterns, torches, and brass or glass lamps. It is more refined, so it will not produce harmful smoke, soot, and other pollutants. Lamp oil must be kept at or near room temperature. Frozen lamp oil may defrost too quickly, posing an explosive risk. It comes in a wide variety of colors and scents.[10]

Lighter Fluid

Charcoal lighter fluid is a highly volatile fluid that can be made from either a petroleum or alcohol base. Great care should be used in storage and use of the product. It can impart an unpleasant flavor to foods cooked with it. Keep the container closed. "Store away from open flames, sparks, heat sources, direct sunlight, strong oxidants, and corrosives."[11] A good replacement for charcoal lighter fluid is a charcoal chimney. Newspapers or canned heat can be used to ignite charcoals in a safer manner using the chimney.

Liquid Paraffin

Liquid paraffin is a distilled form of kerosene and is similar to other lamp fuels, such as coal oil, lamp oil, or kerosene. It is available in a variety of colors and scents. It should not be confused with paraffin wax. Liquid paraffin is highly toxic if ingested, while paraffin wax is chemically benign, which is why it can be used in making homemade jams and jellies. Medicinal liquid paraffin is a highly refined white mineral oil used in cosmetics and for medicinal purposes. Liquid paraffin produces carbon monoxide and carbon dioxide when burned. Good general ventilation should be sufficient to control airborne levels. It should be stored in a cool, dry, well-ventilated area.[12]

Fuel Stabilizers

Fuel deteriorates in storage and becomes gummy, which will plug fuel filters and fuel injection systems and will prevent equipment from operating. An emergency is not a good time for your equipment to fail. Gasoline, diesel, and kerosene can be stored for many years if treated with a high-quality fuel stabilizer annually. One bottle of PRI treats 256 gallons of fuel. PRI has an indefinite shelf life if unopened. Once opened, the manufacturer recommends a 3-year shelf life.[13] After that time, it will begin to lose its effectiveness.

GASEOUS FUELS

Gaseous fuels, under normal conditions, remain in a gaseous form, which allows them to be easily transported through pipes from point of origin to place of consumption. Some may be liquefied for transit or storage. It is possible for these gases to escape and collect undetected, posing an explosive risk. Odors are commonly added to assist in detecting leakage.

Butane

Butane is highly flammable, colorless, and easily liquefied. For our purposes, butane is used in lighters and butane torches, and it is bottled as a fuel for cooking or heating. When burned, it produces carbon monoxide and carbon dioxide. Adequate ventilation must be provided. Butane does not perform well at near freezing temperatures.

Butane cylinders must be carefully stored above freezing (32 degrees) and below 120 degrees away from open flame or heat sources. They are extremely flammable and exposure to heat or fire could result in detonation. Do not store near any oxidizing materials (chlorine or concentrated oxygen). Store in a cool, dry location with adequate ventilation.[14]

Natural Gas

Access to natural gas during a power outage is possible. Some appliances, such as a furnace, require electricity to operate in addition to natural gas. A number of natural gas ranges, fireplaces, and water heaters may work when the power is out depending on the model. Most gas ranges will still work by lighting manually, but do not count on the gas oven working. We recommend you turn off your electricity and experiment. Which of your gas appliances might provide some of your fuel needs during an outage if you still have access to natural gas? We do not count natural gas in our list of storage fuels because the supply may be disrupted. However, it is a great option if it is available.

Natural gas is a colorless gas with an offensive odor added to assist in the detection of leaks. Carbon monoxide poisoning can occur if appliances are not functioning properly or due to poor ventilation. Natural gas is extremely flammable and may be ignited by a simple electrostatic discharge (static electricity). When breathed in, vapors may displace oxygen, resulting in drowsiness, light-headedness or dizziness, impaired judgment, unconsciousness, or death. If you smell the typical rotten egg odor, leave the home immediately and call your local gas company. Gas should be turned off at the meter where the gas supply enters the home if you hear or smell leaking gas in an emergency. The gas should only be turned back on by the gas company.[15]

Propane

Propane is a liquid fuel stored under pressure. It is vaporized into a gas before leaving the tank. It is available in portable one-pound disposable tanks, five-pound tanks, and 20-pound tanks, as well as fixed tanks that hold hundreds of pounds of propane. Propane creates a hot, clean fire. The equipment and tanks are simple to use. The fuel will store indefinitely, but check the tanks for signs of rust or dents. Propane should be stored with service valves closed and plugged when not in use. Propane is heavier than air and may collect in low-lying areas, creating an explosive risk.

When propane burns it produces carbon dioxide, nitrogen, and water vapor. However, incomplete combustion may occur if there is not enough oxygen, which can result in the production of carbon monoxide. Always provide adequate ventilation when using. Touching liquid propane could result in freeze burns. It is "highly flammable when mixed with air (oxygen) and can be ignited by many sources, including open flames, smoking materials, electrical sparks, and static electricity."[16]

SOLID FUELS

Solid fuels are solid materials that release energy through combustion to provide heat. These fuels tend to be safer to store and have a longer shelf life than liquid or gaseous fuels.

Debris

Debris, for our purposes, refers to any available burnable material. In the aftermath of a disaster, there may be debris that can be used as fuel such as wood from destroyed buildings or landscape. Use caution not to burn debris that has paint, varnish, or stain since it may release harmful toxins into the air.

Gel Fuel

PyroPac is an example of a gel fuel that is a great portable heat source. Squeeze the gel onto a fire-safe surface and light it. It can be used in a small fuel tablet stove. A single 1.25-ounce packet will burn for 15 minutes, leaving only tiny white ash behind. Use in a well-ventilated area and do not breathe the fumes.

Instafire

Instafire is a recent creation of wood pellets, volcanic rock, inert minerals, and paraffin wax. It produces an 8- to 10-inch flame for 10 to 15 minutes and will burn in wind, rain, sleet, and snow. Instafire can be used as a fire starter or a standalone fuel source. Instafire should only be used outdoors, but it can be stored indoors safely because it is noncombustible. It will start to get soft at 130 degrees but does not melt until 160 degrees, so storage outside may be acceptable depending on your climate. It has a shelf life of 30 years.

Charcoal

Charcoal burns hotter and cleaner than wood. The briquettes store safely but must *never* be burned indoors. Charcoal consumes a tremendous amount of oxygen and produces a vast amount of carbon monoxide, a deadly poison. Purchase a high-quality charcoal for fuel storage. Do not store ready-to-light varieties. The lighter fluid will evaporate over time and will not be of any benefit. Charcoal will store for an extended period of time if it is stored in an airtight container, such as a sealed 5-gallon bucket. Moisture-absorbing desiccant may also be helpful in keeping it dry. When stored in the original paper bag, it can absorb moisture, rendering it minimally effective or useless over time. Recharge it by laying it out in the sun on a hot day.[17]

Charcoal briquettes are a powerful, inexpensive cooking fuel option.

Coal

Coal is a naturally occurring sedimentary rock that makes a great fuel. It burns hotter and longer than wood. Coal produces carbon monoxide when burned and should only be burned in a carefully maintained coal fireplace. It requires significant oxygen to burn efficiently or the carbon monoxide may escape into the home instead of up the chimney. Coal fires should be started slowly, beginning with newspapers and wood. Small pieces of coal are slowly added to the fire to prevent smothering the fire. It can be purchased in bags or in bulk.

Old-fashioned coal is easy to store and burns hot.

Trioxane Fuel Bars

This is a compressed, solid fuel used for fire starting, cooking, and as a heat source. One bar will burn for seven to nine minutes, creating intense heat. Trioxane fuel bars are designed for military and survival use. They come packaged in a coated, waterproof foil wrapper with each bar scored in thirds. They are a military surplus item and produce very little flame and no smoke. Trioxane should only be used outdoors since it produces toxic gases when burned. It will store indefinitely in a cool, dry place.

Wax

Wax candles are a good old standby to provide light and a little warmth. Store in a tightly-covered container. Paraffin wax and beeswax both can produce carbon monoxide, carbon dioxide, and small amounts of sulfur and nitrogen when burned. Always burn in a ventilated area. Candles will keep indefinitely in a cool, dry, well-ventilated location away from heat or sources of ignition.[18, 19]

Esbit Fuel Tablets

These are small cubes that generate up to 1,400 degrees of intense heat for 12 to 15 minutes. It can be used as a fire starter, for cooking, or as a heat source. Esbit tablets produce very little smoke and leave almost no residue. They produces several toxic gases when burned, so make sure to use outside in a well-ventilated area. Esbit fuel tablets have an indefinite shelf life and are nonexplosive. Store in unopened, original packaging and keep away from moisture and sources of ignition.[20]

Fuel tablets make excellent fire starters or fuel for pocket stoves.

Firewood

Firewood is a great fuel. Wood is one of the least expensive ways to heat your home and one of the safest storage fuels. All wood is not equal. Some varieties pop and smoke, some burn hotter or longer, and some just smell nicer when they burn. As a general rule, hardwoods (deciduous trees such as oak, hickory, and maple) produce more BTUs (heat content) than softer woods (conifers such as pine, fir, and cedar). The best fires are a mixture of softwoods and hardwoods. The softwood starts easily while the hardwood burns longer and produces nice coals. It is best to store wood off of the ground on cement blocks, pallets, or wooden planks. This reduces the risk of insect infestation and wicking moisture from the ground, and improves air circulation. Firewood will store indefinitely; however, after four years, the energy output will begin to decrease.

Seasoned wood works best. Freshly cut trees may be 50–60 percent water. The moisture greatly reduces the available energy. Once the wood is allowed to dry for about six months or so it will produce about twice the BTUs as freshly cut wood. Burning wood causes creosote to form in stovepipes and exhaust systems. Creosote fires can be extremely dangerous and can lead to major house fires. Take precautions to reduce your risk of creosote fires. Inspect your stovepipe and stove exhaust system regularly. Burning wood produces carbon monoxide. It is important to use a well-maintained fireplace or stove that has been specifically designed to burn wood.

Wood is one of the safest fuels to store.

MRE Heaters

MRE heaters are designed by the military to heat MREs quickly and safely without fire. They can also be used to provide localized warmth. They are made from powdered food-grade iron, magnesium, and sodium. When water is added to the chemicals in the heater, a chemical reaction heats up almost instantly. MRE heaters have a shelf life of about five years. Older heaters take longer to heat up. The vapors released by an activated heater contain hydrogen, a flammable gas. Do not place near open flame. MRE heaters are safe to use indoors.

Newspapers

Newspapers are handy to have around. They are great to start fires or charcoal with. Paper bricks can be made out of soaked shredded newspaper. A brick maker forms the soaked paper into a brick shape and squeezes the water out. The bricks are dried for a few weeks and will burn at a rate of four per hour. This method is quite time intensive. Newspaper logs can be created by rolling dry papers around a dowel, tying them with twine, and then soaking for several hours before drying. Another method is to soak the newspapers first and then roll them onto a dowel and tie. The dowel is always removed before drying. It allows air to circulate through the center, speeding the drying process and reducing the risk of mold. Adding a little bit of dish detergent to the water during the soaking process seems to make a better product. Burn a combination of paper logs and firewood for a better fire.

Paper bricks are time consuming to make, but they burn well and are a good use of resources.

Wood Pellets

This fuel is made out of compressed sawdust. Wood pellets are a good solid fuel that burns quite efficiently in a wood pellet stove. Pellet stoves require electricity to operate a hopper, which feeds the pellets into the stove. To be an effective emergency preparedness tool, a backup power system would be necessary. Store a generous amount of pellets since they are difficult to find at times. They come in manageable 40-pound bags and store nicely. Wood pellets have an indefinite shelf life if stored in a dry place out of direct sunlight.

MISCELLANEOUS ENERGY SOURCES

Solar

Radiant light and heat from the sun is referred to as solar energy. It is an abundant source of free energy, which can be a great tool in everyday life as well as during emergencies. We usually refer to solar energy as active or passive, depending on the way it is captured, converted, and distributed. Active solar uses photovoltaic panels or thermal collectors to harness the energy and produce electricity. A sun oven with reflectors, solar-powered battery chargers, and photovoltaic panels mounted on a roof are all examples of active solar.

Passive solar is incorporated in the design of buildings to warm them, take advantage of natural lighting, and improve air circulation. Small changes in the orientation and design of buildings can translate into significant savings. Our chicken coop is an example of a passive solar design. It faces south, sporting a reclaimed industrial glass door and window. The winter sun shines through the glass and warms the four-foot high cinder block wall inside the coop, which provides thermal mass. The wall radiates the warmth back into the coop during the night when temperatures are lowest. During the hot summer months, the overhang prevents the direct sun from shining into the chicken coop so it remains cool. Air vents on both sides at the top of the coop ensure adequate air circulation and ventilation.

Another amazing use for solar energy is for water disinfection. It is possible to kill the nasty pathogens in water by clarifying (removing debris from) it, placing the water in a 2-liter clear plastic bottle, and placing the bottle out in the sun for a day. Solar water disinfection is discussed in detail in chapter 8.

Batteries

Household batteries come in two basic categories: single-use and rechargeable. The chemistry composition is different, so do not try to recharge single-use batteries. Batteries should be stored separately from devices (flashlights, radios, and so on) in a cool, dry place. Heat can lead to leakage, rupture, and capacity loss. Batteries can have a shelf life of 10 to 15 years depending on storage, quality and type of battery.

Single-use or disposable batteries include lithium, carbon-zinc, alkaline, silver-zinc, and zinc air.

You can recharge and repeatedly use rechargeable batteries. Solar battery chargers are a great option for recharging batteries without electricity. To extend the battery life of rechargeable batteries, do not store them unused for an extended period of time. Charge every six to nine months. Nickel metal hydride (NiMH), Lithium ion (Li Ion), nickel cadmium (NiCd), and sealed lead acid (SLA) are examples of rechargeable batteries.

Battery Bank

A battery bank is a collection of two or more batteries joined together to function as one. The purpose of a battery bank is to provide more power than a single battery. This can be a handy tool to provide power during an emergency. A small battery bank, kept charged by using household power, may be enough to run critical medical equipment during a short-term power outage. Battery banks can be charged with standard household power, solar power, wind power, or with a generator. An inverter is used to convert the energy to useable household power. Battery storage life varies greatly depending on the type of batteries used.

Battery banks can be charged by household power, solar, or wind.

Wind

The power of the wind may be harvested using wind turbines to generate electricity. The power can be used immediately or stored in a battery bank to be used when the wind is not blowing. Small turbines are available for home use. A small hybrid system can take advantage of both solar and wind. Go to windpoweringamerica.gov for wind resource maps and information on using wind power.

Portable Electric Generator

A generator may be a useful tool to provide backup power. A couple of hours a day would be enough to maintain a freezer or refrigerator and allow a few hours of convenience. Connect appliances directly to the generator using approved and properly sized power cords. Always operate a generator outside, away from windows or doors where exhaust containing carbon monoxide may enter the home. Read and follow manufacturer recommendations when operating a generator. Never refuel a generator while it's running. Watch your generator closely during use—they are noisy, advertising the fact that you have power, and are a prime target for thieves.

SAFETY FIRST!

We strongly encourage you to have working fire extinguishers, smoke detectors, and carbon monoxide detectors located in strategic places in your home. Know how to turn off the natural gas supply to your home. Have each member of your household practice using a fire extinguisher. Learn the dangers of carbon monoxide and warning signs (see chapter 14). Conduct regular fire and carbon monoxide drills so everyone knows what the alarms mean and exactly what to do. Do not just talk about it—physically do it.

BE WISE: DON'T DO STUPID THINGS!

As we teach classes, we have the opportunity to learn many valuable things from our students. We have also learned things that terrify us. Occasionally, some people are so afraid of being without what they need in the future that they put themselves and their families at serious risk today. Be wise—please be wise, and don't do stupid things!

Here is a list of a few of the not-so-wise and pretty stupid things we have heard about:

- "I store gasoline in used milk jugs in my garage." Never store any liquid fuel in any container other than an approved, labeled one. Plastic milk jugs are engineered to degrade in a short period of time. They are not suitable for water storage, much less explosive fuels.

- "I have 500 gallons of gasoline, which I store on the back of my property only 20 feet from my neighbor's home. Better his house than mine." Be a good neighbor. Good neighbors do not blow each other up. Do not store more than the legal limits of any fuel.

- "I have 200 canisters of propane in my basement." Can you say, "kaboom"? Storing fuel inside of your home may negate your homeowner's policy as well as make a little fire into a dangerous explosive event. Do not risk your life or the lives of firefighters as they fight to save your home.

- "If the power goes out, I'll just bring my Coleman stove in and cook on my kitchen counter." A disaster is the perfect time to get carbon monoxide poisoning, don't you think? Do not burn any fuel inside your home that produces carbon monoxide unless it is in a vented appliance or rated for indoor use. Just because someone else is doing it does not make it safe.

- "No one has the right to tell me what I can do on my own property. Just try and stop me!" That is probably okay if you live all alone in the desert 25 miles away from any populated place. Otherwise, there is a much bigger picture than just you and me, starting with the safety of your family. For most of us, the fuels our neighbor stores might endanger us. Play by the rules and keep everyone safe.

- "The salesman told me this would work great in an emergency." A salesman is interested in making a sale. You are in charge of keeping your family safe. Take time to research and practice. Purchase wisely and use safely. A crisis is a horrible time to be in need of emergency medical care.

FUEL AT A GLANCE

Now that we have discussed each fuel type in detail, the following information is for quick reference. Remember, you do not need to store all of these fuels. Understand what fuels are the best options for your situation and decide what you need. Always comply with local laws and regulations for storing fuel in your area.

Alcohol

Recommended shelf life: Indefinite

What happens after shelf life: Loses potency if allowed to evaporate

Safe storage: Store in tightly sealed original container in a cool, dry place

Cautions: Extremely flammable; evaporates quickly

Batteries (Lithium)

Recommended shelf life: 10 years

What happens after shelf life: Loses potency

Safe storage: Best stored in an airtight container in a cool location

Cautions: Leakage

Batteries (Alkaline)

Recommended shelf life: 3–5 years; may last longer than package expiration date

What happens after shelf life: Loses potency

Safe storage: Best stored in an airtight container in a cool location

Cautions: Leakage

Battery Bank

Recommended shelf life: Varies

What happens after shelf life: No longer holds a charge well

Safe storage: Keep cells filled; keep batteries, terminals, and cables clean; store lead acid batteries in properly vented box

Cautions: Electrical shock; acid burns; batteries may explode

Butane

Recommended shelf life: 8 years–indefinite

What happens after shelf life: N/A

Safe storage: Store in cool, dry place away from heat sources

Cautions: Highly flammable

Canned Heat

Recommended shelf life: 10 years–indefinite if unopened; varies by manufacturer

What happens after shelf life: Loses potency

Safe storage: Store upright, away from heat sources

Cautions: Dispose of damaged or dented cans

Charcoal

Recommended shelf life: Indefinite

What happens after shelf life: May not light or burn well if moisture has been absorbed—dry out on a hot, dry day to restore viability

Safe storage: Store in airtight plastic or metal containers to prevent moisture absorption

Cautions: Produces vast amounts of deadly carbon monoxide; never use indoors

Coal

Recommended shelf life: Indefinite

What happens after shelf life: Air speeds up deterioration and breakdown, causing coal to burn faster

Safe storage: Store away from circulating air, light, and moisture away from home

Cautions: Susceptible to spontaneous combustion; produces carbon monoxide

Coleman Fuel (White Gas)

Recommended shelf life: 5–7 years (unopened); 1–2 years (opened)

What happens after shelf life: Will not burn as well

Safe storage: Store in original container in a dry area with no rapid or extreme changes in temperature; store in detached garage or shed

Cautions: Highly flammable; produces carbon monoxide; never use indoors

Diesel

Recommended shelf life: 18–24 months; life may be extended with a fuel stabilizer

What happens after shelf life: Will not burn as well; gums up equipment

Safe storage: Store in approved yellow containers in detached garage or shed

Cautions: Produces carbon monoxide; jells at low temperatures; do not burn indoors

Firewood

Recommended shelf life: 4+ years

What happens after shelf life: Decreased BTU output

Safe storage: Store off the ground; protect from moisture; allow for plenty of air circulation; store away from the house

Cautions: Termites, pests, and rodents

Fuel Tablets (Esbit, Trioxane, Hexamine, Sterno)

Recommended shelf life: Indefinite

What happens after shelf life: N/A

Safe storage: Store in a dry place in original packaging

Cautions: Use in a well-ventilated area; do not burn indoors!

Gasoline

Recommended shelf life: 6–12 months; may be extended with a fuel stabilizer

What happens after shelf life: Breaks down and becomes ineffective; will gum up equipment

Safe storage: Store in approved red containers in detached garage or shed; best place is in the tank of your car

Cautions: Highly flammable; storing large quantities is hazardous; outdoor use only

Gel Fuel

Recommended shelf life: Indefinite

What happens after shelf life: N/A

Safe storage: Store in a cool, dry place in original packaging

Cautions: Flammable; outdoor use only

Kerosene

Recommended shelf life: 2–5 years; may be extended with a fuel stabilizer

What happens after shelf life: Will not burn as hot

Safe storage: Store in approved blue plastic container in a cool, dry place; store in detached garage or shed

Cautions: Produces deadly carbon monoxide, nitrogen dioxide, and sulfur dioxide; use in well-ventilated area; avoid indoor use

Lamp Oil

Recommended shelf life: Indefinite

What happens after shelf life: N/A

Safe storage: Store in a cool, dry place in original container, tightly sealed

Cautions: Do not allow to freeze; combustible liquid; frozen oil may defrost too quickly, posing an explosive hazard

Lighter Fluid

Recommended shelf life: Indefinite

What happens after shelf life: N/A

Safe storage: Store in a cool, dry place away from open flames

Cautions: Newspaper or canned heat will work in a charcoal chimney and is much safer

Matches

Recommended shelf life: Indefinite

What happens after shelf life: N/A

Safe storage: Keep dry

Cautions: Flammable

MRE Heaters

Recommended shelf life: 5 years–indefinite

What happens after shelf life: Takes longer to heat up and does not achieve high temperatures

Safe storage: Store in a cool, dry place away from water

Cautions: Keep activated heater away from open flame because it produces hydrogen gas and may create an explosive hazard

Newspaper Logs

Recommended shelf life: Indefinite

What happens after shelf life: N/A

Safe storage: Store in a dry place

Cautions: Burns better if mixed with regular wood

Propane

Recommended shelf life: Indefinite

What happens after shelf life: N/A

Safe storage: Store in detached garage or shed

Cautions: Pressurized cylinder of flammable gas; leaks pool in lowest place, creating an explosive hazard; do not use indoors except in appliances rated for indoor use; watch canister or tank for signs of rust or dents—replace damaged containers immediately

Solar Modules

Recommended shelf life: Usually have a 25-year warranty; may work longer

What happens after shelf life: Effectiveness decreases

Safe storage: Keep clean and free of debris

Cautions: None

Wax (Candles)

Recommended shelf life: Indefinite

What happens after shelf life: N/A

Safe storage: Store in a cool, dry place

Cautions: Open flames are dangerous—use in a well-ventilated area with great caution

Wind Turbines

Recommended shelf life: 5–25 years

What happens after shelf life: Output may diminish or malfunction

Safe storage: Periodic maintenance

Cautions: Danger—moving parts

FUEL SAFETY AND STORAGE ACTION PLAN

The first item of business is to contact your local fire department and learn what the fuel storage guidelines and restrictions apply in your local area. Apartment dwellers may have different guidelines than single family homes. Safely and legally build your plan around these guidelines.

Next, contact your insurance agent to discuss your homeowner's policy. Ask for specific information regarding fuel storage. Depending on your policy, storing some types or amounts of fuel may negate your policy. It may be wise to review your written policy also. Follow the guidelines from your insurance policy.

Make a list of the critical items you might need fuel for during an emergency. Explore the different options you have available. This list should include only those things that are necessary for survival. Needs and wants are two very different things. Focus on providing for needs before luxury or convenience items.

Carefully consider where the fuel should be stored. Refer to the detailed descriptions earlier in the chapter to learn storage requirements for different fuels. A few fuels may be safely stored inside a garage, but most should be stored in a detached shed. It would be better to do without than to accidentally start a dangerous house fire.

Armed with the above information, you are ready to develop your personal fuel storage plan. The length of time you want to prepare for is an important consideration. Your goal may be to function through a short-term power outage, make it through the winter, or survive an entire year in the event of a long-term power outage caused by an EMP. Implementing conservation strategies will enable you to consume considerably less fuel. Do not stress over exact numbers. Make educated guesses. As you practice, you will get a better idea of exact fuel consumption and will be able to tweak your plan appropriately.

We have prepared a worksheet to walk you through designing your fuel storage action plan. It can be found at www.theprovidentprepper .org/the-practical-prepper/action-plan-fuel-safety-and-storage. As you plan and prepare, make safety your number one priority.

|| 13 ||

Emergency Lighting
I Can See Clearly Now

It is better to light a candle than curse the darkness.

—Eleanor Roosevelt

Darkness is depressing and potentially dangerous. Stumbling around in the dark can cause injuries. Any injury in a disaster situation has the potential to be life threatening. Living in the city, we are rarely in complete darkness. The utter darkness that comes with a power outage can be unsettling. Our family did not realize how much we depend on our electrical lighting until we could not use it for a few days. We found that when night brought the dark, we were better off going to bed with the sun.

Light elevates your mood and increases productivity. Fears and worries are magnified in darkness. Life looks better in the morning because of the light. We encourage you to study your lighting options and plan to keep your family safe and in the light during power outages. Carefully consider the dynamics of the people living in your home. Should open flame be an option? Would burning fuel indoors compromise the health of the elderly, young, or infirm?

Providing lighting for your family is simpler than you may think. We are going to review a variety of lighting sources. Do not buy every device listed in this chapter! We review them in order to help you select the tools that may work best in your situation. Take time to complete the action plan at the end of this chapter. Inventory what you already have, and then create your plan and work steadily to execute it. It is a great feeling to know you will have light when you need it.

Children find comfort in having their own light source. However, open flames can be extremely fascinating to children and pose a fire hazard.

LIGHTING

Lighting requirements will vary depending on the circumstances. What purpose is the light intended to serve? A headlamp provides great hands-free light, but a lantern would work better to provide light around a table. You may want to think about how you would light your world indoors as well as outdoors. Consider short-term solutions and options for longer-term power outages.

Light intensity is measured in lumens—the higher the lumen, the brighter the light. This little table will give you an idea of the brightness of a few common light sources to assist you in your planning. The bulb makes a big difference in the amount of light produced with the same amount of power.

Light Source	Lumens
Glow stick	4
Candle	13

Kerosene lamp	20–100
3.5-watt light-emitting diode (LED)	150
40-watt standard lightbulb	450
8-watt LED	450
10-watt compact fluorescent lamp (CFL)	500
Propane lantern	830–1500
100-watt standard lightbulb	1600

Power sources for light vary. We have grouped them together into the following categories: flame, electric, chemical, solar, manual, and perpetual.

FLAME LIGHT SOURCES

Let us begin by reviewing light sources that use a flame to provide the light. These sources can be dangerous, and great care should be taken around any open flame. Some situations, such as checking for a gas leak, may necessitate using a sparkless option. It would be wise to plan for a flameless option as well. Store matches, or butane lighters, or some way to ignite the flame. Keeping a working carbon monoxide detector and a fire extinguisher handy is also essential.

Light sources that work by flame are fire hazards. Use caution.

Candles

Many different forms of candles are available. A candle lantern or chandelier may increase safety. Candles provide a soft, low light and burn for a long period of time. Candles are easy to obtain and store. The open flame presents a fire hazard and consumes a small amount of oxygen, so provide a little ventilation. Candles have an indefinite shelf life if stored in a dry, cool place.

One type of emergency candle is the 100-Hour Plus Candle, designed with a plastic base and filled with liquid paraffin. It is smokeless and odorless.

Oil Lamps

Traditional oil lamps or lanterns put out more light than candles. The flame is usually surrounded by glass, which is a nice safety feature. Many are designed to be set on a table or hung for greater distribution of light. Practice using the lamps at dinner to create a cozy atmosphere. Oil lamps can add beauty to the home décor.

Keep wicks trimmed to burn cleaner and provide the best light. Be sure to store fuel, wicks, and matches for these light sources. We will review the common fuels for oil lamps, each of which may produce some carbon monoxide as a by-product of combustion. Burn them in a ventilated area.

Liquid paraffin is great for use in liquid lamps. It is smokeless, odorless, cleaner than kerosene, and slow burning. It can be used in traditional oil lamps and wick oil candles. The flame should be restricted to a half inch for safety purposes. Liquid paraffin is fairly safe and has a long storage life. One quart will provide roughly 200 hours of light.

Lamp oil is a liquid petroleum product intended to burn in lanterns with less soot, smoke, and other pollutants. It is a relative of kerosene. Store at, or near, room temperature. Do not allow to freeze. Lamp oil may explode if it thaws too quickly. Depending on wick size and lamp, one quart might provide 75 hours of burn time.

A **kerosene** lantern with a one-inch-wide wick will burn approximately 45 hours per quart of kerosene. A kerosene lantern uses ¼ as much fuel as a gas lantern. The light is comparable to a 40- to 60-watt lightbulb. Ensure proper ventilation when using indoors since kerosene produces carbon monoxide and some black smoke as it burns. The smoke can be minimized by lighting outside and then bringing indoors.

Gas Lanterns

Gas lanterns are designed to be used outdoors. They produce a nice bright light. The fuels produce carbon monoxide, so while they are great for outdoor use, plan alternative lighting for indoors. These lanterns require both fuel and mantles. Candles will not burn without a wick; gas lanterns must have a mantle to burn. The mantles are fragile, so store several extra.

Outdoor liquid fuel lanterns are a good old camping favorite. The light is adjustable, quite bright, and gives off a fair amount of heat. Liquid fuel lanterns are designed to be powered by specific fuels. Kerosene, Coleman or white gas, or unleaded gasoline may be used depending on the model. Use only the fuel recommended for your specific model. Dual-fuel models are specifically designed to accommodate two fuels.

Never use white gas or unleaded gasoline indoors. They produce much more carbon monoxide and must have adequate ventilation. Burn time varies by lantern and fuel type. A Coleman premium dual-fuel lantern will provide seven hours on high and 14 hours on low from 1.3 pints of Coleman fuel or unleaded gas. Two pints of kerosene in a Coleman one-mantle kerosene lantern may only burn 5.5 hours. Calculate your needs based on your specific lantern and fuel choice. Do not store lanterns full of fuel. It can damage the appliance.

Propane lanterns: These very bright lanterns are fueled by a 1-pound propane bottle. They are available in one- or two-mantle models. Depending on the setting and lantern, one bottle of propane may produce 8–14 hours of light. These perform well in windy and wet weather.

ELECTRIC LIGHT SOURCES

Battery-powered lights are a safe and effective option for most of your lighting needs. Batteries store well and last for long periods of time. We find it easy to rotate through our battery stockpile and keep supplies fresh. Light-emitting diode (LED) bulbs will far outperform standard bulbs in both energy performance and bulb life. Select lighting products that take advantage of this technology. Store extra standard bulbs along with batteries.

Quality is important when selecting your light sources. A dollar-store flashlight will not perform well for any length of time. Name brands, such as Maglite, are made of quality materials that you can depend on for many years. They cost more, but light is a critical resource.

Electric light sources are a convenient and safe way to light up your world.

Handheld flashlights: When the lights go out, the first thought is to reach for a good flashlight with fresh batteries. They provide a quick, reliable source of light and are available in a wide variety of shapes and sizes.

Power failure night-light and flashlight units: We have handy lights in the bedrooms that work as night-lights but are actually small rechargeable flashlights. The unit plugs into the wall and keeps the small flashlight charged and handy when needed. When the power goes out, the flashlight goes on automatically. This way you are not left in the dark when a disaster strikes.

Battery-powered lanterns are designed to provide area lighting. Sizes range from personal to family size. They vary greatly in intensity and efficiency, so shop wisely. The Coleman 8D family-size LED lantern will run for 66 hours on low and 32 hours on high (170 lumens) using eight D batteries. It also comes in a rechargeable model. The charge will last six hours on high and nine hours on low. A similar personal-size model uses four D batteries to produce 23 hours on low or 14 hours of light on high (190 lumens).

LED headlamps: These highly efficient task lights are sometimes also called *headlights*. They are worn around the head and direct the light source to follow your field of vision. Many headlamps can be adjusted to create different lighting effects: area, spot, floodlight, and even red night vision light. Most operate using very little energy due to efficient LED bulbs. Designs and efficiency vary. Three AAA batteries may produce 14 to 30-plus hours of run time. The more expensive models tend to be more efficient.

Headlamps are a great source for hands-free personal task lighting.

Personal Lights: Energy conservation is an important consideration in providing light. Do not use energy to light an entire room if you only require a little bit of personal lighting. Small clip-on book lights may provide enough light for reading or small tasks. The Energizer Trim Flex uses two 3-volt lithium coin batteries and will last for 30 hours between battery changes. The Energizer LED book light will only provide ten hours of run time with two lithium coin cell batteries. Understand the limitations and performance requirements of each light and plan accordingly.

Touch Lights: These are lights that can be mounted, or attached magnetically, in virtually any area to provide some light. They turn on and off by simply pushing the lens. An Energizer Professional 3 LED puck light will provide 50 lumens of light for up to 31 hours with three

AA batteries. The Garrity 3 LED touch light will provide light for up to 16 hours with four AA batteries. Size, brightness, and quality are all important considerations when shopping for lights.

CHEMICAL LIGHT SOURCES

Chemical light sticks are a popular treat at nighttime gatherings. They are a short-term, disposable light source. Quality varies greatly. Military-grade or industrial light sticks provide intense light for up to 12 hours, which can be seen up to a mile away depending on model. Dollar-store glow sticks emit a soft light for 6–12 hours. Purchase the right light stick for your intended use.

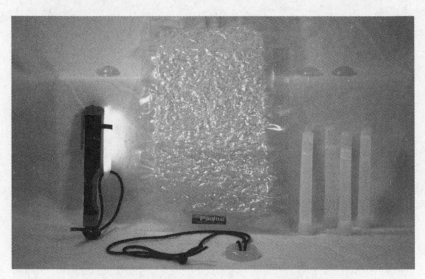

Light sticks and UVPaqlite sources provide a soft, low, functional light. Paqlites can be recharged by any light source. Light sticks are one-time use only.

A **Cyalume light stick** is a plastic stick that comes in a variety of shapes and sizes. Generally, the sticks are four to eight inches in length. Hydrogen peroxide fills an inner glass tube. When broken, the hydrogen peroxide mixes with dye and diphenyl oxalate inside the plastic tube, creating a chemical reaction.

To activate the stick, bend it hard enough to break the glass tube inside and shake to mix the chemicals. Depending on the brand, it will provide a bright colored light for 6–12 hours. It is windproof and weatherproof, does not create sparks for flames, and is safe for all ages.

Light sticks may be purchased online, at sporting goods stores, or at dollar stores. They have a shelf life of four to five years, gradually becoming dimmer over time. These are a safe form of indoor lighting in case of an earthquake or other situation where flammable gases may be present.

SOLAR LIGHT SOURCES

We love using solar products when possible. There is little risk of fire danger or carbon monoxide poisoning. The sun's energy is renewable, free, and readily available. Solar devices capture the sun's energy and turn it into electrical power. This power is usually stored in a battery until ready to be used. We recognize the wisdom in having other light sources available, but we use as much power from the sun as is realistic. Features and capabilities vary depending on the specific model.

Solar-powered lights and battery chargers can be charged by placing them in a south-facing window during the day.

Solar-powered camping lanterns: Choose from a wide variety of solar-powered lanterns, which may be charged with sunlight, an auto adapter, or a UL-listed house adapter. Some models utilize solar, manual winding, or battery backups. The more power options you have available, the greater the chance of having light in any situation. Every model is a bit different.

The Hybrid solar camping lantern boasts six hours of bright light (200 lumens) from an 8-hour charge. See more of their products at www.hybridlight.com. The SolaDyne solar lantern has a dynamo hand crack to backup the solar energy. A full charge provides 16 to 48 hours depending on the setting.

We have two small, basic solar lanterns we bought several years ago. They are kept in a south-facing window to ensure they are charged when we need them. They have survived the abuse of family camping and were well worth the investment.

Solar headlamp: Headlamps can be worth their weight in gold when working in the dark. Hybrid produces a super bright compact headlamp that can be charged using ten hours of sunlight or only one hour if charged via a USB port. Another option might be the Everlite solar clip light with three LEDs. It will provide 20 lumens of bright light for up to 12 hours. An hour of charging will provide one hour of light. The clip light would need to be attached to a hat to work like a headlamp.

Solar landscape, path, and security lights: These handy devices are available just about everywhere in every style imaginable. They are designed to provide interest, beauty, and safety lighting in landscaping. Most are reasonably priced. These lights will emit light all through the night, gradually growing dimmer. Wireless solar-powered motion sensor lights are worth considering. They can provide security lighting outside your home even when the power fails. Keep accent or garden lights charging in the yard but bring them in for light during emergencies.

Solar-powered flashlights: Many solar powered flashlights include other options, such as an AM/FM radio, cell phone charger, or siren to call for help. Goal Zero's solo flashlight is a small rechargeable flashlight with a solar panel and five LEDs. Expose the panel to eight hours of direct sunlight to recharge and it will produce 15 lumens for two hours. The Energizer solar LED flashlight boasts a hand crank for charging at night. Five hours of full sun will power three LED lights for two hours, or one minute of cranking will provide four minutes of light.

Solar battery chargers: If you want to use standard battery-powered lighting devices, consider purchasing rechargeable batteries and a solar charger. The initial investment can be a little bit painful, but the returns are great. Instead of throwing away all those disposable batteries, recharge them using the free energy of the sun.

MANUAL LIGHT SOURCES

These are light sources that require some kind of human energy input for them to work. Frequently, you will find products that use solar power along with manual cranks to enable the device to function without sunlight. The combination lets you enjoy the best of both worlds. Manual devices can be annoying if the emergency lasts for any length of time.

Hand crank lanterns: These are nice for general lighting. They are available with florescent or LED bulbs, which make the batteries last much longer. There is also a battery-less hand crank model available with LED bulbs that claims to last for 20 minutes after 60 seconds of cranking. The Goal Zero lighthouse lantern with USB power hub can provide light and charge your cell phone, MP3 player, tablet, or other device. It charges by AC, DC, and crank for six hours of runtime from four hours of charging time.

Hand crank flashlights: Operated by manually winding, these flashlights come in a wide variety of quality and styles. The Energizer Weatherready 3-LED carabiner crank light will provide three minutes of light from one minute of cranking. The L.L. Bean crank flashlight produces 20 minutes of light from one minute of cranking. Some models will also charge your cell phone or have an AM/FM radio in addition to the light.

Shake flashlights: Some of these flashlights claim they never need batteries or bulbs. They are powered by magnetic field energy that is generated by shaking and charges the internal cell. Thirty seconds of shaking powers the LED bulb(s) for 5–30 minutes, producing up to eight lumens. Quality and performance vary greatly. Some of these are undependable junk, while others may work quite well. Shop carefully.

PERPETUAL LIGHT SOURCES

These are light sources that do not have a limited useable life. They will last close to forever. The sun is the supreme source of light. Natural lighting through windows is amazing and should be used whenever possible. Other than the sun, these sources tend to be dim, although their dependable long life makes them worth exploring.

Natural lighting: Increase the natural light in your home by taking full advantage of sunlight from windows. Decorate using white or light colors to reflect the natural light that enters a room. Mirrors increase the natural light by reflecting it into different parts of the room. Light colors and mirrors will also increase light from other sources (candles, lanterns, and so on).

UV Paqlite products: These light sources do not require batteries, bulbs, electricity, chemical activation, or fuels. There are no mechanical parts to fail, and they are completely waterproof. UV Paqlite products are made from a glow-in-the-dark material called strontium aluminate. It absorbs photons and UV rays to charge, so it can charge in low-level indoor light conditions or by shining a flashlight on it for a few minutes.

4EverLights, made by UVPaqlite, are designed to be a functional light source and are not intended to replace the bright lights produced by lanterns or flashlights. The amount of light emitted is similar to the light given off by glow sticks. They would be a great addition to a survival pack and might prevent injuries from fumbling around in the dark. UVPaqlite products come in a variety of forms. You can find the complete gallery of products at www.uvpaqlite.com.

EMERGENCY LIGHTING ACTION PLAN

We have established that light is vital to emotional well-being and physical safety during a power outage. You do not need to have every cool lighting device available, but you do need to meet your basic needs. Review your risk assessment. What hazards are you preparing for? How long do you need to provide light without electricity? What type of lighting needs do you have? Do you need to take special precautions for members of the household?

We have children in the home, so we prefer to avoid open flame when possible. Each of our children has their own light sticks and flash-lights. We have short-term emergency devices (flashlights, headlamps, candles, and so forth) as well as long-term sustainable methods (natural lighting, solar lights, reusable glow lights, and so on). It sounds like a lot, but it is not. We use many of these devices in our everyday life.

Use the worksheet located at www.theprovidentprepper.org/the -practical-prepper/action-plan-emergency-lighting to brainstorm your emergency lighting needs. Some devices are only safe for outdoor use. Exercise extreme caution when using open flames. Calculate how many hours you need to have emergency lighting. Can you take advantage of natural lighting or solar energy? How many batteries do you need to stockpile? The amount and type of fuel you need will depend on your particular device. Practice using your light sources regularly.

‖ 14 ‖

Emergency Heating
Baby, It's Cold Outside

"Oh, the weather outside is frightful! But the fire is so delightful."[1]

—Sammy Cahn

The need for backup heating depends on where you live. Areas with mild winters, such as Phoenix, Arizona, obviously do not require the same consideration as Cedar Rapids, Iowa, which has an average winter temperature of 23.5 degrees. Keep in mind that unseasonably cold weather can happen anywhere. The record low for Phoenix in January is 29 degrees, but the average range in January is between 46 and 67 degrees.[2] Cold can be deadly if you're unprepared. In this chapter, we will review how you can keep from freezing if your power goes out.

THE EXPERIMENT

We cannot effectively teach something we have not had hands-on experience with. In keeping with that philosophy, our family agreed to turn off the electricity in the dead of winter for a self-inflicted frigid experience.

We have to admit that we cheated right up front—our research project, our rules. We still had a working refrigerator, freezer, and hot water. No other electricity was used, including lights. At the time of the experiment, we had four small children living at home, the youngest of which was not quite two years old. We lived in a well-built two-story home with upgraded insulation and 2 × 6 walls. Allow us to share this cold experience with you.

Day 1

Low of 1°F with a high of 18°F; inside temperature of 51°F

We embarked on this adventure with a great deal of excitement. Our little research assistants thought this was going to be better than camping. We began to make all of the preparations we had researched, turned off the power, and started the game.

We set up two little inexpensive pup tents in the family room, one for the boys and one for the girls, and spread out sleeping bags and blankets inside them. Extra blankets were spread on the master bed where we would sleep. The family room was our designated living area since it had good access to the kitchen and could be isolated from the rest of the house.

*Small tents create a great microenvironment
in which to stay warm.*

Flashlights, candles, glow sticks, and lanterns were gathered and placed in strategic locations in preparation for use at nightfall. We made cardboard inserts for the windows and placed them next to the glass, and then closed the blinds in an effort to retain the heat inside the house.

Meals were simple. We cooked foods over a collapsible stove using canned heat for fuel. We used candles for light in the kitchen, which was a mistake. After several attempts by the children to light various items on fire with the flame from the candle, we gave up and used the battery-powered lanterns and flashlights. At bedtime, we dressed the children in blanket sleepers, gave each one a glow stick, and tucked them in sleeping bags inside their little tents. We went to bed in our queen-sized bed, which was covered with a heavy stack of blankets. We slept comfortably snuggled in our bed together.

During the night, Kylene woke terrified that the little ones were going to freeze to death. She was shocked when she unzipped the first little tent and was struck in the face by a blast of warm air. The twins were sleeping on top of their sleeping bags all toasty warm. The tents had created a microenvironment, which worked like a charm.

Day 2

Low of -1°F with a high of 18°F; inside temperature of 51°F

Breakfast was a little frustrating. Kylene wanted hot cocoa because she was cold and could not use the microwave. Cooking takes much longer when you are dependent on an alcohol stove to heat the water. Eventually, scrambled eggs and hot cocoa filled up tummies, and we proceeded through the day.

Children are resilient. The cold slowed them down only slightly.

Kylene was excited to take a hot shower to warm up. She neglected to think it through very well. After a delightful shower, she returned to the cold with a wet head and no blow drier. She dressed quickly but could not stop shivering, and she was having difficulty thinking clearly. Soon she realized she was in trouble. She needed a heat source quickly, so she took the children across the street to a neighbor's home and warmed up in front of a fireplace in a warm house. Kylene had hypothermia. She knew better but got careless and put herself in serious danger in her own home.

All productivity ended with nightfall. The dark was depressing and difficult to function in. No television for entertainment, only games or reading by dim lights. Bedtime was a blessing and we allowed it to come early.

Day 3

Low of 12°F with a high of 21°F; inside temperature of 49°F

Kylene began day three without a shower. She pulled out the butane stove to cook breakfast on. She was short-tempered and tired of the slow single-can alcohol stove, and she was much too cold to cook outside. At this point, she stopped caring about safety and used a portable butane stove to speed up breakfast.

By late afternoon, Kylene decided to abandon the experiment and called to tell Jonathan, who had been sitting in his heated office at work while she was freezing at home with the children. Of course, he claims he turned off the heat in his office, but how cold can it get in the middle of a heated building? She announced that she had had enough and expected a pat on the back for her valiant effort. Instead, Jonathan told her to put on a hat. (It was a good thing he was several miles away, or he may not have lived to write this book.) After a considerable amount of venting, Kylene put on a hat. She was much warmer.

Day 4

Low of 16°F with a high of 28°F; inside temperature of 46°F

As a reward for mostly good behavior, we got to experiment a little with heat sources. We had a gas fireplace that worked without electricity. It was nice to sit up against because it would warm our backs, but it did not affect the temperature in the room. The blower fan did not work without power. We tried the Mr. Buddy propane heater (UL-rated for indoor use), and Kylene was one happy mama. She put it on the kitchen table and for the first time in days enjoyed playing games with the children.

Kylene enjoyed a shower with the Mr. Buddy propane heater on the bathroom counter. It heated the little bathroom nicely. The house felt significantly colder that day even though the outside temperature had increased.

LESSONS LEARNED

We learned valuable lessons from this experience. Kylene had originally agreed to go for one week without electricity. It was harder than she thought, so she bailed. Jonathan, wisely, agreed to call it good. The cold had not brought out the best in her. We had intentionally avoided using alternative heat sources until the fourth day, because we wanted to see how cold the house would get and if we could survive. Here is what we learned:

- You can survive without electricity.

- Cold results in survival mode. Keeping warm becomes an all-consuming activity.

- Dark is depressing. Productivity started with sunrise and ended with sunset. Safe alternative sources of light are important.

- Open flame is dangerous. Children are fascinated by the flames in candles. Accidents happen quite easily.

- Store easy-to-prepare foods. Hot cocoa, hot apple cider, soups, hot cereals, and other warm foods are wonderful for warming from the inside out.

- Wear a hat.

- Store *lots* of blankets. Blankets were used to cover windows and separate rooms, as well as for bedding. Many more blankets are required to stay warm without a heat source.

BASIC PRINCIPLES OF HEAT LOSS

When organizing priorities, we refer to the rule of threes. You can survive three minutes without air, three hours without shelter, three days without water, and three weeks without food. That puts air and shelter at the top of the list. For the purposes in this chapter, we define shelter as the ability to maintain appropriate body temperature.

Let us review the basic principles of heat loss. We lose heat in five basic ways:

- **Conduction** is heat loss through the ground. Avoid sitting or lying on a cold surface where heat is literally sucked out of your body. Sitting or sleeping on foam pads can significantly reduce heat loss due to conduction. Wear thick wool socks and shoes.

- **Convection** is heat loss due to air movement. We often hear about wind chill factor. It can be 30 degrees outside, but it may feel like it is only 15 because of the wind pulling heat away from your body. Wearing windproof jackets can significantly reduce heat loss.

- **Radiation** is heat loss to the environment. Thirty percent of body heat is lost through the head and neck. Clothing keeps you warm by creating a barrier and reflecting radiant heat back to your body. Mylar blankets reflect up to 90 percent of body heat back.

- **Respiration** is heat loss through breathing. Every time you exhale, you breathe out warm air. Inhaling replaces that lost warm air with cool air. Increased respirations decrease body temperature as well as dehydrate the body.

- **Evaporation** carries away the heat along with the water. Perspiration encourages heat loss as water conducts heat hundreds of times faster than dry air. Have you ever tried to take a hot pan out of the oven with a wet cloth? The water in the cloth will turn to steam almost instantly—ouch! A dry cloth would not have burned you as quickly. It is critical to stay dry.

COLD-INDUCED ILLNESS

Cold weather brings with it sickness. Exposure to cold can suppress the immune system. Viruses spread more readily in dry, chilly air. According to the Harvard Health Letter of January 2010, "Blood pressure increases during the winter, and, by some reckonings, 70% of the wintertime increase in the death rate can be traced back to heart attacks, strokes, and other cardiovascular causes of death."[3] The elderly, infirm, and very young are especially susceptible to cold.

Preventable cold-weather illnesses include carbon monoxide poisoning, frostbite, and hypothermia, all of which can each lead to serious illness and death. The good news is that they are largely avoidable. The first step is to understand the illnesses themselves and the conditions that create them. Then take the necessary steps to prevent them from occurring.

Carbon Monoxide Poisoning

Carbon monoxide is a deadly by-product of burning some fuels. Charcoal, gasoline, diesel, Coleman fuel (white gas), kerosene, natural gas, and wood all produce this deadly gas as a by-product of combustion. It is possible for any flame to produce carbon monoxide if sufficient oxygen is not present for complete combustion. Always provide adequate ventilation.

Carbon monoxide is an odorless, colorless, tasteless gas. It is known as the "silent killer" because people often have symptoms that are attributed to other causes. Symptoms include dizziness, headache, weakness, nausea, impaired judgment, confusion, irritability, and flulike symptoms. Carbon monoxide interferes with the blood's ability to carry oxygen to the cells of the body. It may reach toxic levels in minutes or hours. Carbon monoxide replaces oxygen in the blood until suffocation occurs. Incidences of carbon monoxide poisoning cases increase dramatically following a disaster. Primary sources of poisoning are gasoline-powered generators and charcoal burning devices. Unvented kerosene heaters are another cause of carbon monoxide poisoning after disasters.

Carbon monoxide poisoning is preventable. Keep a working carbon monoxide detector with a digital readout and battery backup in your home. Provide adequate ventilation when burning anything. Learn about fuels and use them appropriately (see chapter 12).

Hypothermia

Hypothermia is a serious, life-threatening condition. The victim is usually is not aware of his own dangerous situation. Hypothermia occurs when core body temperature drops below 95 degrees Fahrenheit and the body is losing heat faster than it can produce it.

We usually associate hypothermia with the outdoors. Mild hypothermia can be developed indoors after extended exposure to cool temperatures. The elderly and infirm are at greater risk than the young and healthy. Hypothermia may be a risk when the temperature in homes is less than 60 degrees.

The first warning sign is shivering, and then uncontrollable shivering. But a stop in shivering is a sign that death is approaching. Symptoms may include clumsiness, stumbling, slow or slurred speech, confusion, difficulty thinking, drowsiness, false sensation of feeling warm, apathy, progressive loss of consciousness, weak pulse, or slow and shallow breathing.

Treatment involves slowly warming the victim to normal body temperature. Reduce heat loss by getting into a warm sheltered environment and dry clothing. Share body heat using skin-to-skin contact and cover with blankets. Cover the head. Increase heat production by drinking warm liquids (no alcohol or caffeine) if alert. Do not apply direct heat. Get medical help as soon as possible.[4]

Hypothermia can develop rapidly and progress quickly. The best protection is to recognize the threat and actively work to prevent it. Put on a coat before you get cold. Stay out of wet and cold weather. Plan for ways to stay warm during cold weather without electricity. If you do not have the ability to stay warm in your home, where can you go to keep warm? Make contingency plans.

Frostbite

When the skin and the body tissues underneath it freeze, frostbite will occur. When body parts are exposed to temperatures below freezing for too long, blood flow stops to the exposed area and body tissues are damaged. The nose, cheeks, ears, fingers, and toes are most often affected.

Frostnip is the first stage of frostbite. It will irritate the skin, causing numbness without resulting in permanent damage. Symptoms of frostbite include a prickly feeling, numbness, burning, hard and waxy-looking skin, discolored skin (red, white, grayish, or yellow), and cold skin.[5] Frostbitten skin may be red, swollen, and painful when it warms up. Severely frostbitten skin may become blistered or turn black. Seek medical care since frostbite can lead to complications including infection and nerve damage.

Avoid frostbite by wearing warm clothing that protects against windy, cold, and wet weather. Dress in layers of loose clothing. Avoid tight shoes or clothing, which may restrict blood flow. Completely cover your ears. Mittens provide better protection than gloves. Always carry emergency supplies when traveling in cold weather. Drinking alcohol causes your body to lose heat quickly, so avoid it. But hot cocoa and other warm nonalcoholic drinks will help keep you warm.

TIPS FOR INCREASING BODY TEMPERATURE

Body heat is produced by metabolizing the food we eat and the liquid we drink, and by exercise. It can also be acquired from an external heat source such as a fire or another warm body. Let's review some common-sense ideas for staying warm:

Stay Hydrated

Drink plenty of tepid water. You may not feel thirsty, but you need to drink between ½ and 1 gallon every day. Do not eat snow or drink ice water. Cold drinks will reduce your core temperature. Dehydration thickens your blood, placing you at an increased risk of hypothermia.

Eat

Food is like the wood and kindling in a fire. Your body gains the energy to stay warm from the foods and beverages you consume. Eat foods high in protein, carbohydrates, and fats. Fats keep your thyroid and metabolism functioning properly and will help you stay warmer. Warm foods will help you warm up from the inside out. Hot cereals, broth, soups, stews, chili, beans, hot cider, and hot cocoa are great foods for a chilly environment.

Be Active

A healthy body is more tolerant of cold. Twenty minutes of exercise can warm you up and keep you warm well after you stop moving. Exercise increases blood flow to the extremities, preventing frostbite. Avoid overheating by adjusting layers of clothing. Sweat can dampen your skin and clothes, which can quickly wick heat away from your body. Wet clothing is a dangerous enemy.

Keep Your Core Warm

Keeping your core warm helps the entire body stay warmer. We define the core as your head, torso, and halfway down your thighs. When the body gets cold, natural defenses kick in, constricting blood vessels in the skin to keep blood flowing to the vital organs.

We are amazed at how a homeless person can survive subzero temperatures in the dead of winter. Although some die from exposure, we can learn from watching them. We have observed that they wear layers of clothing. Some insulate by stuffing wadded newspapers, rags, or other materials inside their coats. They always wear hats and dress warmly from the beginning to maintain body temperature instead of waiting to be chilled before dressing. If they can survive, you can too.

Clothing is your first line of defense. Layers of loose lightweight clothing allow you to adjust to changing temperatures. Tight-fitting clothing can restrict your circulation. Most heat is lost through the head and neck, so keep them covered. Protect hands by wearing gloves or mittens. Wear shoes, slippers, or at least socks, even in the house. Avoid cotton and keep the neck area loose to allow moisture to escape.

Blankets

Always have extra blankets on hand. Even if you have to store them in boxes in the rafters, keep a stash of several blankets. If the power goes out, blankets have a multitude of uses. You cannot have too many warm blankets.

Mylar blankets or sleeping bags are light, highly portable, and great for survival kits. They provide a wind and vapor barrier, returning the majority of radiant heat to the body. Remember the five ways your body loses heat? Radiant heat loss and convection account for less than half of the heat loss mechanisms. Mylar blankets cannot effectively replace standard blankets or sleeping bags for insulating value.

Social Interaction

People are social creatures. An increased sense of well-being and happiness is found through interacting with others. Make the effort to dust off the games, relax, and play together. Invite the neighbors over, if you live alone or even if you do not. The laughter and fun will elevate the mood and result in increased body temperature from the interaction. It will give the depressing aspects of the current situation a new healthy perspective.

HOW NOT TO FREEZE WHEN THE LIGHTS GO OUT

An earthquake shakes your home on a cold, windy January evening. Your home is in relatively good shape with the exception of a few broken windows, no gas, and no electrical power. You are left without electricity for an undetermined amount of time. It may be hours. It may be weeks. How will you keep your family from freezing?

Taking the time to think through various scenarios is not intended to frighten, but to provide opportunities to plan for a variety of possible situations. We cannot anticipate every possible crisis; however, with thoughtful planning we will have the knowledge and resources to survive most of them.

Consider the following ideas as part of your "Winter Power is Out Action Plan."

Secure the Home

Immediately after the event, take a few minutes to look around and carefully evaluate your surroundings. Is the structure stable? Cosmetic damage, such as broken windows, that leaves the foundation and walls intact might indicate the structure is stable. Fractured, tilting, or collapsed walls or ceilings suggest the structure is not safe to stay in. Do you smell natural gas? What dangers are present? Are all family members accounted for? Is it safe to stay? It may be better to camp in your backyard than stay in your home if there is any concern about the safety of the structure.

If you determine that it is safe to stay in your home, begin to secure your home. Cover broken windows with heavy polyethylene plastic sheeting (clear or opaque, at least 4–6 mil thick) and secure with duct tape or painter's tape. Windows may be intact enough to leave in place. Multiple layers of plastic may help to increase insulation value. If you have not stored plastic sheeting, you may need to get creative. Plywood, cardboard, aluminum foil, or even newspapers could be used, if you get desperate. The goal is to keep the cold out and the heat in.

Select One Living Area

It is not realistic to heat the entire home using emergency heating methods. Unless, of course, you have a wood-burning stove and enough wood to fuel it, or a similar backup heating system. It may still be a good idea to limit the space you heat to conserve fuel.

Select one area to heat and separate it from the rest of the home. Confine emergency heat to a small area. Consider the following when selecting the room:

- Is there a fireplace or built-in heat source?

- Are kitchen or restroom facilities accessible?

- A south-facing room could take advantage of passive solar heat.

- Avoid rooms with large windows or uninsulated walls.

- Basements are good because the earth acts as a natural insulator.

- Isolate the room from the rest of the house by keeping doors closed, hanging blankets over doorways, or putting up temporary partitions of cardboard or plywood. Anything to isolate the living area from the rest of the home to conserve heat. Bring important items into this living area such as blankets, warm clothing, sleeping bags, survival packs, games, and so on.

Our friend's family survived the winter after the 1964 Alaskan earthquake by setting up a tent in the living area inside their home. Their wood-burning stove was damaged by the earthquake and was unsafe to use. The tent created a microenvironment, providing a warm place to sleep and recreate. This is an excellent example of using the resources you have on hand to make the best of a situation. Stop and think, "How can I keep the heat in and the cold out?"

Cold Weather Clothing

Do you have enough coats, jackets, sweaters, boots, gloves, hats, long johns, and so on to keep your family warm in the dead of winter without any additional heat sources? Wool is a great option. Purchase winter clothing a year ahead. We buy the children's coats, boots, and gloves at the end of the season to take advantage of clearance prices. Dress warm before you get chilled. Put on a hat and warm clothing.

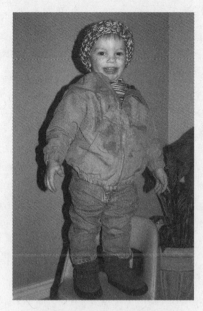

Young children need more changes of clothing than adults. Plan for several changes of outerwear.

Jim Phillips has designed foam clothing and sleeping bags that perform quite well in cold weather and may be worth your consideration. You can find more information at jimsway.com.

Hand and Foot Warmers

Hand and foot warmers can be great tools. Air-activated hand warmers will last between one and ten hours. They gradually lose heating ability in storage. It is probably not realistic to store enough for an entire winter, but a box or two could come in handy. Store a few in your vehicle survival kit. Moisture can render the warmers useless.

As with everything else, use carefully. Our nephew put a few warmers in his boots before a Scout hike and came home with burn blisters. He had placed them next to his skin and did not realize they were so hot until after the damage was done.

Insulate Windows

Windows are a weak spot when it comes to insulating the home. The efficiency of insulation in a home is often measured in R-value (resistance to heat flow through a material). The larger the numbers, the better the insulating value. Windows typically have an R-value of only one or two, compared to exterior walls with an R-value of 13 to 19 or ceilings with an R-value of 30 to 50. Can you see why windows are an area of concern?

However, windows also allow light into the home. If located on the south side, the sun shining through them can warm the home. It may be wise to allow the light and sun in through south-facing windows during the day and insulate them at night. Storm windows and hurricane shutters can help improve efficiency.

Insulating blinds and curtains can reduce heat loss. Covering windows with layers of clear plastic sheeting or bubble wrap will allow light in but will insulate against heat loss. It can also be an acceptable temporary fix for broken or cracked windows. Windows could also be covered with cardboard, blankets, plywood, shower curtains, foam board, or anything that will keep the cold out and the heat in.

Expedient Insulation

The north side of the home is a weak point because there is no solar heat gain. Consider stacking bales of straw or even piling snow outside the walls on the north side of the house to help insulate it from the cold.

ALTERNATIVE HEATING METHODS

As you decide which of the alternative methods to use to heat the living area in your home, use great caution. It would be a tragedy to survive the earthquake only to have your family die from carbon monoxide poisoning or in a house fire because of a well-intended mistake.

Any flame may produce carbon monoxide as a result of incomplete combustion. Always have a working carbon monoxide detector near when burning anything in your home. We will explore a few options for providing a little extra heat during a power outage. Whatever option you choose, practice with it to ensure it works the way you intended it to and to become confident in how to use it appropriately.

Alcohol Heater

The Heat Pal 5100 is a good example of an alcohol heater and stove combination. It can be used to cook as well as heat. Alcohol is a good option to burn indoors. While any flame has the potential to produce carbon monoxide if there is not enough oxygen, the natural by-product of burning alcohol is carbon dioxide. Always ventilate (open a window or door an inch or so) when burning anything to replace oxygen consumed by the flame. Alcohol is a good storage fuel because of its indefinite shelf life.

The Heat Pal 5100 functions as a heater as well as a stove. It can be used indoors.

Kerosene Heaters

We personally do not plan to use a portable unvented kerosene heater in our home, especially during an emergency. Some available kerosene heaters are rated for indoor use. Kerosene produces deadly carbon monoxide, nitrogen dioxide (which may cause throat and lung irritation), and sulfur dioxide (which can impair breathing) when burned. Klean-Heat, an odorless kerosene alternative, still produces the same by-products as standard kerosene when burned. Adequate cross ventilation is required for safety. That means opening a window a few inches on each side of the room to allow the air to move through the room. They are frequently used in other countries, but why risk it when we have safer options available?

That being said, vented kerosene heaters are an option worth exploring. The difference is they are vented to the outside and do not release toxins into your home—similar to a fireplace. Purchase the best grade of kerosene available. Kerosene is a good storage fuel with a 5-year shelf life that can be extended with fuel stabilizers.

Portable Propane Heater

Mr. Heater Buddy (Portable or Big) is rated for indoor use. We really like these heaters. They can use a 1-pound propane canister or be connected to a 20-pound propane tank by a propane hose. The 20-pound propane tank must remain outside and be connected to the heater through a window or door inside. The larger heater utilizes batteries to power a fan. The portable version is perfect to carry around the house and warm whatever space you are in.

The fuel should always be attached to the heater outside and brought in. Propane is a great storage fuel with an indefinite shelf life. Never burn indoors unless the appliance is rated for indoor use. Propane is heavier than air. If a leak occurs, the gas will pool in the lowest spot and create an explosive hazard. Use caution.

Propane heaters that are rated for indoor use are a good solution for emergency heating.

Wood-Burning Stove or Fireplace

A wood-burning stove is a wonderful way to heat a home during an emergency as well as every day. We saved for several years in order to purchase one. It is quickly paying for itself. We use it all winter long to warm the house as well as for cooking. It gives the home a pleasant cozy feeling.

Fireplaces and wood stoves vary significantly in their efficiency. Pellet stoves require electricity and will not work well for emergency heating without backup power. Research and plan carefully before making a purchase. Are you using it primarily for heating or do you want it to be used for cooking as well?

Wood is a perfect, safe storage fuel. The amount you may need to store depends upon your climate, stove efficiency, and usage. We tend to go through two cords during a winter. Our neighbors go through four to five in a similar-sized home. Store dry seasoned wood along with kindling, matches or lighters, and fire starters. Chimneys should be cleaned annually to prevent buildup, which may cause chimney fires or result in carbon monoxide being forced into the home.

We enjoy our wood-burning stove throughout the winter for both heating and cooking.

Terra-cotta Pot Heater

Sometimes a little creativity is required to keep warm in an emergency. As you will learn in the next chapter, canned heat is one of our favorite indoor fuels. It is inexpensive, burns clean, and stores safely. You can create a small heater using a couple of different-sized terra-cotta pots, a portable folding stove, and canned heat. Set up the folding stove. Then place the smaller pot upside down on top of the stove. Cover the hole with something nonflammable to prevent the heat from escaping. A piece of foil works well. Then place the larger pot on top the same way. Remove the lid from the canned heat, place it inside of the stove, and light it.

The heat is channeled through the pots and a convection current is created, providing a nice, localized heat. This will not heat an entire room. It provides a nice source of heat to warm your hands and may heat a very small space. A terra-cotta pot heater might be a good emergency option for someone who lives in a small apartment. The alcohol fuel and stove can be used to cook as well as provide a little warmth and would not take up much space. For details on construction and design, visit www.theprovidentprepper.org/terracotta-pot-heater.

This terracotta pot heater utilizes canned heat, two different-sized pots, and a portable folding stove to provide a hand warmer and a little bit of space heating.

Passive Solar Heating

Let the sun help heat your home. Passive solar heating utilizes the sun's energy to provide warmth. When combined with thermal mass, this energy is stored and helps reduce temperature fluctuations. Thermal mass can be concrete, bricks, tile, rocks, water, and similar materials. Six inches is enough to do the job well.

When possible, open blinds and drapes on the south side of the home when the sun is shining. Effectiveness may be increased by placing thermal mass in the path of the sunshine to absorb the heat. Be sure to close the blinds or drapes when the sun is not shining to increase the insulation (keep hot air in and cold air out). Use caution not to place more weight on the floor than the structure can handle. Even placing water bottles in the direct sun can help.

PREPARE YOUR HOME

Winterize your home now. Many utility companies will perform a home energy audit at no charge. That is a great way to have a professional give you a list of what things need to be taken care of. Our home performed well without power because it was well insulated.

Install weather stripping around windows and doors. Check the insulation in your attic, basement, and exterior walls. Do they meet or exceed local building codes? How about installing storm doors or windows? Can you install energy-efficient blinds or curtains? Check for cold air entry ports around exterior wall electrical outlets, switch plates, and gaps around windows or doors. Clean the chimney and vents. Keep the roof in good repair. Insulate pipes exposed to the cold in the exterior walls or attic.

Go to the Database of State Incentives for Renewables and Efficiency at dsireusa.org and click on your state to find what financial incentives may be available to help you make your home more energy efficient. There are grants, rebates, and tax credits to help lessen the financial hit. Low-income programs may also be available to improve energy efficiency at little or no cost if you qualify. Take time to investigate what opportunities you may have to make your home more energy efficient.

LANDSCAPE FOR ENERGY EFFICIENCY

One way to prepare your home is to landscape with energy efficiency in mind. Strategic landscaping can reduce energy bills now as well as help during challenging times. Convection created by the wind can suck warmth from your home. Plants can be used as insulating blankets for your home.

Trees, fences, or other structures can create windbreaks to shield your home from direct wind. Windbreaks on the west, north, and east of homes may cut fuel consumption an average of 40 percent. Fuel consumption can be reduced by 25 percent in homes with windbreaks on the side of the prevailing winds.[6] Plant deciduous trees on the south side to allow for solar heat gain in the winter.

Well-planned landscaping is a great investment. For useful information on landscaping for energy efficiency, go to landscapeforlife.org.

SPECIAL NEEDS

Consider the special needs of each member of your household. Is there anyone who is highly sensitive to the cold? The very young, the elderly, and individuals with compromised heath cannot tolerate cold temperatures or toxins produced by inappropriate burning in the home. Are there children who may be fascinated by open flame or heating appliances? Is there an elderly person in the home who is a little forgetful and could accidently leave a flame burning? How can you protect them and prevent an accidental fire?

Remember that open flame of any kind increases the risk of house fires. Use great care to keep all combustibles away from the heat source. Review chapter 12 and store fuels safely and legally.

EMERGENCY HEATING ACTION PLAN

The title of this chapter might be emergency heating, but our real goal is to keep from freezing until life returns to normal. What risks are you preparing for? How long could you be without power? Consider each category on the worksheet at www.theprovidentprepper.org/the-practical-prepper/action-plan-emergency-heating and decide how to best prepare to survive the cold. Practice using alternative heat sources to ensure they work as intended. Always have working smoke detectors, carbon monoxide detectors, and fire extinguishers to increase your safety.

|| 15 ||

Emergency Cooking
No Power? No Problem!

"A house is not a home unless it contains food and fire for the mind as well as the body."

—Benjamin Franklin

It is five o'clock on a winter afternoon. Suddenly the power goes out in your home. It does not take very long before you realize that you cannot make dinner. The outage may only last a few hours. Cold sandwiches will work for tonight. But what if it should last for days, weeks, or longer? What will you do? Are you ready?

In this chapter, we will focus on alternative energy solutions for cooking. We will discuss a variety of fuel options along with cooking devices and methods. It is important to have a backup plan or a series of options so that no matter what the scenario, you will be able to take care of yourself and your family. For instance, if you must stay indoors because you are sheltering-in-place, you will need a different set of options than if you have the ability to cook outdoors. A Camp Chef and 20-pound propane tank would be difficult to take in an evacuation scenario. You do not need to have all of the options we share with you. Come up with a few that would work well for you. Have fun with them and practice on a regular basis. Develop a strategy that will ensure you are able to cook in several different types of emergency situations, including evacuation, indoor, outdoor, summer, winter, and so on. Always put safety first!

We were challenged to have a one-year supply of fuel on hand.

For years we had faithfully stored food but had not considered how we would cook it without electricity or natural gas. There is wisdom in having a year's supply of fuel, but there are also huge safety issues and appropriate laws prohibiting the storage of large amounts of potentially dangerous fuels. Jonathan, being an engineer, did the math and had serious concerns that we could realistically accomplish this in an urban setting. We took the challenge and began a journey of research, experimentation, and discovery. Could we realistically store a year's supply of fuel safely and cost-effectively? Absolutely! The solution lies in a variety of energy sources and the conservation of those resources.

CRISIS COOKING

The first order of business is to simplify the menu. Any crisis brings a multitude of challenges that will occupy much of your time. Meals should be simple, nutritious, and comforting. Heating canned foods or boiling water to make mashed potatoes out of potato flakes may be all you can manage at times. Keep a supply of foods on hand that can be eaten without cooking or with minimal effort. Prepare only what will be consumed during one sitting as you cannot refrigerate leftovers. Now is not the time to waste any food.

SAVING PERISHABLE FOODS

During an extended power outage, the valuable food in your freezer could possibly spoil within a few days. Keep your freezer closed as much as possible. If you have a generator, you can keep food frozen by running it for only a couple of hours a day. A full freezer will maintain temperature much longer than one that is partially empty. Consider storing jugs of water in the freezer to take up the extra space and help it run more efficiently. Water expands when it is frozen, so allow a little extra space at the top for expansion to avoid splitting. This water may come in handy during an emergency.

With a little planning, you may be able to save much of your frozen food. Meat, vegetables, and fruits can be preserved and made shelf stable for months. Processed foods, such as frozen entrees or ice cream, should be consumed first.

Meat can be bottled by pressure cooking in canning jars. Recipes are available from local extension offices or home canning books. Store canning jars, lids, and a pressure canner, along with a heat source such as a Camp Chef and some propane. Smoking meat will increase its longevity by slowing down the growth of bacteria and spoilage of fat, enabling it to stay safe to eat for an extended period of time. Jerky would also be another option. Remove the fat from the meat, cut it into very thin slices, marinate it, and dehydrate it into jerky. Preserving meat with salt is also possible, if you have stored enough. Salt draws out the moisture and prevents bacteria from surviving while the meat is hung to dry.

Frozen vegetables and fruits can be bottled or dehydrated. Contact your local extension office or find a home canning book for detailed information on bottling fruits and vegetables. An electric dehydrator will not work without power, but other options include placing the fruits or vegetables in an unused vehicle, on dryer sheets placed out in the heat, or in a solar dehydrator. Fruits and vegetables will require less time to dry if they are cut into small, thin pieces.

Processing previously frozen foods will not produce the highest-quality product. However, during a crisis, food becomes precious and waste should be avoided. Safely preserving the food in your freezer may be a good idea. Plan now. Explore the options available and decide which is best for you. Invest in the necessary supplies and learn the skills and techniques that will ensure you are ready to act when the time arrives.

Remember, do not risk your health by eating any food that is questionable. An disaster situation is not a good time to need emergency medical services because they will not likely be available.

ALTERNATIVE COOKING METHODS

Always make safety your number one priority when using any cooking device. It is possible for any flame to produce carbon monoxide if there is not enough oxygen for complete combustion to occur. Read directions and comply with all manufacturer safety recommendations. Possible dangers from cooking with liquid and gaseous fuels include fires, burns, poisoning by breathing or ingestion, and explosions. Please exercise great care and wisdom in fuel use and storage.

Let us explore some possible fuels, strategies, and cooking devices you may want to consider as you develop a plan to cook during an emergency.

Conservation Methods

Conservation is critical, particularly when fuel is limited. Plan ahead by baking in the solar oven during the day, or prepare your main meal early enough to use the sun oven to prepare it (best solar cooking is between 10 a.m. and 4 p.m.). For example, bring a pot of stew to a boil while cooking breakfast and place it in a hay box to finish cooking until dinnertime. Using a pressure cooker can save up to 70 percent of the normally required cooking time, conserving precious fuel. Use only a few charcoals in a paper box oven instead of many in traditional methods. Experiment with these techniques now. You will be amazed how easy it is to use less fuel every day.

Hay box, fireless cooker, insulation cooker, wonder box, and **thermal cooker** are all different names for the same concept. These cookers have been used throughout history to make the most of limited fuel but do not actually "cook." The food is brought to a good strong boil and placed in an insulated box or container. The food continues to simmer for several hours due to the excellent heat retention. Insulation can be hay, Styrofoam beads, blankets, towels, or anything that will insulate the pot, with at least four inches on each side as a general rule. You cannot have too much insulation.

The trick is to insulate well against outside temperatures. For example, we have experimented creating hay boxes with rigid packing insulation in a cardboard box with an old bean bag placed on top. We also snuggly pack a pan into an ice chest with old blankets and towels to create a hay box. They both work great. Over time, the insulation will start to smell bad due to the high moisture level. It is preferable to use something washable. See http://theprovidentprepper.org/thermal-cookers-no-power-slow-cookers/ for instructions on creating your own.

This method takes about four times as long to cook but uses much less fuel. Soups, chilis, and stews are ideal candidates for this method. Large roasts are not ideal because even if the liquid is boiling on the outside, the center of the roast is cool. Starting the food in a pressure cooker and then placing it in a hay box combines the best of both tools. Resist the urge to peek. You will lose significant heat if you do. Just trust that it is working. We were skeptical when we first tried the hay box, but when dinnertime arrived, we removed a steaming hot pot from all of the homemade insulation. The meal was fully cooked and too hot to eat. Our record for maintaining appropriate serving temperature is 14 hours.

A word of caution: It is possible to create an environment where bacteria can flourish if this is not done correctly. Food should still be hot (above 140 degrees) when you take it out, not merely warm. If the food has fallen below 140 degrees, heat it back up to boiling to kill any bacteria that may have been breeding. Adding additional insulation should solve this problem in the future.

Heated food is nestled in layers of blankets inside of an ice chest to create an effective insulated cooker.

A **pressure cooker** is an airtight pot that cooks food quickly under steam pressure. This is a must when it comes to conserving energy. Pressure cookers cook food up to ten times faster than standard methods, which translates into significant savings in fuel. They are available in many different sizes and styles, but stainless steel is highly recommended. A pressure cooker can soften up tough older beans in just ten minutes. When fuel is limited, consider bringing the food just up to where the rocker on the top of the cooker starts to rock. Remove it from the heat and insulate it, either in a hay box or covered with a few towels or blankets. Using a pressure cooker will result in considerable fuel conservation.

A **thermal cooker** is a commercial version of a hay box. A thermal cooker, vacuum insulation cooker, or magic cooker has a stainless steel cooking pot and lid for heating food. The pot is placed in a double-wall vacuum-insulated outer container to finish cooking or to hold it at temperature for up to six hours. We wrap ours in a small blanket and tuck it in a box to significantly increase efficiency. Honestly, it doesn't work as well as our homemade hay box, but it is very convenient. An added little bonus is it will keep cold things cold too, like the hay box.

Commercial thermal cookers are convenient.

Vacuum-insulated bottle cooking: Start with a quality, wide-mouthed, stainless steel, vacuum-insulated bottle (such as Thermos or Stanley). It will hold the heat well and is mostly unbreakable. When possible, preheat the bottle by filling with hot water. Dump out the water just before placing the ingredients in the bottle and add the boiling water. Quickly secure the lid and shake for 20 to 30 seconds. Place the bottle on its side and allow it time to work its magic. Foods cooked in liquids—such as rice, pasta, soups, and hot cereals—are good candidates for a vacuum-insulated bottle.

Cooking with Alcohol

Alcohol is a great cooking fuel because it burns clean, lights easily, and stores indefinitely in a tightly sealed container. It does not burn as hot as some fuels. However, it is not explosive like other fuels. Pure forms of alcohol can be safely burned indoors with a little ventilation. Use caution—some forms may be toxic, such as methanol (wood alcohol), which can be harmful if absorbed through the skin or inhaled.

Denatured alcohol is a good alcohol fuel and is available in hardware stores in the paint section. Ethanol or ethyl alcohol (Everclear) is a grain alcohol that can be purchased at a liquor store and is about 95 percent alcohol. Both of these forms burn clean, making them great choices for cooking fuel.

Rubbing alcohol (isopropyl) is a good second choice. It may be purchased in different strengths. The higher the percentage of alcohol, the better it will burn. There are two common strengths of rubbing alcohol readily available, 70 percent and 91 percent strength. The 91 percent strength will burn better due to the higher alcohol content, whereas the 70 percent strength contains 30 percent water. Use it if that is all you have, but plan for a better option. Isopropyl alcohol produces a yellow sooty flame and is safe to burn indoors with proper ventilation.

Alcohol space heater/stove: The Heat Pal 5100 provides a safe, non-pressurized heat source that doubles as a single-burner stove. It holds one quart of alcohol and will burn for up to five hours. It is relatively light (5.1 pounds) and compact yet puts out up to 5200 BTUs. This stove was designed as a marine device but works great as a small indoor heater or stove.

This alcohol stove doubles as a heater.

Alcohol burner/stove: A quick search of the Internet will deliver a variety of plans for homemade alcohol stoves created from recycled cans. These stoves are usually small and are frequently used by Boy Scouts and backpackers. A military alcohol burner can be purchased at a military surplus store. It is almost indestructible and quite convenient to use. It can be filled with alcohol, lit, and placed under a Sterno portable folding stove. The fumes escape from a ring of small holes, which creates a nice even fire. Smother the flames to extinguish. If you blow on them, you just might lose your eyebrows. Do not screw the lid back on until it has completely cooled off. Two ounces of alcohol will burn in a stove for 10–15 minutes depending on the stove and type of alcohol.

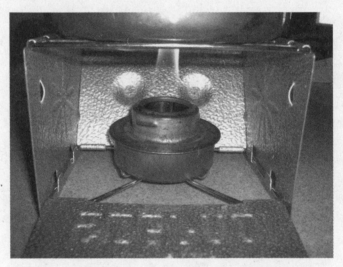

Alcohol burners are durable and refillable. This burner is being used in a Sterno folding camp stove.

Canned heat: A wide variety of canned heat options are available and will burn anywhere from two to six hours. The cans are filled with forms of alcohol or petroleum gel, which are flammable but do not burn quickly. It puts out a visible flame and a good amount of heat. The heat and flame go straight up, with little spread, concentrating the heat in one spot, thus requiring frequent stirring to avoid scorching the food.

Canned heat is safe to burn indoors with adequate ventilation, is lightweight, stores nicely, and is good for heating foods. Canned heat can be used with a Sterno portable folding stove, chafing dish (similar to a double boiler), or fondue pot. The number of cans used will determine the amount of heat output. We can use up to four cans of Safe Heat in an EcoQue portable grill (formerly known as Pyromid).

Four cans of Safe Heat in the base of an EcoQue portable grill creates a hot fire.

A good place to purchase canned heat is by the case in the catering section at warehouse stores. They come in flats of twelve and stack nicely for storage. The shelf life varies depending on the manufacturer and ranges between a few years to indefinite. Store cans between 40 and 120 degrees, upright, away from heat sources, and dispose of damaged or dented cans.

Cooking with Butane

Butane is a convenience fuel. It is a bit expensive, but it performs nicely in many conditions. Butane does not vaporize well at near freezing temperatures and may sputter or misfire. The recommended shelf life for a butane canister is eight years. Store with care since the fuel is highly flammable. Butane releases carbon dioxide when burned. It is heavier than air, so leaked fuel may pool and pose an explosive risk.

Butane stove: Caterers use these stoves because they are lightweight, convenient, and safe to use indoors with adequate ventilation.

Butane stoves should be placed on a stable heat-resistant surface. Most stoves have excellent flame control, and many come with an automatic piezo-electric ignition. These are lighter and more portable than liquid fuel stoves. One eight-ounce butane canister will provide two hours of burn time at maximum output and up to four hours on low. They are easy to use and require no special cookware.

Cooking with Charcoal Briquettes

Charcoal briquettes are one of the least expensive fuels (per BTU) you can buy. They store safely but must *never* be burned indoors!. Charcoal consumes a tremendous amount of oxygen and produces a vast amount of carbon monoxide, a deadly poison. A charcoal chimney (available at most sporting goods stores) provides an excellent way to start the charcoal. Remember to store matches and newspapers or lighter fluid to start the charcoal. Canned heat may be utilized under the charcoal chimney to start the charcoal.

Charcoal chimneys make lighting briquettes much easier.

Start by purchasing good-quality charcoal. For fuel storage, do not store ready-to-light varieties—the lighter fluid will evaporate over time and will not be of any benefit. Charcoal will store for an extended period of time if it is stored in airtight containers. Moisture-absorbing desiccant may also be helpful in keeping it dry. When stored in the original paper bag, charcoal can absorb moisture, rendering it minimally effective or useless over time. An inexpensive way to store charcoal briquettes is to use powdered laundry soap buckets and caulk the lid shut to ensure it is airtight. If charcoal has absorbed moisture, it can be easily restored by laying it out in the hot sun for a day to remove the moisture. Place it immediately in an airtight container to keep it from doing what it does best, absorbing moisture. It will store indefinitely in an airtight metal or plastic container.

Paper box oven: Similar to the apple box oven (see below), this small homemade oven is just big enough to bake a 9 × 13 pan. It is made using a box that contained reams of letter size paper. It is simple and inexpensive to make. It uses less charcoal than the apple box oven to achieve the same results and is easier to bake in. Coals must be placed on an inverted cookie sheet or pie tin on the bottom of the box. If coals are placed directly on the bottom of the box, it will burn. Remember to put fresh coals in before starting to cook any additional foods. (See www.theprovidentprepper. org/paper-box-reflector-oven for detailed instructions.)

A paper box oven uses less charcoal than an apple box oven. It fits a 9 x 13 pan or small cookie sheet.

Apple Box Oven: Inexpensive but efficient, this oven is constructed using an apple box (free for the asking at most supermarkets), heavy-duty aluminum foil, spray adhesive (optional), a cooling rack, and a blanket for insulation in cold weather. It bakes using only 10–14 charcoal briquettes. Use one coal for each 35 degrees desired. For example, ten coals will heat the oven to 350 degrees. More coals are required in cold weather. Place started coals on the foil surface, position food on the rack, and place the oven on top. The oven can maintain temperature for 45–55 minutes. *Never* use this indoors. An oven bag can be utilized to create a window in the oven; however, the window lacks clear visualization, tends to tear, and creates some heat loss. Using two boxes inside each other will create a sturdier oven. Covering the box with a blanket or towels will insulate it and increase its efficiency. See http://theprovidentprepper.org/apple-box-reflector-oven/ for detailed instructions.

*This oven is made from an apple box and will bake
foods using charcoal briquettes. For outdoor use only!*

Dutch Oven: Many amazing meals are created with this classic cooking method. It is a great way to prepare meals, breads, and desserts. With a little experience, anyone can become an expert. Dutch ovens are easy to use and store, and they will last for many years when cared for properly. To make Dutch oven cooking even more energy efficient, you may want to try a Volcano Grill.

Dutch ovens are the perfect way to create a tasty feast when the power goes out.

Volcano Grill: This great device can be used with charcoal, wood, or propane. It will use one-third of the typical amount of charcoal to create the same delicious Dutch oven meals. The airflow is regulated and the heat flow is channeled to the sides of the pot, enabling it to use less fuel. It can also be used as a portable fire pit.

Cooking with Kerosene

Kerosene is a fairly safe and efficient fuel. It stinks and smokes when igniting and extinguishing, but burns nicely. It should be used outdoors whenever possible because it produces carbon monoxide, nitrogen dioxide, and sulfur dioxide when burned. We do not recommend indoor use. If using indoors, ensure proper cross ventilation by opening a window on each side of the room at least one inch. Kerosene has a five-year shelf life. There are generally two types of kerosene stoves: wick and pressure. There are many variations available.

Kerosene Pressure Stove: This stove burns kerosene vapor. The fuel must be preheated with a couple of tablespoons of denatured alcohol. The burning alcohol heats the brass burner and you use a manual pump to create pressure. The kerosene rises inside the burner and is vaporized. Once the stove starts, the heat from the flame creates enough heat that pumping is no longer necessary. It is a little trickier to use than the wick stove, but it is lighter and can be broken down into smaller pieces, so it is much more portable. Like all of these tools, deciding which to use is a matter of personal preference.

Kerosene Wick Stove: One popular version of the kerosene wick stove is the one-burner "Sockwick," which will burn for 13 hours on one gallon of kerosene. It produces a nice hot flame of 9000 BTUs per hour. The advantage to the kerosene wick stove is that it is easy to light and extinguish. It keeps burning until you run out of fuel.

Cooking with Miscellaneous Fuels

Miscellaneous fuels serve a variety of purposes. Some of these are great ideas for a portable evacuation bag but poor choices for daily cooking due to cost or other limitations.

Fuel tablets are used in tiny folding stoves.

Gel Fuel: PyroPac gel fuel is a safe and easy heat source. It is used by squeezing the gel onto a fire-safe surface or in a fuel tablet stove and lighting it with a match. One packet can provide 15 minutes of burn time. It is portable and has an indefinite shelf life.

Gel fuel lights quickly and burns hot.

InstaFire: InstaFire is a blend of wood pellets, wax, and volcanic rock. It can be used as a fire starter or a stand-alone fire. One cup provides up to 30 minutes of burn time. It comes in a plastic bucket and has a shelf life of 30 years when stored in a cool, dry place. A quick homemade stove can be constructed with a few bricks, a #10 can, or a Sterno portable folding stove.

MRE Heaters: These are designed to heat MRE meals quickly and safely without fire. You can also heat up other watertight food containers (but nothing plastic) that are small enough to fit in the bag. Alternatively, you can place a heater in a small ice chest with sealed food to be warmed. MRE Heaters are made from powdered food-grade iron, magnesium, and sodium. When water is added to the heater, a chemical reaction produces heat almost instantly. It only takes a few minutes for an MRE to heat up. One drawback is that they have a shelf life of only about five years. We found that older ones did heat up, but they took longer. Activated heaters release hydrogen vapor, a flammable gas. Do not use near an open flame.

Solid Fuel Tablets (Esbit): These half-ounce tablets are designed to work in a pocket stove. One cube will generate up to 1400 degrees of intense heat for 12–15 minutes and will bring one pint of water to a rolling boil in less than eight minutes. They are non-explosive, portable, smokeless, and easy to light. Fuel tablets must be used outdoors, and they are not appropriate for cooking large amounts of food. They are, however, great for lighting fires or charcoal briquettes. Fuel tablets have an indefinite shelf life if stored in a dry place.

Trioxanne Fuel Bars: These bars are compressed, solid fuel made for military and survival use as a heat source or for cooking food and boiling water. They are non-explosive and do not create smoke, sparks, or residue. One bar will burn for seven to nine minutes at over 14,000 BTUs. They light easily and can be broken in pieces so that you use only what you need. Trioxanne fuel bars must only be used outdoors and make great fire starters. They have an indefinite shelf life.

Cooking with Propane

Propane comes in pressurized cylinders and is highly flammable. It burns very hot. Propane is heavier than air and may pool in a low area, such as a basement, creating an explosive risk. It is a great storage fuel with an indefinite shelf life. The tanks need to be closely watched for signs of rust, dents, or anything that may result in leakage. Use in a well-ventilated area and store carefully away from the home.

Camp Chef: A favorite propane cooking tool, it is available in a stove/oven combination or as a stand-alone stove. It is portable enough to take camping and sturdy enough to process jars during home canning. We process our jars in the garage on the Camp Chef, which keeps the heat and mess out of the house. One 20-pound propane tank may provide up to 15 hours of cooking time. This would be perfect when cooking for a family or large numbers of people.

Propane Barbecue: A weekend backyard barbecue can come in handy during an emergency if propane bottles are full. Many have a side burner, which can make a nice stove top in addition to the ability to grill or bake.

Propane Stove: These are great for camping and outdoor cooking. They are similar to the Coleman stoves, which use white gas. They are lightweight and portable. Ovens are available to put on top of the stove for baking.

Cooking with Solar Energy

Sunlight is a great fuel source. It's free, abundant, and relatively safe. Optimal solar cooking hours are between 10 a.m. and 4 p.m. Solar cooking is possible throughout the year in many parts of the world. For example, we used our sun oven to bake bread on a ten-degree, clear winter day. There are many ways to harness the sun and cook your food with solar energy. The basic idea is to collect the light on a reflective surface, absorb the heat with dark colors, and retain the heat in enclosed containers, oven bags, and so forth.

Parabolic Cooker: This amazing but bulky cooker uses highly focused light intensified by large solar collectors to achieve high cooking temperatures. The shape of the reflectors resembles an open umbrella. These cookers are a little complicated and can be potentially dangerous. Beware of stray reflected solar rays; they can be hard on your eyes and a possible fire hazard.

Parabolic cookers use highly focused light to achieve high cooking temperatures.

Solar Funnel Cooker: Inexpensive to make and easy to use, this unique design is adapted from Dr. Steven Jones's solar funnel cooker. It works well for pasteurizing water and making simple meals. The lid on the black canning jar acts like a pressure cooker, decreasing the amount of cooking time required. With a little practice, this is a great cooking device. Foods may require a little longer cooking time. (See http://theprovidentprepper.org/solar-funnel-cooker/ for detailed instructions.)

Inexpensive solar funnel cooker.

Solar Inner Tube Cooker: This cooker is not as efficient as other versions, but it can be made quickly out of readily available materials. Begin with a stable bottom surface that is either reflective or covered with aluminum foil. Place an inflated black inner tube on the surface and place your cooking vessel in the center. A dark-colored pot works best. Cover with a sheet of glass or other transparent material.

Solar Oven (Box Cooker): You can find plans for homemade solar ovens on the Internet, but there are commercial brands available. A solar oven uses the power of the sun to cook. It even works reasonably well on partly cloudy days. The Global Sun Oven is a good option. It reaches temperatures up to 400 degrees Fahrenheit but can consistently reach 325–350 degrees. It is easy to use, safe, portable, and fun. Some directional adjustments are required during the cooking process to take best advantage of the sun. A solar box cooker is great for everyday use, not just in an emergency.

Brownies baking in a Global Sun Oven.

Cooking with White Gas

White gas (used in Coleman Fuel) is an explosive fuel that produces deadly carbon monoxide. It should never be used indoors. However, it burns hot even at subzero temperatures. Coleman fuel stored in an unopened container—in a dry place with a stable temperature—has a shelf life of five to seven years. A previously opened container in the same area should be used within one to two years. Use caution when storing this fuel.

Coleman Stove: This camping favorite burns white gas, which is relatively inexpensive and widely available. The stove is portable and produces a nice, hot fire. Coleman also makes a "dual fuel" design that will also burn unleaded gasoline. This is a great option—it may be easier to obtain unleaded gasoline than Coleman fuel during an emergency. One quart will burn for about two hours with both burners on high.

Cooking with Wood or Debris

Wood (or debris) is a great option for both everyday and emergency cooking. It is one of the least expensive and safest fuels to store. Disasters often produce debris, which can be collected and burned. Use caution and be sure that any debris you choose to burn is free from substances that might release toxins into the air, such as paint or plastics.

Biomass or Rocket Stoves: These stoves will burn wood, charcoal, or any flammable biomass material for fuel. The fuel is fed into the stove through a small door at the base. The cooking pot sits on top. The chimney effect creates a nice, hot fire using minimal fuel. The only drawback is that it requires fairly continuous tending to keep fuel fed into the stove. Plans for homemade versions are available on the Internet.

*Biomass stoves create a nice hot
fire using minimal fuel.*

Debris or Zip Stoves: These little stoves come in various styles and generally employ either a fan or a chimney system to improve combustion and heat production. They utilize small scraps of debris, lumber, nutshells, twigs, bark, pine cones, charcoal, and so on. Zip stoves are great for cooking for one or two people and may be a good option for an evacuation bag.

Portable Grill: A portable grill with legs can be placed over a fire and serve as a good cooking area. Food may be cooked directly on the grill or in pots and pans over the flame or hot coals. These grills are inexpensive ($10–15) and are valuable, versatile tools.

Wood Burning Stove: Whenever possible, using a wood burning stove is highly recommended. A quality stove can be quite expensive, but it comes with a big payoff. Choose wisely and select one designed to cook as well as heat your home. While the heat from the stove can be comforting in cold weather, it is miserable in warm weather. Be sure to plan for alternate methods of cooking during the summer. Cooking on a wood stove takes a little longer because the fire must be started and managed. Cast-iron cookware works best, but heavy steel will do also. It is easy to scorch foods if you use thinner metals. Make sure you have adequate seasoned wood and clean your chimney annually.

This is simply a sampling of the options available. You only need to have a few to be ready to cook when the lights go out. Safety should always be your first priority. Make sure all appropriate safety precautions are clearly understood and applied. Always have working fire, smoke, and carbon monoxide alarms, and use caution with open flames. Never inappropriately use any device or fuel that produces carbon monoxide. It would be a great tragedy to survive an initial catastrophe only to risk carbon monoxide poisoning.

We are ordinary people making preparedness a priority. We love to experiment and have learned a tremendous amount. The burnt meals and failed ideas have sparked a greater desire in us to succeed. The successes have been sweet and immensely satisfying, and the failures have been great learning experiences. Now it's your turn. Use your creativity and get excited about the learning process. Incorporate alternative cooking methods into your daily life now, while food is cheap and Wendy's is still open.

CREATING YOUR PLAN OF ACTION

Our plan to provide one year of cooking and heating fuel is on the chart below. We have chosen not to calculate the actual number of required cooking hours because the wood burning stove we use to cook from October through May will also heat our home. The solar ovens provide us with an unlimited number of cooking hours whenever the UV index is seven or greater. Conservation methods are regularly employed in our cooking strategies. We have planned alternatives to ensure that we will be able to cook in a wide variety of situations. Depending on the type of foods you have stored, two to three hours of fuel a day may be a reasonable place to start if you use your fuel wisely. Your plan should be unique to your circumstances.

Jones Family One-Year Cooking and Heating Fuel Storage Plan

Fuel	Size	# Needed	# Hours	Cost
Alcohol	Quart	8	40	$25
Canned Heat	6-hr can	36	216	$40
Charcoal	15 lbs	10	180	$150
Propane	20 lbs	5	75	$55
Wood	Cord	4	Oct-May	$400 or less
Solar	Oven	2	Unlimited	FREE
				$670

COOKING FUEL PLANNING GUIDE

We created a Sample Fuel Planning Guide to help you understand how much fuel you might use to cook basic storage items. This will useful in calculating fuel requirements. The section on dry beans is included from the chart below. You can find the complete table at http://theprovidentprepper.org/the-practical-prepper/action-plan-emergency-cooking/ along with a worksheet to assist you in developing your action plan.

Due to a wide range of variables, it is not possible to calculate exact fuel requirements. We offer this chart as a starting point. As you practice, you will be able to get a much better feel for what your specific requirements will be. Exact fuel requirements vary with weather, temperature, altitude, and food products. For instance, a loaf of homemade bread may take 30 minutes to bake one day and 40 minutes another day in the same oven. Experiment and discover what your usage will be.

Cooking Fuel Planning Guide

Food Item	Possible Cooking Device Options
Dry Beans Older beans can take much longer to cook. Sometimes they won't soften up unless cooked in a pressure cooker. Transferring boiling beans to a hay box or wonder box will significantly decrease your fuel consumption. Cooking larger batches will not take significantly more fuel.	**Butane Stoves** require 1–2 canisters (1–2 hours burn time on one 8-ounce canister). **Camp Chef propane stoves** require 1.5–2 pounds of propane (15 hours in a 20-pound tank). **Coleman Stoves** require 1 pint (2 hours with both burners on high will burn 2 pints). **Dutch Ovens** using charcoal briquettes require 46–60 briquettes (15 coals on top and 8 on bottom for 350 degrees, replacing coals a couple of times). **Dutch Ovens in Volcano Grills** require 12–15 briquettes (12 coals for 350° will last up to 3 hours). **Heat Pal 5100** using denatured alcohol burns 1–2 cups of alcohol (1 quart lasts for 5 hours). **Kerosene Sock Wick Stoves** burn 1–2 cups of kerosene (one gallon burns for 13 hours). **Wood Stoves** require 1–2 hours of cook time (approximately 4–6 logs). ****Make the Most of Your Resources**** **Pressure Cookers** reduce cook time, resulting in fuel savings. Total cook time will be less than 20 minutes. Once it comes up to pressure (13–15 minutes), cook time is only 1–3 minutes. Release pressure naturally. **Global Sun Oven** cook times will vary depending on UV index. Plan on 2–4 hours of cook time in lower temperatures.

Be sure to calculate fuel requirements for all of the items on your menu. If the menu includes beans, rice, and corn bread, each item will consume fuel. One-pot meals such as stew will require less fuel overall. Develop your action plan by taking into consideration the unique circumstances of your location, resources, and needs.

Take time to write your plan down on the worksheet provided at http://theprovidentprepper.org/the-practical-prepper/action-plan-emergency-cooking/. Adjust the plan as your needs change. Practice the cooking methods that appeal to you. One cooking concept may sound perfect but not quite work out like you had thought it would. We learned that it was much easier to use the solar oven on sunny days than to start charcoal and use an apple box oven. Whatever you choose, start safely accumulating the required cooking devices and fuels now. Try to make one meal a week using an alternative cooking source. Most importantly, make steady progress and enjoy the journey.

‖ 16 ‖

Shelter
Come In out of the Storm

"The time to repair the roof is when the sun is shining."

—John F. Kennedy

According to the rule of threes, you can survive only three hours without shelter in a harsh environment. Maintaining body temperature is critical. You must find a way to stay out of the sun, wind, rain, snow, and cold. Ideally, our homes provide a comfortable, climate-controlled atmosphere. In this chapter, we will discuss shelter options during emergency situations.

DISASTER-RELATED HOME REPAIRS

You may be able to stay in your damaged home as long as it's structurally sound. After any disaster, supplies are in high demand and short supply. If you have the ability to store a few tools and supplies in your garage or shed, you can quickly make temporary repairs to keep the elements and looters out until permanent repairs can be made.

Cordless power tools such as a drills and saws will speed up repairs. Ladders, crowbars, handsaws, chainsaws, hammers, staple guns, axes, shovels, razor knives, pliers, and screw drivers are everyday tools that may be quite helpful. Supplies to consider stocking might include sheets of plywood, nails, screws, staples, heavy plastic, tarps, duct tape, rope, bungee cords, and so on. Think about your home and the supplies you might need to cover broken windows or patch holes in the roof or walls. These supplies may enable you to safely stay in your home.

SHELTERING-IN-PLACE

We often refer to emergency sheltering inside of your home or workplace, as *sheltering-in-place*. In the event of a chemical or biological hazard or hazmat spill, it may be too dangerous to attempt to evacuate. The safest option might be to stay where you are and prevent the toxins from harming you.

Chemical and biological substances usually hover close to ground level. An ideal room to shelter-in-place would:

- Have access to a bathroom and running water

- Have limited ways for air to enter, such as windows, doors, and air vents

- Have access to a telephone

- Be an upper-level, inner room

Carbon dioxide can build up in a sealed air-tight room. A basic guideline is to allow for ten square feet of floor space per person per five hours. Under normal atmospheric conditions, chemical threats should dissipate within a few hours, though it is possible for a continuous leak or an industrial fire to extend the danger.

All entry points must be sealed to prevent contaminants from entering. These events usually occur with very little warning. It is best to have plastic sheeting precut and labeled to expedite the process and prevent exposure. Before preparing the room, turn off central air, close the fireplace damper, and close and lock all doors, windows, shutters, curtains, and blinds. Gather family members, pets, and last-minute supplies (cell phone, entertainment, snacks, prescription medication, emergency kit) into the designated room before sealing it up.

Seal all cracks around window and door frames with wide duct or painter's tape. (Painter's tape does less damage to surfaces.) Seal anything air might enter through, including keyholes, vents, fans, and exterior-wall electrical outlets. Cover windows and exterior doors with plastic sheeting and seal with tape. Soak a cloth or towel and use it to seal the gaps underneath doors. If you get caught without supplies, use whatever you can—heavy-duty garbage bags, masking tape, and anything else that can create a barrier against chemicals.

If your risk factor is high for this hazard, you may want to create a special kit for sheltering-in-place and keep it in a closet or under a bed in the designated room. Each situation is unique. You may still have public utilities, but there is always a possibility those services will be disrupted. Have a backup plan in the event you are without power. Items in your kit might include:

- Precut 4–6 mil plastic sheeting for each window, door, air vent, or fan.

- A large roll or two of duct tape or wide painter's tape.

- Scissors or a knife to cut the sheeting and tape

- Towel or cloth to wet and roll up under the door

- Emergency equipment—first aid kit, fire extinguisher, and so on

- Communication equipment—amateur radios, FRS radios, battery-operated radio, extra batteries

- Sanitation kit

- Water and food; can opener

- Light source

- Entertainment

- Blankets

- Plastic bags, containers, and cleaning supplies (if required for waste)

Listen for instructions from local authorities. When the event is over, open windows and doors and turn on your ventilation system. If it is safe to do so, go outside until all the air inside the building has been exchanged with clean air from outside.

SELF-IMPOSED ISOLATION

There may come a time when you need to hunker down in your home and prevent contact with others. This quarantine may be due to a pandemic—to prevent exposure to germs—or civil unrest, where venturing out of your home could be dangerous. This is a self-imposed isolation to ensure the health and safety of your family. The length of the quarantine will vary depending on the nature of the hazard.

With pandemics and other outbreaks, it's difficult to determine the exact amount of time you may need to isolate yourself. Viruses cannot survive without a host. If it were possible for everyone to isolate themselves, the duration of a pandemic would be relatively short. Currently, they tend to expand in waves before finally resolving in a year or two. In a pandemic, the entire household must isolate itself from society. If one person goes to work or to the store, that person risks bringing home the germs to everyone.

Periods of civil unrest could last days, months, or even years. The danger may be localized or widespread. In either of these scenarios, it is possible that public utility, transportation, medical, and emergency services may be interrupted. You may need to consider relocating depending on where you live and how dependent you are on public utilities.

Gathering the supplies and financial resources to last a year is a realistic goal. Consider the following ideas to prepare for a time when going out in public could be dangerous:

- Store food, toiletries, and supplies. Develop the ability to produce at least some food to supplement your food stores.

- Store water and have a way to transport and purify it.

- Store enough fuel to stay warm, light your home, and cook your meals in the event power is disrupted. Consider sustainable options such as solar and wind.

- Learn basic medical care and first-aid skills. Stock important medication and first-aid supplies.

- Purchase communication equipment and learn to use it well. Provide backup power for communication devices.

- Cabin fever can make you crazy enough to venture out and regret it. Plan ways to stay entertained. Accumulate a good selection of books and games.

SHELTERING AGAINST RADIATION EXPOSURE

A nuclear event can produce radioactive fallout. Protecting yourself from dangerous levels of radiation requires special shielding. If a nuclear power reactor fails and you have adequate notice, it may be best to relocate out of the affected area until the situation is resolved. In the event of a nuclear attack, the radiation could cover much of the country. Radiation is deadly and cannot be detected by any of our physical senses—special tools such as a radiation survey meters (Geiger counters) are required to detect and measure radiation levels.

Radiation poisoning is the result of exposure to a large dose of radiation over a short period of time. It is a serious and often fatal condition. The amount of radiation absorbed determines how sick a person will become.

Protecting against radiation is very different from protecting against chemical or biological threats. *Fallout* includes dust, dirt, or other particles that have been contaminated with radiation. Fallout can be carried hundreds of miles downwind from ground zero. As it travels, it becomes less and less dangerous. Protecting against radioactive fallout requires placing barriers between you and the particles until the radiation has decayed to a safe level.

The basic elements of radiation protection involve time, distance, and shielding.[1]

- **Time:** Fallout radiation decays and loses intensity rapidly. Minimize exposure time. It's most critical to avoid exposure during the first few hours and days after an event.

- **Distance:** The further you are from the fallout particles, the less radiation you will be exposed to.

- **Shielding:** Put material between yourself and the source of the radiation. The greater the amount of shielding, the less your exposure. Heavy, dense materials like concrete provide the best protection.

Our favorite resource for information on nuclear survival is *Nuclear War Survival Skills* by Cresson H. Kearny. Other valuable, free online information can be obtained at:

- **TACDA Academy:**
  http://www.tacda.org/index.php/tacda-academy/

- **Good News about Nuclear Destruction:**
  http://www.alertsusa.com/reports/goodnews.pdf

- **When Ill Winds Blow from Afar:**
  http://www.alertsusa.com/reports/illwind.pdf

- **What to Do if Nuclear Disaster Is Imminent:**
  http://www.alertsusa.com/reports/whattodo.pdf

It is a good idea to print a hard copy of any information you find useful and keep it in your reference library so you have it in the event of an emergency.

An underground shelter is ideal for protecting you from many hazards, including radiation. If you have the resources to construct one, do so. If not, it would be wise to understand how to construct a temporary shelter to provide protection from radiation in an emergency. The first few hours and days are the most critical, but it may take weeks before it is completely safe to venture out.

Study the sources above to determine the best places in your home, school, and workplace to minimize radiation exposure. Prevent radioactive particles from entering your home by turning off ventilation systems and closing windows, doors, and vents. Seal up any areas that may allow contaminated dust particles into your home. You will likely have to shelter for a few weeks, so unlike when you're sheltering from biological and chemical agents, this should not be an airtight seal.

The more mass you place between you and the fallout, the less exposure you will receive. There is no way to predict the amount of radiation you may need to protect against. A very high level of protection calls for five inches of steel, sixteen inches of solid brick or filled concrete blocks, and three feet of water or loose dirt or two feet of packed dirt. Do the best you can with the resources you have available.

An emergency radiation shelter can be constructed using available materials and a sturdy table. If you do not have a table, remove a door from its hinges and place it on top of sturdy supports such as dressers. Stack bricks, wood, water, food storage, books, magazines, and other thick objects on top of the table and around all of its sides. Do not put more weight on the table than it can safely support. The best protection is in the middle of all that mass. It might be difficult to stay in such a small space, especially when the threat is invisible. Take your emergency kit, communications equipment, bedding, and entertainment with you into your little cocoon until you are absolutely certain that the danger has passed.

PORTABLE SHELTER

What about shelter in the event you have to leave your home? Hotels can be an awesome choice if and when they are available. Recreational vehicles or trailers can be kept stocked and ready to leave at a moment's notice. Store enough fuel to make it to your intended destination without stopping for gas. This will keep you out of long lines and away from desperate individuals.

A sturdy tent provides a lot of options. Consider how many people you want to shelter. A four-person tent will realistically hold only two or three adults and a little gear. Buy quality. A cheap tent will provide a false sense of security and leave you without shelter when you need it most. Purchase a repair kit and the necessary tools to keep your tent in good repair. These are a few of the basic options available:

- **Wall tents** are made with heavy canvas and strong poles. They are designed to be a comfortable, longer-term living space. Vented stoves can be used for heating and cooking inside of a wall tent.

- **Teepees** might be a good option. When made out of heavy canvas and sturdy lodge poles, they provide great long-term living space for a family. They are easily set up and taken down. The design creates a chimney effect, which allows the smoke from a small fire in the center to escape out the top.

- **Family or dome tents** are designed to be lightweight and sleep more people. They often have fabric room dividers for increased privacy.

- **Backpacking and expedition tents** are light and highly portable. They may be a good option for an emergency kit.

- **Shelters of expedience** may be created using a tarp, plastic sheeting, and rope.

There are many reasons why storing a tent is a wise idea. Portable shelters can protect you from winter cold as well as summer heat. They can provide shelter in your backyard if your home is destroyed. You can even set up a tent in the middle of your family room during a power outage to create a warm microenvironment.

BUG OUT LOCATIONS

We discussed bug out locations in chapter 4. A bug out location is a place that has been prepared as a home away from home in the event of evacuation or disaster. It should be well stocked and far enough away that the same hazard would not affect it. Some hazards may not provide enough warning to safely travel to your bug out location. If you leave too late, you might get caught out in the hurricane you were trying to escape. Once a nuclear event occurs, travel may expose you to dangerous levels of radiation. Always have a contingency plan.

SHELTER ACTION PLAN

The rule of threes establishes shelter as a top priority. In reality, you may not have the luxury of three hours to find safe shelter. A nuclear or chemical event may provide only a few minutes of advanced warning. Fatal exposure can occur in minutes. What is your plan for sheltering? Take time to brainstorm the possibilities and develop your plan using the worksheet provided at http://theprovidentprepper.org/the-practical-prepper/action-plan-shelter/.

17

Keeping Cool
I'm Melting!

"If you can't stand the heat, get out of the kitchen."

—Harry S. Truman

Cities such as Phoenix, Arizona, rely heavily on air conditioning to keep the population cool and comfortable. A widespread power outage on an average summer day could be devastating. Even more dangerous are record temperatures in normally temperate climates where people are not used to severe heat and do not have the knowledge, skills, and tools to stay cool. According to the Centers for Disease Control, more people in the United States died from extreme heat between 1979 and 2003 than died from hurricanes, lightning, tornadoes, floods, and earthquakes combined.[1]

Those of us who live in urban areas are at greater risk of extreme heat than those who live in rural areas. Higher temperatures in cities can be attributed, in part, to greater vehicle and building heat exhaust, fewer trees, and more dark, paved areas. The heat absorbed by rooftops and the fact that heat rises contribute to increased temperatures for those living on upper floors of buildings. The young, elderly, obese, and disabled are the most vulnerable to extreme heat. In this chapter, we will discuss a few recommendations for staying cool when things get dangerously hot.

UNDERSTANDING CONDITIONS

A heat wave is a prolonged period of dangerous heat, often combined with high levels of humidity. The heat index combines both the air temperature with relative humidity to indicate how hot it feels, similar to calculating the wind chill factor. A heat index of 90 degrees or greater dramatically increases the risk of heat-related illnesses. A heat wave combined with drought conditions can be extremely dangerous. Poor air quality frequently accompanies a heat wave, contributing to respiratory problems.

Guidelines for declaring a heat emergency are specific to your location. A heat emergency may be declared when the heat index climbs to 105° with nighttime temperatures at 80° or above for several days. Go to http://www.weather.gov/ for current conditions and forecasts in your area.

HEAT-RELATED ILLNESS

Heat can be just as deadly as freezing temperatures. Learn the signs of heat-related illnesses and understand how to act quickly.

Heat Cramps: Muscle aches and spasms from heavy exertion in extreme heat. Sweating depletes the body's salt and fluid levels. Low salt levels in muscles can cause painful cramps. They are often a first sign of other heat-related complications. Treat by drinking clear juice or sports beverages and resting in a cool place.

Hyperthermia: The ideal body temperature is 98.6 degrees Fahrenheit, or 37 degrees Celsius. Hyperthermia occurs when the body absorbs or produces more heat than it emits. Prolonged exposure to heat can be deadly. Any body temperature above 104 degrees can be life threatening; the brain begins to die at 106 degrees. Hyperthermia is a contributing factor in heat exhaustion and heat stroke. Symptoms of hyperthermia include rapid pulse, elevated body temperature, thirst, dilated pupils, dizziness, nausea, vomiting, headaches, confusion, seizures, coma, and hot, dry skin.

Heat Exhaustion: Mild shock that results from inadequate body fluids due to extreme heat and extreme exertion. Blood flow to the skin increases, which decreases the blood flow to vital organs. Body temperature rises, which increases the risk of a heatstroke. There are two types of heat exhaustion: salt depletion and water depletion.[2] Symptoms may include pale, cool, or moist skin; profuse sweating; muscle cramps or pain; fainting or dizzy; headache; weakness; thirst or nausea; core temperature of over 100 degrees Fahrenheit; dark-colored urine; and rapid heartbeat.

Allow the victim to rest in a cool area, away from heat sources. Drink plenty of fluids (avoid caffeinated beverages and alcohol). Remove tight or restrictive clothing. Have the victim take a cool bath or shower, or sponge down with a cool cloth. Contact a doctor if the victim does not improve within 30 minutes. Avoid heat and heavy exercise for at least two days.

Heatstroke is a life-threatening condition that occurs when the body fails to regulate its own temperature. Symptoms may include unconsciousness, temperature over 104 degrees Fahrenheit, seizure, difficulty breathing, confusion, severe restlessness, anxiety, fast heart rate, heavy sweating or absence of sweat, vomiting, diarrhea, and red, hot, or dry skin.

This is a medical emergency and requires immediate medical care. Get the victim out of the sun and into a cooler location. Expose as much skin to the air as possible. Cool by spraying with cool water or sponging with a cool, damp cloth. A fan can help with cooling. Give fluids if the victim is awake and alert and in an upright position. Apply ice packs to the neck, armpits, and groin. Do not place in an ice bath. Fever-reducing medications, such as aspirin or acetaminophen, should not be given.[3] They are not effective in treating heatstroke.

Heat Rash: This is a skin irritation that looks like a cluster of small blisters or pimples. It is usually caused by heavy sweating in hot, humid weather. The most commonly affected areas are the neck, upper chest, groin, and the areas under the breasts and inside elbow creases. Treat by keeping the area dry and providing a cooler, drier environment.

Sunburn: People flock to water sources on hot days to cool off. This exposure to the sun increases the risk of sunburn. Second-degree sunburns can burn the deep layers of skin and damage nerve endings. Avoid sunburns by using sunscreen or keeping skin covered with lightweight clothing and a wide-brimmed hat. Protect lips by wearing lip balm with sunblock.

Treat mild sunburns by taking cool showers or baths and by applying cool cloths to the affected areas. Applying lotions with aloe vera or topical steroids may reduce pain and swelling. Increase fluid intake and rest in a cool room. Severe sunburns may require medical attention.

TIPS FOR KEEPING BODY TEMPERATURE COOL

Keeping cool is not just an issue of comfort—it can truly make the difference between life and death. Heat-related illnesses are highly preventable. We have collected some ideas to help you stay cool when faced with times of extreme heat:

- Drink plenty of cool water, even if you do not feel thirsty. Avoid caffeine and alcohol. Caffeine is a mild diuretic. Alcohol blocks the release of the antidiuretic hormone, which results in increased urination. Your body eliminates more water than it gains when you drink alcohol.

- Fill a spray bottle with cool water to spray on your skin. Remember to spray your face and wrists. Mist your sheets with water before going to bed. These benefits increase when you use a fan.

- Take a cool or slightly warm bath to lower your body temperature.

- Stay indoors in a cool place during the hottest parts of the day. The lowest level of a building tends to be the coolest. Basements are ideal.

- The best foods for hot weather are salads, sandwiches, fruits, vegetables, and cool but not ice-cold beverages. Foods rich in potassium have a natural cooling effect on the body because potassium regulates water and mineral balance throughout the body.[4]

- Slow down, take frequent breaks, and avoid strenuous activities. Exercise increases your core body temperature. Do not work up a sweat.

- Avoid direct sun. Work outside or exercise before the sun comes up in the morning or at night.

Fans

Battery- or solar-powered fans are helpful in moving air when the power is out. Fans can be used near a window to exhaust hot air to the outside and bring cooler air inside. They are most effective if you can have a window open on each end of the home to create a cross breeze. Keep windows closed during the heat of the day. When the outside temperature drops below the inside temperature, use fans in the windows to draw cooler air inside. Early morning is usually the ideal time to do this. Directing a fan toward a wet hanging towel can act as a crude evaporative cooler.

Small battery-powered fans can move the air around in your personal space and make you feel cooler even when the power is out. Fans will not prevent heat-related illness when temperatures are in the 90s or above. Do not blow extremely hot air on yourself; it can increase the risk of heat exhaustion. Use fans to provide circulation.

CLOTHING

Wear cool, lightweight clothing around the house. Outside clothing should be loose, lightweight, and breathable. Cotton or linen will work well. Cover as much skin as possible with long-sleeve shirts and pants. This will protect the skin from the sun and act as an insulator from the heat while wicking sweat away from the body. The right clothes will keep you much cooler.

Wear sunglasses to protect your eyes. Wet sweat bands on your head and wrists can help reduce body temperature. Commercial cooling collars or towels also work well. Cooling scarfs soaked in water and then wrapped around your neck, forehead, or wrist can keep you cool for several hours as the water evaporates. A variety of specially designed cooling hats, vests, and bandanas are available online. Wear a breathable hat with a flap or neck cover. A wide-brimmed hat will also offer good protection from the sun.

PREPARE YOUR HOME

The temperature inside your home can be substantially reduced by following just a few simple guidelines. Start by making your home as energy efficient as possible. Visit http://www.dsireusa.org/ to find rebates and other incentives to help soften the financial blow.

- Outdoor temperatures are coolest during the early morning. Open windows during the night or in the coolest part of the morning to let cool air in. Placing a box fan in the window to suck cool air in can help exchange the air faster. Create cross ventilation by having windows open at both ends of the home. Close windows as soon as the outside temperatures start to rise above the temperature inside the home.

- Windows are a weak point. Keep blinds and curtains closed to increase insulation. Hang blankets or sheets over the windows if necessary.

- Check your home for hot-air entry points. Apply weather stripping or insulation to prevent hot air from entering.

- West-facing windows heat up the home. Install thermal curtains or blinds in west-facing windows or place aluminum foil over those windows to reduce heat gain.

- Strategically landscape your home to prevent solar heat from being absorbed through the windows and roof. Temperatures directly under trees can be as much as 25 degrees cooler than air near black-top. Take special care to protect the west side of the home from direct sun with shade trees and bushes.

- Research passive solar home design. Small changes can translate into a higher level of comfort without using electrical devices.

- A whole-house fan can inexpensively exchange the air inside the home with cooler air. It moves the hot air inside the house out through the attic, reducing the entire home's temperature. These fans are installed in the ceiling. Our whole-house fan draws only 36 watts, which could easily be provided by a small solar backup system. It exchanges the air in the home at a rate of 1265 cubic square feet per minute.

- Consider using a small alternative energy system, such as solar or wind, to produce enough energy to power your fans.

SPECIAL NEEDS

Some individuals are especially vulnerable to extreme heat. It may be wise to evacuate the young, elderly, or infirm during an extreme heat wave, especially if electricity is unavailable. You may not have to travel far to find a place with tolerable temperatures. Carefully consider the people in your care and plan for ways to take care of their needs. An air-conditioned shopping mall, library, movie theater, or public building would be a great place to hang out during the heat of the day.

HEAT WAVE ACTION PLAN

Armed with this information, it is now time to develop your action plan to stay cool and prevent heat-induced illnesses. Surviving heat is not always an emergency; for many of us it is an annual event. This is just good common sense. Visit http://theprovidentprepper.org/the-practical-prepper/action-plan-keeping-cool/ to complete a worksheet that will assist you in developing an action plan to keep you and your family cool during a heat wave without power.

|| 18 ||

Home Protection and Security
Safe at Home

"A child has the right to feel that in his home he has a place of refuge, a place of protection from the dangers and evils of the outside world."

—David O. McKay

Home is where we want to stay. Our goal is to be safe and protected within the walls of our homes. In order to achieve this, we must physically fortify our home against possible hazards, including criminals, periods of civil unrest, and desperate individuals as well as man-made and natural disasters. While it's impossible to protect a home from every threat, there are many things within your control that can strengthen your home and prevent it from being an easy target. In this chapter, we will discuss how to make your home safer and explore a variety of ideas on how to secure your home against intruders.

OPERATIONAL SECURITY

Operational security is the process of identifying potential threats and taking action to eliminate or reduce them. As applied to emergency preparedness, it means taking the time to learn who lives in your neighborhood and what the potential threats are in your area. It also means being observant and careful.

Secure your home with layers of protection to discourage trespassers from breaking into your home. Do not make your home an obvious fortress, or someone will wonder what you have that's so valuable. We will discuss ways to secure your home and still blend in with your neighbors later in this chapter.

The Women's Army Corps anti-rumor slogan in 1941–1945 was "Silence Means Security." The security of the nation depended upon silence. Small conversational slips can compromise your security as well. Who might be listening to your conversations, monitoring your social media, or noting the supplies taken into your home? If you let people know you have food storage and supplies, you have made yourself into a target. Take care not to put your family in danger through careless conversation. Downplay your level of preparedness and share details on a need-to-know basis only. We encourage you to be prepared and willing to share during tough times, but do so anonymously for your own protection.

KNOW YOUR NEIGHBORHOOD

The first step is to get to know your neighborhood—both its physical layout and the people who live there. Take special note of possible areas of concern on your commute to work or school. Consider the following questions:

- Are there areas with concentrations of graffiti or gang activity?

- Are there places where traffic is easily congested?

- Where are the hazardous cargo routes through highways, interstates, and railroads?

- Are there chemical plants, refineries, or fuel storage facilities nearby?

- Are there possible terrorist targets near your home?

Take a map and mark all of these areas as well as any other threats or dangers. What are the possible alternate routes in and out of your neighborhood? Try exploring different routes during your normal daily travels. Mark alternate routes on your map. If you need to evacuate, a strategically marked map will help you think clearly when adrenaline is flowing during a crisis.

Neighborhoods are made up of a diverse group of people. They differ in age, race, marital status, family size, income, resources, physical abilities, and level of preparedness. Most people are basically good and interested in the welfare of others. Sadly, it only takes a few bad eggs to ruin a peaceful neighborhood. Selfish, dishonest, destructive, and even dangerous people are a reality that must be dealt with. We encourage you to get to know your neighbors. Reach out, serve, and help whenever possible. Building relationships now will translate into greater security and resources during difficult times.

It is always a good idea to be friendly with local law enforcement officers. Take good care of the families of first responders in your neighborhood. Be observant. Report any criminal activity. Learn more about who lives in your neighborhood by visiting http://www.familywatchdog.us/ to find registered sex offenders. Graffiti indicates local gang activity; learn about local gangs and what graffiti symbols mean. There are local organizations and police officers who can assist you in learning how to stay safe from street gangs.

The relationship you have with your neighbors can make a big difference in the security of your home. Neighbors watching out for each other is a highly effective layer of protection. We encourage you to join a neighborhood watch program or create one in your neighborhood.

HOME SAFETY

Accidents are common in most homes. Many accidents can be prevented with a little bit of proactive maintenance. Any injury can be painful and annoying, but in a disaster, a small scratch has the potential to become life threatening. Let's begin by exploring your home for possible hazards.

Perform a home safety inspection as though you were a stranger. We are so familiar with our home that we step over obvious hazards on a daily basis without even noticing. Grab a clipboard and an inspector's hat and recruit deputy inspectors (children love this authority) and begin in the street in front of your home. Keep going until the entire property has been inspected inside and out. Write everything down. Don't take time to fix anything now, just write!

What are some of the obvious hazards? Blocked doorways, missing shingles, broken steps, broken windows, low hanging branches, and trip hazards are a few. Write them down. Are there two forms of escape from each room? Are there working smoke detectors in each bedroom? Are there working carbon monoxide detectors on each floor and in the garage? Is there a working fire extinguisher on each floor, in the kitchen and in the garage? Do all of the exterior doors and windows lock? Are combustible or flammable materials stored near the water heater? Are vents blocked? Are firearms stored safely? Keep going and record absolutely everything that may pose any type of dangerous situation.

Do you have earthquake and fire safety measures in place? Are water heaters strapped to the wall? Is tall furniture (book cases, entertainment centers, heavy pictures or mirrors) secured? Is the shut off wrench stored close to the gas main, but out of sight? Are there any frayed or exposed wires? Is the dryer vent blocked with lint? Are the chimneys clean? Does the furnace need servicing? Continue writing everything down until the entire home and yard has been critically inspected.

Enlisting the help of family members to conduct a home safety inspection increases awareness and promotes cooperation.

Now that you have your list, reward your team of inspectors and take a deep breath. Do not let the list overwhelm you. We are going to break it down into small manageable pieces and before you know it, you will have made significant progress.

Carefully review the list and divide it into categories. Some items will require immediate attention, such as the front door not locking properly. If you have the skills, this could be classified as a simple repair; if not, classify it as "involved." You will either need to learn how to fix it by watching DIY videos online, checking out DIY books at your local library, recruiting the assistance of a talented friend, or hire the work done. It is vital to the security of your home that all doors are secure. This is an example of an item that must be completed immediately.

Toys scattered on the front walk are a tripping hazard. They may be classified as "Immediate Simple." They should be picked up right away to avoid injury and it is an easy task to accomplish. Relocating combustibles next to the water heater may be "Immediate Simple." Delayed items should be addressed, but can realistically wait, such as a drippy faucet or a fence repair.

Classify each item on your inspection list according to the worksheet provided at http://theprovidentprepper.org/the-practical-prepper/action-plan-home-protection-and-security/.

Once you have categorized the safety items, get to work on the "Immediate Simple." Assign out tasks as appropriate. Cross each item off your list as the task is completed. Next, review the "Immediate Involved" list and develop a plan to address the items on the list. Continue working the list until all items have been completed. Then get your team of inspectors together again and conduct another home safety inspection. Praise the wonderful progress that has been made. The new list should be surprisingly short and manageable. Annual safety inspections will ensure your home environment stays safe.

ORGANIZATION

One of the biggest obstacles for many preppers is the tendency to keep everything because "someday I might need that." This mentality creates a pack rat environment with piles of stuff that does not do anyone any good because you cannot find what you need when you need it. The reality is less is more. You do not own stuff. Stuff owns you. Simplify your life. Get rid of items that take up space and energy without serving a useful purpose.

Consider what items are truly useful and create a permanent home for them. A place for everything, and everything in its place. That is the ideal. Unfortunately for our family, it is not always our reality. We struggle with keeping things "just in case." We have systems in place which seem to help. Every year we go through each closet. Out-grown clothing is either boxed up, labeled, and stored for a younger sibling or given to charity. Worn out sheets or towels are immediately cut into useable rags, bandages, reusable toilet paper, or disposed of. Old food storage is fed to the chickens or composted. No more storing mountains of stuff "just in case."

Be sensitive to the feelings of others when sorting through and disposing of stuff. Kylene has boxes of pictures and memorabilia from the children that are completely off limits when it comes to downsizing. Jonathan has his tools and spare parts. Some things just need to be organized and boxed up. Respect stuff that is valued by another regardless of the whether or not the reasoning makes any sense to you. Our daughter collects rocks. Every day she comes home with pockets full of "special" rocks. We reached an agreement that she could collect all the rocks she wants if she keeps them in a rock garden in the window well outside her bedroom. Compromise can work organizational miracles.

In disaster situations, it is vital to know where critical items are immediately. Where is the wrench to turn off the main gas line? How about the first aid supplies? Plastic sheeting and duct tape? Keys to the storm shelter? Batteries for the radio? Get rid of the clutter and create permanent homes for the important stuff. Organized and clutter free is an amazing feeling.

HOME INTRUDER INSPECTION

The Federal Bureau of Investigation reported 8,975,438 property crimes nationwide in 2012. Victims of property crimes suffered losses totaling $15.5 billion.[1] These numbers indicate it is worth the time and effort required to secure your home and valuables.

Let us begin by changing hats and looking at your home from another angle. Put on dark clothing and cover your face with a bandana, nylon stocking, or ski mask. This time when you inspect your home, you are the bad guy who wants to gain access to your home. Get everyone involved in the adventure. It can be quite educational.

Begin out in the street in front of your home around dusk. What can you see through the windows? Are valuables such as televisions and computers easily visible and tempting? Would a stalker be able to see family members and observe activities inside the home? Scan your surroundings. Where could a bad guy possibly hide? Are all points of entry visible and well lit? Look at the borders of the property. Could someone gain easy access by hopping a fence or opening an unlocked gate? How could the home be made more secure and less inviting to possible intruders?

Challenge your family to gain access to the home without using the garage code, key, or breaking anything. You may learn a trick or two from your kids. You may be surprised how easy it is to find an open door or window. Is there a key hidden in a traditional hiding place? Find the vulnerable areas of your home and write them all down. Remember, no amount of extra security can replace actually locking the doors and windows.

Conduct a home intruder inspection and discover weak areas in your home security.

Congratulate your team of masked bandit volunteers for a job well-done. Review the notes from the inspection and enlist the help of your team to come up with an action list to fortify your home. A truly secure home requires the buy-in of everyone who lives there.

Take a moment to record the results of the inspection. These are important action items to increase your home security. You can use the worksheet located at http://theprovidentprepper.org/the-practical-prepper/action-plan-home-protection-and-security/ to help organize your action items.

HOME SECURITY

Unfortunately, recent crises have demonstrated that human nature can bring out the best in some people and the inner monster in others. Harden your home to protect your house from robbers now and looters after a disaster. Let us explore the most common entry points and how to secure them, along with valuable ways to fortify your home. Remember, no amount of additional security can take the place of actually locking doors and windows!

Securing your home is about creating layers of protection. If someone really wants to get into your home, they could easily drive a piece of heavy equipment right through the front door. Our goal is not to withstand a military assault, but to make the home a less desirable, more difficult target for criminals or anyone who would want to cause harm or take resources. The first priority is to protect the family, then precious resources. Never make your home so secure that you are unable to escape during an emergency. Let us look at some smart changes you can make to add layers of protection to your home security. Many of them do not take much time or money.

APPEARANCE

Appearances matter. Does your home look like it may be full of expensive items? Do you park expensive vehicles in the driveway? Are valuable toys in the front yard? Avoid having anything in plain sight which might make someone think you are rich. Be careful not to advertise new high-ticket items by placing the empty boxes in the garbage can in front of the home. Discretely dispose of them or take them to a recycling center.

The same thing applies to your food storage and supplies. Use a little discretion when hauling cases of canned goods or buckets of food storage into your home. An NRA sticker in the window advertises that you have guns in the home. You might think that advertising you own guns might deter thieves. Guns are a prized target for criminals who may consider the valuable weapons worth the risk.

Make your home look secure, but not like a fortress. It should deter potential burglars but stay under the radar. You invite criminals when your home appears to have high-ticket items inside. Park vehicles inside the garage. Blend in with your neighborhood and stay as invisible as possible.

LIGHTING

Thieves hate bright lights. Proper lighting can prevent someone from using the dark or shadows for concealment. Install exterior lighting to ensure all doors and windows are visible. Mount motion sensitive security lighting in strategic locations. These fixtures enable the lights to respond to activity without having to be left on all night long. Solar powered security lights are great for areas without access to electricity and will work during a power outage.

Place interior and exterior lights on a timer when you go on vacation to make it appear that someone is home. Always leave some exterior lights on at night. Consider using motion-sensor night-lights inside your home. They light your path through dark halls at night and turn on whenever someone walks past them.

SOUND

Sound is another way to discourage a thief. Security alarms use sound to disorient and discourage intruders. A television or radio playing will give the impression that someone is up and about. Barking dog alarms use microwave and radar technology to detect motion outside a door. Some sound like a German Shepherd and the barking becomes more intense if motion continues. Look around and you will discover a wide variety of security gadgets which use sound to add a layer of protection.

DETERRENTS

Deterrents are intended to make an intruder think twice before breaking into a home. A dog can be a great deterrent. It does not need to be a trained guard dog. A dog with a deep, threatening bark is our top choice, but the bark of any good dog can alert you to an intruder and give you a few extra seconds of response time. A barking dog will attract attention and may encourage someone to move right past your home. This is only an additional layer of protection. During times of civil unrest, when people are desperate to survive, a father trying to feed his starving children may not be phased by a barking dog.

Alarm systems and remote control cameras can be an effective layer of protection to add to your home. They discourage an intruder and can provide a few seconds of advanced warning. Monitored alarm systems automatically alert the company, who in turn contact local law enforcement. Actual response time can be very slow. Alarms will not stop someone who is determined to get in. System batteries wear down quickly when the power is out. It is best not to plan on the protection of an alarm system during an extended power outage.

What is the plan if your security alarm goes off? Should the children stay in their rooms or go to a different room? Should they call 911? Do they have access to a phone and know who to call? Have a written, practiced plan in place.

Security cameras are an excellent way to track intruders, or your surroundings, from inside your home. Small, inexpensive cameras are easily installed. Consult a crime prevention officer from your local police or sheriff's department for advice on strategic placement of cameras. Post a generic alarm company sign in your yard or window, whether or not you have an alarm. Avoid specific signs such as "Protected by ADT." They may provide enough information for a burglar to disable it.

The best deterrent is to keep your doors and windows locked. Locking all points of entry forces an intruder to forcibly enter the home. Rekey locks if a key has been missing long enough for someone to make a copy of it. Never hide a spare key under the doormat or flower pot, above the door frame, in a fake rock by the front door, or on a window ledge. If you must hide a key, consider the following ideas:

- Inside a mean-looking dog's house.

- Buried in the ground inside a short PVC pipe that has been capped on both ends.

- Left with a trusted friend or neighbor.

- Inside a properly installed, coded lock box mounted out of sight.

LANDSCAPE

The landscape itself can invite or deter trespassing animals and humans. Keep windows and doors clear of trees or shrubs where someone could hide. Trim tree branches away from the home to prevent access to second story windows. In front of the home, keep hedges shorter than three feet to avoid providing a screen for someone to hide behind. Make it difficult for someone to conceal themselves while breaking in.

A thorny or prickly shrub strategically planted under windows will discourage even the most determined of intruders. Rugosa Rose is a beautiful bush with vicious thorns, perfect to create an uninviting place to hide. Its mature size is between four to eight feet high and spreads four to six feet. There are many varieties and sizes of roses, most with delightfully sharp thorns. Plant a shorter variety directly under windows. Be sure to consider the mature size and plan accordingly. Roses add beauty, while creating another layer of defense.

*Rose bushes under windows add another level of
protection to the security of your home.*

Secure the borders of your property using landscaping. Thorny shrubs and bushes create the perfect barrier as a hedge, or along a fence line, to detour intruders from accessing your land. Consider planting a combination of plants, such as bamboo trees with spiky holly bush underneath. The bamboo creates a physical barrier while the holly makes access painful. A few great thorny candidates include juniper, blue spruce, common holly, firethorn, purple berberis, oleaster, and fuschia. Select thorny varieties from a local nursery that grow well in your climate.

Edible shrubs or bushes serve a dual purpose of securing the home as well as feeding the occupants. Consider planting boysenberries, raspberries, goji berries, gooseberries, blackthorn bushes, citrus trees, pomegranates, and wild plums. Some of these plants can be purchased in a thornless variety. If you are using them for security purposes, make sure to get the thorniest ones available. Purchase only varieties that thrive in your climate. Prickly pear, a bushy cactus, is great for some desert climates.

Thorny bushes planted along a fence discourage potential criminals from climbing over the fence and into your yard.

Well-planned landscape can create a beautiful environment while adding another layer of security to your home. Properly done, it can be almost as effective as a barbed wire security fence, without attracting attention or looking frightful. Install a tall sturdy privacy fence, whenever possible, along with heavy duty locks on sturdy gates and keep them locked.

DOORS

Doors are a vital point of entry to secure. Exterior doors should be made of solid wood, fiberglass, steel, or aluminum to withstand significant force and provide the greatest protection. The frame, strike plate, and hinges are just as important as the door itself. Replace the standard short screws with three-inch screws that will go clear through the frame and sink deeply into the stud. Door hinges should be high quality and sturdy. Install a wide-angle peephole in the front door to enable you to clearly see who is at the door before opening.

Replacing standard screws with three-inch screws in the strike plate is a quick, inexpensive way to strengthen doors.

The door knobs and locks are also vital. We recommend American National Standards Institute (ANSI) Grade one locks. They cost more, but they are worth the money. Install both a deadbolt and a quality knob on all exterior doors and on the door between your home and garage. These locks meet commercial building requirements and provide the best residential security available.

Storm doors or security doors can add another layer of protection. Storm doors are designed to increase energy efficiency but can also help secure the home. Security doors are designed to intentionally prevent forcible entry and can offer some protection against storms. They are expensive but worth considering.

A quality home security bar such as the Buddy Bar Door Jammer can prevent access through a door. This device is used to secure the door by wedging it under the handle with the base on the floor. The concept is similar to wedging a chair under the door handle to prevent it from opening. It provides additional security against unwanted intrusions, making it extremely difficult to gain access through the door. Portable versions are available for use while traveling.

Door barricades or crossbars can be a great tool to effectively deny access through a door. The bar is secured to the wall on both sides of the door, preventing the door from opening. Some bars are completely removable, while others only lift up while not in use. Sometimes they are referred to as Katy Bars. They do a great job of protecting from hurricane force winds as well as providing excellent security.

Sliding glass doors can be a weak point. Some can be simply lifted right out of their tracks from the outside. The locks are easily pried open, unhooked by wiggling the panel, or cut with a hacksaw. Adequate security devices may include a track lock, hinged door bar, insertion pin lock, or a metal or wooden dowel in the track. However, none of these will prevent someone from breaking the glass to gain entrance. A security door will greatly increase the security of a sliding glass door.

Consider installing secure locks on bedroom doors. In the event an intruder gains access to your home, it may provide a few extra moments to prepare to defend yourself or escape out a window while he tries to break down the door.

WINDOWS

Windows are a vulnerable point of entry. It is easy to break glass or pry windows open. Some sliding windows can be lifted out of their track from the outside. It is well worth the effort to secure the windows of your home. Keep windows closed and locked when you are not home. Keep in mind you may need to escape out a window during an emergency. Never compromise safety in the name of security.

Replace worn-out window putty on wooden windows. Double hung windows can be "pinned" by carefully drilling holes angled slightly downward in the outer sash. Be careful not to go totally through the sash or compromise the thermal seal. Insert a nail or bolt to prevent window from being opened. Do not do this on vinyl or metal windows. Horizontal sliding windows can be secured by placing a wooden dowel in the lower track or pins at the top and bottom as with the double hung windows. Permanently seal any window not needed for ventilation or as an emergency exit.

Window locks are relatively inexpensive. We avoid key-operated locks because we do not want safety compromised during an emergency exit when we cannot locate the missing key. Window latches and sash locks are easy to install and effective. Visit your local home improvement store for a wide variety of options.

Keep blinds or curtains closed after dark. Do not let burglars know exactly who is home or what to expect if they get inside. Install blinds, curtains, or reflective film on garage windows to prevent contents from being visible. An empty garage may tip off a criminal that no one is home. Do not give them that advantage.

These expensive weapons are highly visible from the street at night.

Storm windows or hurricane windows are made to withstand debris flying into them at 100 miles per hour through a lamination process at the factory. They will break, but not allow entrance. Security film should be professionally installed and is similar to window tinting. It is installed on the inside of the window. The glass will break, but the film holds the pieces together to prevent entry. Businesses commonly have security film installed to protect against smash-and-grab thefts. Tempered glass is four times stronger than standard glass, but will break and allow entry. It is not a good choice for security.

Glass panels and sidelights less than an arm's length from a door knob should be fitted with glass brick, grates, or grills. You can solve this problem by installing a double cylinder deadbolt that requires a key to open from both the inside and outside. It is important to keep a key handy, but out of arm's reach, in the event you need to evacuate quickly.

Storm shutters that are controlled from the inside and roll into place are a great but pricey security option. Window guards, steel bars or grills can effectively secure windows, but may pose a risk if needed for an emergency exit. Do not use on bedroom windows. Security window well covers are a great way to protect basement windows. They can be secured from deep inside the window well with a simple cotter pin or other locking device. The cover prevents access and provides for a quick easy escape in an emergency. Make sure the occupant of the room has the strength to slide the cover off and climb out of the well.

Review your notes from your home intruder inspection. What can you do to increase the layers of security for your home? Are there areas of weakness that need to be strengthened? The goal is to make your home difficult to access and uninviting so anyone with bad intentions will move on to an easier target.

SECURE VALUABLES

In the event an intruder makes it through your layers of protection and into your home, make your valuables as inaccessible as possible. They are usually in a big hurry. Store valuables, firearms, vital documents, and food storage in unlikely places. Most criminals will search a master bedroom first, so do not store valuable items there. Bathrooms, kitchens, hallways, mudrooms, and laundry rooms are your best bets. Firearms, cash, and vital documents are best kept in a large fireproof safe. Wherever you store valuables, keep a record so you will remember where you put everything.

Interesting ideas for creative places to store valuables include:

- Inside an empty package of frozen food, re-glued shut and stored in the freezer

- Sealed in a #10 can labeled as food storage

- Behind framed photos (vital documents)

- In a "dummy" electrical outlet

- Inside of a toy

- In false walls or under floorboards

- In faux air vent storage units

- In a recessed medicine cabinet disguised to look like a painting

- Inside of hollow books on a book shelf

- Inside an old canister vacuum cleaner

- In empty food containers inside a kitchen cupboard or pantry

- In plastic VHS boxes stored with videos

- Inside a floor safe

- In storage boxes that blend in with your other storage items marked as something uninteresting

Does that stimulate your creative thinking? Where could you stash valuables? These techniques only work if you keep it a secret from everyone. Remember, children love to share information with their friends, who tell their friends and parents and teachers and soon everyone knows. Do not make yourself into a good target by spreading the news. It might be wise to engrave valuable items with "This Property Stolen From . . ." and include your driver's license number. Marked property is much more difficult to fence and easier to return to the rightful owner if it is stolen.

TIPS FOR APARTMENT DWELLERS

You may not have much control over the level of security in a rental unit. It can be a little challenging to secure an apartment if you do not have the ability to make changes. Contact your landlord and explain your security concerns. They may be willing to secure it for you or allow you to make the necessary improvements.

It is important to know your landlord's or management company's key control system. Chances are good there are other keys to your rental out there. Managers are often given master keys, as well as maintenance personnel. Just who has a key to access your home?

It should be possible to increase the security of your doors without anyone being the wiser. Replace the screws on the hinges and strike plate as discussed earlier with three-inch screws. Purchase a door jammer. They are effective and you can take it with you to your next home. Use window locks which do not require any screws that may damage windows. There are DIY alarm systems which can be installed and easily moved from place to place. Other security gadgets you might want to consider such as door-stop wedge alarms, door handle alarms, and glass breaking alarms, if nothing else is allowed.

Garden apartments are more susceptible to burglary than high-rise apartments. An upper floor apartment is easier to secure as the only entrance may be the front door or fire escape. But it also comes with a host of other challenges. Security is important. You may have to go ahead and make the changes and be willing to pay for removal and restoration when you vacate the rental.

Join an apartment watch. It is similar to a neighborhood watch, but consists of an organized group of tenants who are on the lookout for suspicious activity and report it immediately. If safe, get to know your neighbors.

HOME PROTECTION AND SECURITY ACTION PLAN

Your home is a great source of protection. It can protect you from harsh weather, dangerous people, and be a place of refuge. We prefer to stay in our home and face the challenges from our home territory that has been carefully secured and stocked with provisions whenever possible. Consider your individual circumstances and come up with a realistic plan to add layers of protection and increase the security of your home. We have created a helpful worksheet at http://theprovident-prepper.org/the-practical-prepper/action-plan-home-protection-and-security/ to help you organize your action plan.

|| 19 ||

Personal Safety
Don't Mess with Me!

I am responsible for my own safety.

The surest way to stay safe is to avoid dangerous situations all together. However, that may not always be possible. It is critical to know how to defend yourself, build physical skills, and use the weapons of your choice. This chapter will focus on personal safety skills.

AVOID DANGER

Learn how to be safe while you are out and about. Pay close attention to your surroundings and follow your intuition. There may be times of civil unrest where it will be highly dangerous to be out among people. When this happens, avoid going out in public if at all possible. If you must venture out, blend in with the crowd and do not do anything to attract attention to yourself.

We cannot emphasize enough the importance of practicing operational security. Do not make yourself a target by advertising your weapons, supplies, or preparedness status. If everyone around you is dirty and hungry, do the best you can to blend in to prevent becoming a target for desperate people.

SELF-DEFENSE TRAINING

Personal self-defense training can give you the skills and confidence to protect yourself in dangerous situations. Your body can be an effective defensive weapon if you develop the skills and train regularly.

Criminals are cowards and look for easy targets. You may be protected simply by the confident way you carry yourself or respond to an initial confrontation. Training and skill development can help you cultivate that confident air.

There are many different forms of self-defense training. Select one that meets your objectives and fits with your personality and skill level. You will be much more likely to stick with something you enjoy. Kylene could never tolerate the violence of kickboxing, but is a certified radKIDs instructor and teaches self-defense classes for children. Our friend takes Elite Yoshukai Karate along with her son in a family oriented program. Programs are available for everyone, from young children to seniors with limited strength and mobility. Find one that works well for you.

Self-defense training increases confidence, muscle memory, and your ability to defend yourself.

Repetition of physical skills increases muscle memory. Some skills seem quite awkward and difficult at first. Practice enables the body to react without taking the time to engage the brain. This is critical when adrenaline is pumping and your safety is on the line. Confidence is gained when you have a plan and the skills to take care of yourself in a physical confrontation. We strongly encourage everyone to take some form of self-defense training.

CHILD SAFETY AND SELF-DEFENSE TRAINING

Children can be little disasters just waiting to happen. They are frequently referred to as tornadoes for a good reason. It is critical to create a safe environment for them. Keep weapons, chemicals, and dangerous objects out of reach. Install child resistant locks on cabinets and doors to limit access to potentially harmful areas.

Take time to teach children how to be safe. Never assume they know something. Gently remind them of the importance of following important safety procedures. Educate through discussion and hands on practice. Make preparedness into an exciting game. Play "what if?" What would you do if mommy did not come to school to pick you up one day? What would you do if someone tried to give you a ride in their car? How would you respond to a student at school who pushed you down and told you not to tell?

RadKIDs classes teach children how to be safe and avoid danger as well as how to escape an abductor.

We highly recommend every child go through a radKIDs training program. You can learn more about the program or find programs near you at www.radkids.org. This program enhances the ability of children to utilize knowledge, skills, and power to protect themselves from violence and harm. They learn vital physical self-defense skills. Children become empowered and learn to replace fear, confusion, and panic in dangerous situations with confidence, personal safety skills, and self-esteem. They are in charge of their own safety. They always have a plan.

WEAPONS

The list of potential weapons is endless. When we think of weapons we often list firearms, knives, batons, pepper spray, mace, Taser guns, brass knuckles, crossbow, and other items traditionally labeled as weapons. However, many common household items can be used as weapons: baseball bats, kitchen utensils, and even newspaper. Football hooligans in England crafted "Millwalll bricks" by tightly rolling sheets of newspaper and folding to create a handgrip and curved head. They do as much damage as bricks. The possibilities are endless, but we will focus on a few of the more common weapons used for personal protection.

COMMANDING VOICE

Your most effective weapon is your voice. A strong, loud "NO, STAY BACK" or other command response can often prevent a situation from occurring. It draws attention from others and may throw an attacker off guard. Any police officer will confirm that using a powerful, commanding voice frequently prevents them from having to resort to using other weapons. Practice using your voice as a weapon. It does not come naturally to most of us.

FIREARMS

The choice to use firearms is a very personal one. Many factors come into play in deciding whether or not to own a firearm. Use these weapons legally and responsibly. Store firearms correctly in a quality gun safe out of the reach of children. Educate family members on gun safety. Train each person on every weapon in the home. We require each of our children to go through a hunter's safety program and learn to safely handle the weapons we own. Firearms are part of our environment, and they need to learn how to be safe around them.

Assume every gun is loaded and handle it accordingly. Never point a gun at anything you do not intend to kill. Keep your finger off the trigger unless you are ready to shoot. Be sure you know what you are shooting and what is behind your target. Practice shooting and handling the weapons regularly. Carrying a gun you are not physically and mentally prepared to use can be a highly dangerous choice.

Most experts will recommend three types of firearms: rifles, shotguns, and handguns. Each has a different purpose when it comes to personal defense. The key is versatility and common calibers so ammunition is easy to obtain. Understand your national and state laws about using, transporting, and storing firearms. Using this deadly weapon should be a last resort, not the first.

Avid gun enthusiasts have strong preferences. Consult a professional for advice on purchasing the best weapon for your personal needs and abilities. We offer this list of general options for the beginner.

- Revolvers are simple handguns. Each bullet is placed into a cylinder individually. They are especially good for beginners, because they are easy to use, maintain, and are reliable.

- Semi-automatic pistols are good for advanced users. There is a greater incident of jamming, making reliability an issue.

- Rifles are probably better suited for hunting, but they can definitely provide protection.

- Shotguns are often the choice for home defense because they are more forgiving when it comes to precision shooting. The spread of the pellets is one inch per foot. If the intruder is eight feet away, the spread is eight inches. They provide exceptional stopping power, are inexpensive and simple to operate. Shotguns recoil and can provide the shooter with a pretty good kick. Most experts recommend a 12-gauge shotgun for home defense, but a 20-gauge will kick less.

PEPPER SPRAY

An alternative weapon is pepper spray. The active agent is oleoresin capsicum. This is a derivative of cayenne peppers. It is an inflammatory agent. The discomfort and debilitating effects last for between 20 and 90 minutes, gradually decreasing over several hours.[1] Pepper spray units can be fired repeatedly and shoot 8–20 feet depending on the model. It is available in small bottles which can be kept on a key chain clear up to large one pound bottles effective against multiple attackers.

The body reacts immediately to the spray. It causes temporary blindness, tears, saliva, a runny nose, coughing, and difficulty breathing. It is effective even on those under the influence of drugs or alcohol. We like to use 17 percent pepper spray for self-defense. This grade is strong enough to disable just about any attacker without permanently damaging or killing him.

A three ounce bottle is easy to use and tucks nicely away in drawers. There is not the great fear of children getting seriously hurt as there is with firearms. The effects are painful, but not life threatening. The small .05 ounce bottles are small enough to take out walking or jogging. It is very effective against attacking animals.

If you get sprayed by accident, do not rub as it will significantly increase the burning sensation. The Pepper Spray Store recommends applying whole milk to the affected area by spraying it on with a spray bottle, splashing it on the skin, immersing it, or saturate a clean towel with the milk and lay it gently over the area. To remove the oil from your skin make a solution of 25 percent Dawn dishwasher detergent and 75 percent water. Wash the affected area at least seven or eight times. You can put it in a large bowl and immerse your face for 10–15 seconds at a time. Do not wipe the solution away. Just let it sit. Remember touching will increase the burning. It will take 15–45 minutes before symptoms subside.[1]

You may consider carrying Sudecon decontamination wipes in the event of accidental exposure. They are individually packaged and easy to carry. The manufacturer claims the wipes can reduce the burning sensation in 7–15 minutes.

OTHER WEAPONS

There are many other self-defense weapons you might choose to use: Taser guns, stun guns, batons, and a variety of knives. Whatever your choice of weapon, make sure that you know the laws, are trained, and that you are skilled and practiced at using it. You must be mentally and physically prepared to use it or it can be used against you.

PERSONAL SAFETY AND SECURITY ACTION PLAN

Now it is time to create your plan. What are your goals? One of our goals is to train each member of our family in a self-defense program that is appropriate for individual ages and mental and physical abilities. Which weapons will work in your budget and circumstances? Develop a realistic action plan to keep you and your family safe. Go to http://theprovidentprepper.org/the-practical-prepper/action-plan-personal-safety/ for a worksheet to assist you in your planning.

20

Medical
The Doctor Is Out

"Laughter is the best medicine—unless you're diabetic, then insulin comes pretty high on the list."

—Jasper Carrott

Our world is a dangerous place, full of difficult unforeseen events. In a matter of a few precious moments, life can change dramatically. During a large-scale crisis, those faithful emergency response teams we depend upon will be so overwhelmed they will probably be unavailable to assist you and your loved ones. Hospitals and clinics will suffer from staffing and supply shortages. They will be inundated with numerous serious casualties. You may need to depend on yourself, your family, and your neighbors to make it through the initial crisis or even longer. Are you ready?

In this chapter, we will explore important aspects of taking charge of your own medical needs. Allow the ideas to stimulate your thought processes and carefully consider steps you can take to insure the health of those you love.

PHYSICAL HEALTH PREPARATION

Any type of crisis situation can be quite physically and emotionally taxing. It is important to keep yourself in the best condition possible so the challenges will have minimal impact on your health. Build your immune system. A physically strong, healthy body makes life more enjoyable and will give you better odds during a disaster.

We recommend you follow these basic guidelines to ensure you are physically ready for whatever may come.

- Eat a balanced diet loaded with whole grains, legumes, fruits, and vegetables. Store a supply of healthy foods and rotate regularly to maintain freshness and insure maximum nutrient content.

- Exercise regularly to strengthen your body and maintain a healthy weight.

- Get at a minimum of 15 minutes of sun exposure every day.

- Visit your health care provider for regular preventative check-ups and follow recommendations.

- Monitor and treat chronic health conditions. Take prescribed medications as directed by your health care provider.

- Keep up-to-date on all immunizations.

- See your dentist regularly to maintain healthy teeth.

- Learn and incorporate stress relieving and relaxation techniques into your life.

- Prepare and maintain a personalized survival kit that can sustain you during the first several days of an event. Remember to include daily medications and a quality water purification unit. See chapter 5.

PROTECTING YOUR HEALTH DURING A CRISIS

During the first few days of any crisis, it is important to consciously think about taking care of your physical needs. If you compromise your health, you will become part of the problem instead of part of the solution. Here is some basic advice.

- Drink plenty of clean, safe water. You may not feel thirsty. Drink anyway. Dehydration prevents your brain from working properly. It can make you feel groggy, slow, and "out of it." Your kidneys will not function well, allowing toxins and waste to back up, making you feel crummy.

- Remember to eat. Chances are you may be quite busy and may forget to eat due to many urgent demands. Headaches, dizziness, fatigue, abnormal heart rhythms, nausea, or muscle aches can develop if you go without food for too long. Take time to eat regularly.

- Do not allow yourself to go long periods without sleep. Sleep deprivation weakens your body, making you more susceptible to disease as well as decreasing your ability to react quickly in dangerous situations. Judgment may be impaired along with overall ability to function.

- Carry a current list of medications and dosages in your wallet or purse. Wear a Medic Alert Bracelet or dog tags, if needed, to alert caregivers to any medical condition you may have. It would be a good idea to put emergency contact information on the tag as well.

EDUCATION

In a disaster, professional responders will almost certainly be overwhelmed and unavailable to help you and your family when you need them. It makes good sense for everyone to become educated on basic lifesaving techniques. Contact your local American Red Cross at http://www.redcross.org/take-a-class for information on classes in your area. The following are some classes we recommend taking:

- **Basic First Aid Training** should cover a variety of subjects, including bite wounds, bruises, burns, choking, cuts and scrapes, electrocution, fractures, head injuries, nose bleeds, and puncture wounds. It is frequently combined with CPR training.

- **Cardiopulmonary Resuscitation (CPR) Training** teaches you how to respond to breathing and cardiac emergencies. CPR helps oxygenated blood to circulate to vital organs such as the brain and heart. CPR started by a bystander may double the chances of survival for cardiac arrest victims.

- **Automated External Defibrillator (AED) Training** teaches CPR-certified individuals how to safely use an AED to provide care for cardiac arrest victims. This course is frequently combined with CPR training. AED is a portable defibrillator that automatically analyzes the heart rhythms to determine if a shock is required.

It gives audio and visual prompts that guide trained operators in delivering safe and effective emergency care.

- **CERT (Community Emergency Response Team) Programs** educate individuals "about disaster preparedness for hazards that may impact their area and trains them in basic disaster response skills such as fire safety, light search and rescue, team organization, and disaster medical operations."[1] This training prepares community members to take care of their own needs and respond in the event that professional responders are not immediately available. Contact your local fire department for information. We highly recommend becoming a member of your local CERT team.

CURRENT MEDICAL INFORMATION SHEET

Depending on the situation, you may not have access to your regular physician. Medical records may be temporarily unavailable. It is important to keep an updated medical information sheet for each member of your family. This can serve as valuable information for health care personnel. You may want to staple a copy of important health related documents or more detailed information for those with a complicated medical history to the back of the medical information sheet. Remember to include the following information:

- Name

- Birth date

- Drug and food allergies

- Prescription medications (include doses and schedules)

- Current medical condition(s)

- Chronic conditions (diabetes, high blood pressure, heart disease, asthma, and so on)

- History of serious hospitalizations

- Current immunizations including date of last tetanus immunization

- Health care provider's name and contact information

- Dentist's name and contact information

- Hospital preference

- Medical insurance information

- Emergency contact names and numbers

FIRST-AID SUPPLIES

It is important to have a good first-aid kit in your home, car, office, and in your survival kit. A comprehensive first-aid manual is also a must. **First-aid supplies are limited by the knowledge and skills of the user.** Regularly update first-aid skills.

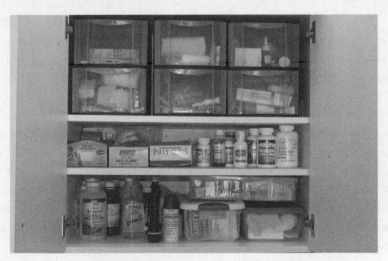

Our family first-aid supplies are kept organized
in a kitchen cupboard for quick access.

Commercial kits are available for every conceivable need from hiking to trauma to emergency surgery kits. These are great foundational kits and contain important specialized tools. We supplement our kits and purchase frequently used items in bulk.

Our family first-aid supplies are kept in an accessible kitchen cupboard ready for any emergency. The main kit is an opaque fishing tackle box stocked with Band-Aids of various sizes, shapes, characters and colors, steri-strips, alcohol prep pads, iodine prep pads, anti-bacterial wipes, antibiotic ointment, hydrocortisone, super glue, tweezers, cotton swabs, scissors, syringe for washing, small gauze pads and tape. This kit is intended to have everything to take care of common minor wounds. Our children frequently access this kit without adult supervision.

We also keep two clear plastic shoeboxes stocked with sterile pads, dressings, gauze wrap, eye pads, triangular bandages, roller bandages, finger splints, wraps and other large injury items in the same cupboard. These are intentionally separated from the main kit to protect them from contamination.

Plastic drawers, kept on the highest shelf, are organized with various medications and medical supplies out of the reach of young children. Gloves, alcohol, hydrogen peroxide, hand sanitizer, flashlight, and other important supplies are right there for when we need them. Having all of the necessary supplies together in one place makes treating an injury much easier. All containers are portable in the event we need to take the treatment to the patient. Always over estimate the amount of supplies you may need.

Our neighbor's dog was hit by a car and sustained serious injuries. We went through six bottles of hydrogen peroxide just during the initial cleaning before he was able to be seen by the vet. A little friend crashed into a barbed wire fence, which resulted in numerous lacerations that had to be cleaned and bandaged. Some required steri-strips to close the wounds. His injuries required a huge amount of supplies. Be prepared with more first-aid supplies than you think you need. In a disaster, there may be several victims with serious wounds. Supplies will be used up quickly.

GENERAL STORAGE MEDICATIONS

During a crisis, we may experience shortages or temporary unavailability of important medications. Drug production and distribution may come to a halt due to shortages of basic materials and staff. Thoughtfully evaluate the needs of your family and store medications accordingly. Consult with your health care provider about storing a supply of antibiotics and other prescription medications.

Prescribed daily critical medications (those for chronic medical conditions such as diabetes, hypertension, emphysema, chronic bronchitis, asthma, coronary artery disease, hypothyroidism, etc.) should be a top priority. It may be prudent to work toward storing a six month supply of critical medications. Discuss this with your physician and enlist his or her help. Be sure to rotate supplies each time a new prescription is obtained.

OVER-THE-COUNTER MEDICATIONS

Many of our needs can be met with over-the-counter medications. We update our supplies annually. We have our own little personalized pharmacy at home designed to meet the unique needs of our family. This supply eliminates the need for late night trips to purchase a needed medication.

Here is a list of a variety of medications to stimulate your thought process as you plan:

- Prescribed, or over-the-counter, daily critical and non-critical medications

- Vitamins, minerals, and other nutritional supplements

- For allergies, runny nose, itchy skin, and so on: diphenhydramine (Benadryl), loratadine (Alavert, Claritin), chlorpheniramine (Chlor-Trimeton), antihistamine

- Congestion relief: pseudoephedrine (Sudafed)

- First-aid ointments: Bacitracin, Lanacaine/Lanabiotic, Neosporin/ Neomycin, Triple-Antibiotic Ointment

- Heartburn relief: ranitidine (Zantac)

- Induce vomiting: syrup of ipecac

- Itchy skin relief: hydrocortisone cream (Cortaid)

- Nausea, vomiting, and diarrhea relief: bismuth subsalicylate (Kaopectate, Pepto Bismol), loperamide (Imodium AD), meclizine (Antivert, Bonine, Dramamine)

- Pain and fever relievers: acetaminophen (Tylenol), ibuprofen (Motrin, Advil), aspirin, naproxen sodium (Aleve)

- For radiation exposure: Thyroid blocking agent for radiation emergencies—potassium iodide See http://thyroid.org/wp-content/uploads/patients/brochures/NuclearRadiation_brochure.pdf for detailed information on use.

- For skin infection prevention: bacitracin ointment

- Sore throat or cough relief: cough drops and throat lozenges, cough suppressant—dextromethorphan/DM (Robitussin DM Cough Syrup)

- Stomach discomfort relief: antacids (TUMS, Rolaids, Maalox, Mylanta), H2 blocking agents (Pepsid, Zantac), proton-pump inhibitors (Prevacid, Prilosec OTC),

- Yeast or fungal infection treatments: Clotrimazole (Gyne-Lotrimin, Lotrimin)

- For severe allergic reactions: EpiPen (epinephrine—requires prescription)

Children require special pediatric formulations of medication. Be sure to stock medications that are age appropriate for the members of your family.

ANTIBIOTICS

Antibiotics require a prescription for good reasons. It is always best to take antibiotics under the care of a knowledgeable physician. Conditions and injuries respond differently to various types of antibiotics. We do not recommend self-medicating. A doctor who understands you are storing a few antibiotics for an emergency may be willing to assist you, if you have built a level of trust and honor that trust. Your doctor knows your health requirements best and can prescribe correct dosages and courses of antibiotics.

Cynthia J. Koelker, MD, at www.armageddonmedicine.net, wrote an article entitled "Seven Antibiotics to Stockpile and Why." She recommends you ask your personal physicians to help you stockpile an assortment of antibiotics. No antibiotic is effective against everything. Some people are intolerant or allergic to various antibiotics. Dr. Koelker suggests the following generic antibiotics; her top three to stockpile would be Cephalexin, Ciprofloxacin, and metronidazole.[2]

- **Amoxicillin** (Amoxil, Trimox, Moxatag, Larotid)—used to treat respiratory infections, strep throat, some strains of pneumococcal bacteria. Common infections treated with amoxicillin include infections of the middle ear, tonsils, throat, larynx, bronchi, lungs, urinary tract, and skin. It is safe for children and pregnant women.[3]

- **Cephalexin** (Keflex)—works similar to amoxicillin, but is stronger against Staph aureus. Common infections treated with cephalexin include skin, bone, middle ear, tonsils, throat, larynx, bronchi, and pneumonia. Dr. Koelker would choose to stockpile cephalexin over amoxicillin, if she had to make a choice.

- **Ciprofloxacin** (Cipro, Proquin XR)—works on anthrax, urinary tract and prostate infections, pneumonia, infectious diarrheas, and bronchitis. Not usually used for women or children.[4]

- **Doxycycline** (Vibramycin, Oracea, Adoxa, Atridox)—useful for respiratory infections (Hemophilus influenza, Streptococcus pneumonia, or Mycoplasma pneumonia), tick-borne diseases, plague, and some urinary/prostate infections. It is used to treat Rocky Mountain spotted fever, typhus, chancroid, cholera, brucellosis, anthrax, syphilis, and acne. Not usually used by pregnant women or children.[5]

- **Erythromycin**—performs similar to amoxicillin. It is used to treat upper/lower respiratory tract infections, skin infections, acute pelvic inflammatory disease, etc. Penicillin-allergic patients may be able to take it. Causes cramps and diarrhea. Safe for children and pregnant women. Examples of common uses are strep throat, pneumonia, diphtheria, whooping cough, listeriosis, syphilis, gonorrhea, chlamydia, Lyme disease, acne, and tetanus.[6]

- **Metronidazole** (Flagyl)—targets specific infections. Used for certain sexually transmitted diseases, anaerobic bacteria, certain parasites, and some ameba. Amebic dysentery, amebic liver abscess, anaerobic infections, bacterial vaginosis, clostridium difficile infection, Giardia, helicobacter pylori, pelvic inflammatory disease (PID), trichomoniasis, and rosacea are examples of conditions treated with metronidazole. Should not be used by children.[7]

- **Sulfamethoxazole and trimethoprim** (SMZ-TMP)—used for urinary tract infections, respiratory bacteria, and resistant staph (MRSA).

Your individual antibiotic needs will vary greatly depending on age, allergies, sensitivities, and medical condition. Once again we highly recommend working with your doctor to stock medications which are appropriate and safe for your individual needs.

MEDICATION STORAGE AND SHELF-LIFE

Drugs should be stored in original packaging in an airtight plastic container at room temperature (unless otherwise specified by manufacturer). Store in the dark and away from moisture. Humidity, extreme temperatures, sunlight, and air can cause drugs to deteriorate. Hot, humid bathrooms are not a good location for storing medications. Monitor the expiration dates printed on the labels and rotate to ensure a fresh supply. Ask your pharmacist what happens to your prescription medications after the expiration date and use accordingly. Always store medications out of the reach of children.

Some storage temperature requirements depend on the composition of the individual drug. For instance, MedicineNet.com recommends that amoxicillin capsules and 125 and 250 mg dry powders should be stored at or below 68 degrees F (20 degrees C), and chewable tablets and 200 and 400 mg dry powders should be stored at or below 77 degrees F (25 degrees C). Refrigeration is preferred for powder that has been mixed with water, but not necessary. Once mixed, it only lasts 14 days.

Expiration dates on medication bottles indicate the time the drug is guaranteed to be good, not when it is no longer safe to use. Medications may be stable and safe to use for several years past the expiration date. Cynthia J. Koelker, MD, in an article entitled "Using Expired Medications—Antibiotics and Antiviral Medication," suggests that "most tablets and capsules are very likely safe and quite likely effective for several years beyond the printed expiration date. Using expired medications may do for a decade beyond the end of the world as we know it."[8]

A study conducted by the US Food and Drug Administration for the US Military on more than 100 drugs showed that 90 percent were safe and effective far past the original expiration date. "Joel Davis, a former FDA expiration-date compliance chief, says that with a handful of exceptions—notably nitroglycerin, insulin and some liquid antibiotics—most drugs are probably as durable as those the agency has listed for the military."[9] A study published in JAMA Internal Medicine in 2012 entitled "Stability of Active Ingredients in Long-Expired Prescription Medications" reported, "Ongoing studies show that many medications retain their potency years after their initially labeled expiration dates."[10]

We are not advocating routinely using expired drugs. Rotate your medications regularly and dispose of them properly. Consult your doctor before taking any prescription medication while you have access to care. We make this point only to illustrate that if medical care, or access to critical medications, becomes unavailable in an emergency situation, you could have an antibiotic to treat an infected wound or other potentially fatal illness. The drug will likely be effective long after the expiration date printed on the bottle.

HYDRATION

A common treatment provided in hospital emergency rooms is an IV solution to hydrate the patient. Dehydration can be caused by inadequate fluid intake, diarrhea, vomiting, fever, excessive sweating, and may cause serious complications such as swelling of the brain, seizures, kidney failure, coma, and death. Children are especially vulnerable to dehydration from diarrhea. Many injuries and illnesses benefit tremendously from proper hydration.

Be prepared with ingredients to make an oral rehydration solution. The World Health Organization recommends making a solution using 4 ½ cups clean water, ½ teaspoon salt, and 6 teaspoons sugar. Use exact amounts. Too much sugar can make diarrhea worse and too much salt is harmful. Consume within 12 hours at room temperature or within 24 hours if refrigerated.[11]

MEDICAL EQUIPMENT AND SUPPLIES

If you depend on medical equipment (such as glucose and blood pressure monitoring equipment, an air compressor for a nebulizer, or an air concentrator for oxygen therapy) or depend on medication that requires refrigeration, make sure you have good supply of fresh batteries or an alternative source of energy to run your equipment. Practice using back-up energy sources to ensure they will work when you really need them to.

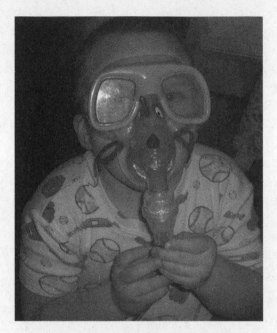

*Back-up power is a critical consideration
for those who rely on medical equipment
for survival.*

Next time you have an injury which requires medical equipment, consider hanging onto that equipment. Braces, walking boots, crutches, walkers, shoulder slings, immobilizers, and other medical equipment may be in short supply in a disaster and could greatly facilitate the healing process. Clean them and store medical equipment together where you will remember where they are when you need them.

Remember to plan for special needs, including glasses, contacts and solution, denture care supplies, extra batteries for hearing aids, and so on. If you have a member of your family that is disabled, or has medical needs which require special care, train alternate caregivers in the event that the primary caregiver becomes unable to provide care during a disaster.

SELF-QUARANTINE

There may come a time when your best course of action will be to isolate yourself, and your family, from other people such as in the case of a pandemic. This means not attending school, work, church, or other activities. In order to do this, you must have sufficient supplies (food, fuel, medication, money, and so forth) on hand so that you can stay secluded. One trip to the store could result in exposing your entire family unnecessarily.

A serious outbreak of a highly contagious disease will mean your best defense lies in completely avoiding other people. Individuals may be contagious days before exhibiting any symptoms. Helping neighbors could be accomplished by leaving food or supplies on their porch at night. Do not risk your entire family by accidently coming in contact with anyone.

If you work in a critical field, you may be required to stay at work or in another location to protect your family from exposure. What would you do? Where would you stay? Would it be possible to telecommute? Does your employer have a plan in place? Explore your options now and prepare accordingly.

It is likely there will be a temporary breakdown in food delivery, electric, gas, and water services. Public order may break down due to widespread illness and death. Could you be completely self-sufficient for three to six months or maybe longer?

BRINGING IT HOME

A stomach virus hit our family with a vengeance. It started with our five-year-old son and systematically worked its way through the entire family with nausea, vomiting, diarrhea, chills, aches and pains, weakness, and a mighty headache. Experiences such as these are a great opportunity to evaluate our level of preparedness for a crisis such as a pandemic.

We learned valuable lessons, including a deep appreciation for a working washing machine, warm running water, and a flush toilet. We were well stocked with sports drinks, crackers, water, and medications. A neighbor knocked on our door late one night needing to borrow a thermometer for her little girl. Fortunately, we had an extra one to lend her. We would expect that to happen during a pandemic and have purposely stocked extra supplies to ensure that our family has enough and some to share.

MEDICAL ACTION PLAN

During any type of disaster, medical care and pharmaceutical supplies may be difficult to obtain. It may be necessary for you to provide care for your family at home. In the olden days, it was Grandma who knew how to take care of the sick and injured. Her wisdom was quite valuable to family and neighbors. We challenge you to develop those skills and that knowledge yourself. Without proper treatment, even minor wounds may develop life threatening infections.

It may be of value to explore some possible alternatives to traditional western medicine. Herbs can be used to treat illness and facilitate healing of injuries. Consider exploring the benefits of colloidal silver, homeopathy, essential oils, energy work, and other beneficial methods of healing.

Armed with the information in this chapter, use the worksheet at http://theprovidentprepper.org/the-practical-prepper/action-plan-medical/ to brainstorm your action plan to care for the first-aid and medical needs of your family if medical care is not available.

21

Community
We're All in This Together

"No man is an island."

—John Donne

No matter how well we prepare for possible hazards, if our community is not prepared, we are in trouble. You may not have the ability to motivate your entire city to prepare, but you may have great influence over your neighborhood or social groups. Throughout history, people have lived in small groups or tribes, clustering together for protection, friendship, division of labor, food, and shared skills. Rarely do you hear of one family intentionally isolating themselves from the group. Banishment is a death sentence. The benefits of the group might mean the difference between life and death.

A group of people will have a variety of necessary skills and resources. It is difficult for one person to have all of the necessary expertise like medical, emergency response, communications, small engine repair, carpentry, physical defense, baking, preserving, and gardening. Combine the skills of ten families and you will be amazed at the diverse skill set you have access to. It would make survival much easier.

The same goes for resources. Financial resources and time allow an inventory of valuable tools to be accumulated. A mature couple in the neighborhood may have acquired many tools, but may not have the physical strength and stamina to make the best use of them. A younger couple may be in the opposite situation: full of strength and energy but without money for tools. Working together both can benefit greatly from the relationship.

As a society we have become isolated, living on the same street or apartment building for years and never getting to know our neighbor. This voluntary isolation contributes to lack of a sense of community, depriving folks of great benefits. Life can be much richer when neighbors reach out and get to know one another, help each other, and build relationships.

SUCCESSFUL COMMUNITIES

Successful communities are deliberately built through planning and effort. They have long standing traditions, close relationships, and a culture of self-sufficiency. Everyone is considered family. They look out for each other and maintain ties that keep the group strong. Some areas are routinely struck by disasters. The citizens choose to stay there and rebuild over and over again. That crazy determination comes from a love of a community and the residents.[1]

In a perfect world, your immediate neighborhood could be built into an ideal community. There are times and places where that is not a possibility. Sometimes it may be dangerous to develop close relationships with neighbors who participate in illegal drugs or other illicit activities. Use wisdom in everything you do. Do not put your family in danger. Most neighborhoods can be greatly improved by building and strengthening relationships.

If you live in a dangerous neighborhood, build a network of like-minded people outside of your local community. Many preppers have a bug out location where they plan to evacuate to if the city gets too intense. It may work for you to buy some land with some friends and create a well-stocked home away from home. In either case, that community of people is critical to your survival. A plan to ride the trouble out all alone is not generally a successful one.

RELATIONSHIP BUILDING

It can be a little awkward to approach a neighbor you have lived next to for five years without ever saying hello to before. Both of you may have developed preconceived ideas about each other. We suggest it is time to cowboy up and get the job done. You can use the direct approach and flat out tell them you think it is about time you both became more neighborly. Then again, you could make up some excuse to go knock on their door. You should be on a first name basis with neighbors on both sides of your street for at least five houses down in each direction.

Extend small courtesies to your neighbors. Pick up an overturned garbage can or wave at them when you pass. Consider hosting a neighborhood block party to make awkward introductions easier. Make it a point to reach out, lend a helping hand, take them small gifts during the holidays, and invite them into your home.

Camaraderie promotes group resilience and survival. People in supportive social networks tend to have stronger immune systems and are happier. The healthier the culture of the group, the better the members deal with the stress of disasters and are able to recover sooner.[2] We encourage you to help one another and be prepared to share resources and skills to benefit your group.

FORMAL NEIGHBORHOOD ORGANIZATION

Strengthening relationships within your neighborhood is a great place to start. Formally organizing the group may provide structure, direction and improve efficiency during a disaster. Community Emergency Response Teams (CERT) are citizens who receive formal training to respond in emergency situations. Their training enables them to assist when emergency responders are overwhelmed. The formal organization we mention is in line with their recommendations.

A large group will need to be officially organized into smaller groups or blocks to increase efficiency. This works well for a single neighborhood or for organizing 1,000 people. Divide neighborhoods into groups, or blocks, using geographical boundaries that make sense. People should be able to see each other. Create divisions through back fences. Think of it this way: in the event of an emergency, could each house or apartment have quick access to the others? Line of sight is important.

Groups of ten homes create the ideal group. Adjust the size as necessary. It would make sense to leave a cul-de-sac with twelve homes in one group. If there are sixteen homes on a street, divide it into two groups of eight. Assign each group a group a block captain and co-captain. Leadership is important. Make sure the captains are willing and able to fulfill their responsibilities. Large organizations should establish a chain of command and communication. We will focus on individual blocks.

Strong leaders are critical to the success of a group. A good captain will earn power and respect from members by a calm, credible nature. He or she is aware of details, decisive, open to opinions, but able to make quick decisions in a crisis. A great leader works to be educated, but recognizes the value and unique contribution of each member of the group. No leader is perfect. Members must be willing to forgive and work toward the common good.

THE FIRST MEETING

The block captain and co-captain should organize a group meeting. Do not make it into an intense end-of-the-world seminar. This is about neighbors helping neighbors. We suggest that you organize the meetings as a block party with food and games. Building relationships and socialization is critical to the success of your group. Meet with the adults (and interested youth) for no longer than 30 minutes. Make the meeting efficient and productive. If you drag it out, your next get-together will not be well attended. We recommend you address these issues:

Neighborhood meetings should be fun, productive, short, and designed to build relationships.

- Introduce the captain, the co-captain, and the neighborhood emergency plan. The goal is to organize yourselves and prepare to work together in the event of any disaster to see to the safety of every member of your group.

- Participation is completely voluntary. Disclosure of resources is optional. Most preppers practice operational security and will not be willing to disclose details of their personal preparations. Do not put pressure on anyone to disclose resources or information. You want them in the group. Ask for members who would like to volunteer to help to see you after the meeting.

Create a comfortable atmosphere for socializing.

- Determine communication routes. What is the best way to communicate to group members? Social media? Neighborhood blog? Email? Text? Phone? In person? Posting signs? Newsletter? Radios? What frequency, station, or privacy code? This is specific to the dynamics of your group. Take each person into account. You may need to·use several methods to cover everyone. Excellent communication is critical!

- Identify specific needs within the group. Everyone is important!

  - Elderly who need to be checked on

  - Young mothers with several children

  - Preschool or daycare in a home

- Handicapped individuals, and specifically what services they might require

- Other unique circumstances

- Structural concerns with buildings

- Hazardous materials

- Pets

- Specific assignments given in writing to each individual with specific due dates. Do not force or coerce any person to participate. Some may be skeptical. A strong group with an important purpose will encourage participation eventually. Sample forms can be found at http://theprovidentprepper.org/the-practical-prepper/action-plan-community/.

  - Individual preparation suggestions

  - Group skills and resources survey

  - CERT training workshop dates and times

  - Family information sheet with important numbers and information—names, ages, contact information (e-mail, cell, home, work, and so on), special needs, and critical information. This sheet will be kept in a binder at the captain's home to be used only for emergencies. It should contain enough information to contact all members of the household and emergency next-of-kin contacts.

- Date and time of next meeting. Space meetings carefully; too much time, and the group does not take things seriously. Meetings held too close together will not allow enough time to make progress.

- Thank each member for attending. Formally end the meeting, but encourage feedback and participation from each group member. This will enable the meeting to be short and still allow for interested members to explore ideas and build relationships.

IDENTIFY GROUP NEEDS AND RESOURCES

The captain and co-captain, along with all interested group members, should sit down and debrief shortly after the first meeting while information is fresh. Make lists of information and develop a strategy for the organizing the group. Lists might include:

- Specific needs of individual group members

- Useful skills. Consider inviting group members to serve as specialists in areas of expertise. A nurse would be a great medical specialist to train and design an emergency medical plan, but may be unable to actually help during an event because of obligations at the hospital. Who needs to feel a part of the group? Who would be overwhelmed by one more thing to do? Do not underestimate the contribution of teenagers in your group. Consider the following:

  - Communications specialist

  - Medical specialist

  - Fire suppression specialist

  - Education specialist—provide short 10–15 minute workshops at each meeting to teach preparedness skills. This person could teach the workshop or arrange for a special speaker to attend.

  - Resource coordinator

  - Personal or self-defense specialist

  - Neighborhood watch coordinator

These positions are limited only by the needs of the group and your imagination. When possible, try to involve every member to help them feel a part of the group. People may surprise you with what they can do.

- Resources (keep confidential)

- Communication plan

- Establish a social media site for members of the group. Some of the best, most accurate, and most timely information following a disaster is found on local neighborhood sites.

- Decide on a staging area for everyone to gather after a disaster. A large, flat front lawn area or tennis court may work. Take shelter into consideration for events during inclement weather. It should be able to accommodate the entire group. After a disaster, everyone should report there. If anyone is missing, help from within the group would immediately search for the missing to ensure their safety. This area is intended to be the hub of activity. Details to follow later in this chapter.

FOLLOW-UP MEETING

Remind each family a few days before the next scheduled group meeting and collect completed assignments, if possible. Extend invitations to participate in specialist positions. Make the meeting into another social event and ask them to bring something to share. Potluck desserts, homemade ice cream, barbecue, salad bar, or whatever a neighbor would like to bring—just entice them to attend and provide opportunities to build relationships.

Start the meeting after everyone has had a chance to enjoy themselves for a while. Remember to keep it short, direct, and productive. Come to the meeting organized and well prepared. People appreciate when their time is considered valuable. This will greatly add to your credibility. You may want to share the following information:

- Review the emergency plan using storyboards. These are posterboard-sized display boards that allow you to visualize the plan. It does not have to look professional. Use a large piece of cardboard and markers if you need to.

- Announce the specialists and their duties. Ask for help in specific areas, if needed.

- Discuss the staging area and how it works. Invite feedback and ideas to improve it.

- Remind members to work on their individual preparedness plans.

- Congratulate members who completed CERT training and announce upcoming training dates.

- Schedule a date and time for next meeting.

- Thank everyone for their attendance and support.

It's that simple. The block captain and co-captain should meet shortly after the group meeting to evaluate the information that was received, modify documents, and strategize on what to do next. Continue to follow this pattern as you build your group.

MOCK DISASTER

Once systems are mostly in place, it is time to host a mock disaster. This drill accomplishes several purposes. It helps members clearly understand their roll and responsibilities. Provides physical, hands-on learning opportunities. Exposes flaws or holes in the plan so they can be corrected and the plan made more efficient.

Plan the scenario in advance. What is the disaster? What information do you have? Who are the victims? What care do they need? Is the incident localized and emergency responders expected to arrive, or are you own for the foreseeable future? How will you initiate the disaster? Consider these scenarios or build your own:

- Earthquake (7.5) epicenter is 20 miles from your neighborhood on Sunday at 3 p.m. Structural damage is moderate. Older homes in your neighborhood are hit the hardest. Ruptured gas lines are fueling fires throughout the city. Localized flooding and raw sewage is flowing due to ruptured water lines. Your street remains intact. What do you do?

- Hazmat spill on Wednesday at 1 p.m. results in a cloud of toxic gases expected to arrive in your neighborhood in 15 minutes. How do you make sure everyone knows it is coming and what to do?

- Severe winter storm has resulted in a wide spread power outage of unknown length. Roads are inaccessible. What needs to happen to make sure the members of the group are all safe and warm?

- A severe heat wave of unseasonably warm weather has produced black outs due to high energy demands. How could the group meet the needs of individual members?

- Heavy rains resulting in mudslides and flooding are threatening the homes in your neighborhood. What should your group do?

- An elderly gentleman in your group is diagnosed with cancer. He is a widower and has no children to care for him. Would it be possible to enlist the group to help meet his needs?

Sometimes we may think that only large scale disasters may make all this effort and planning worth it. We do not agree with that philosophy. Life itself can be a series of disasters sometimes. Developing a close neighborhood group can prevent crime, create a safer environment for children, and provide a network of assistance for mini disasters which plague each of us. These are the neighborhoods where people want to stay forever. They create an island of safety and peace in the middle of a crazy urban area as neighbors band together and look out for each other.

SOMEONE HAS TO STAND UP

The sad truth is this, if you leave it up to someone else, it likely will not get done. We encourage you to stand tall and initiate the process. It is your neighborhood and you have the ability to make it a safer, better place. You do not have to do everything, just lead out and keep the momentum going. Once the plan is in place, it takes very little to maintain a healthy neighborhood. Get-togethers could be held as often as every six months and still accomplish the desired effect.

COMMUNITY EMERGENCY RESPONSE TEAMS

The best training available for community volunteers is a free program sponsored by FEMA. They are referred to as CERT members. This training teaches your average citizen and trains them in disaster preparedness and basic disaster response skills. The training is usually offered through a local fire department or sheriff's office. Go to http://www.citizencorps.gov/cc/searchCert.do?submitByZip to find a class near your home.

Think about what a difference it could make to your family, as well as your neighborhood, if you were trained in fire safety, light search and rescue, team organization, and disaster medical operations. The classes provide hands on training in fire suppression, first aid, along with other valuable skills. At the end of the training, each student participates in a mock disaster. CERT members are trained not to risk their safety like professional responders do.

We strongly encourage everyone to become a CERT member. Teenagers may participate in classes geared especially toward them. The knowledge you gain may save the life of a loved one someday. Do not let gender, age, or physical condition stop you from participating. You may not be able to do everything in the training. Do what you can and learn as much as you can. Knowledge is power.

COMMUNITY RELATIONSHIP ACTION PLAN

Now that we have reviewed how to build a strong network or community, it is time to develop a written action plan. You may not be in a position to organize your community. Do what you can to build strong relationships and make your neighborhood better because you live there. Your immediate neighbors may be a poor choice to build a survival team from and you may need to expand your geographical circle to find a better support system.

Remember that protecting life always comes first. Everything else is just stuff. Close neighbors can be a great asset or potentially a dangerous threat because of the close proximity of homes. Work on these relationships. Build trust and learn to serve one another through regular seemingly insignificant acts of service. Have fun together. Proactively help each other routinely so you will be ready to help each other survive. Trust the group's collective decisions.

Develop a survival team, whether from individuals in your neighborhood or comprised of like-minded people you can trust. Look for a variety of skills, experience, and resources to balance out your group. The best characteristics for group members might include integrity, resilience, strong work ethic, adaptable, willing to learn, and a strong desire to contribute to the welfare of the entire group.

Go to http://theprovidentprepper.org/the-practical-prepper/action-plan-community/ for a worksheet to help you develop your community relationship action plan. We have included a few standard forms at that link that you may wish to hand out at your neighborhood meetings.

- **The Individual Family Checklist** is a basic list of preparedness steps each individual family should complete. Every household should take basic preparedness steps that will strengthen them as well as the community. Depending on your location you may want to include basic safety measures for wild fire, extreme heat, earthquake, flooding, and so on. This form is intended to give you a basic format to consider. Apartment dwellers will have different capabilities and needs than a group living in single-family houses.

- **The Pre-Disaster Assessment Form** helps the captain understand what possible skills and resources may be available during an emergency. This form should be kept highly confidential and neighbors should not be forced to disclose anything.

- **The Emergency Contact Form** can be quite valuable for communicating. This form should be kept in a binder at the block captain's home. The information should be used only in the event of an emergency. If there is a house fire, medical emergency, or other need to contact family members, this list is priceless. The emergency contacts should be a next-of-kin contact who lives outside of the home.

We encourage you to make building a strong community network a part of your life. It just might make the difference in whether or not you survive a disaster someday, and it can definitely improve the quality of everyday life.

‖ 22 ‖

Financial and Legal
Getting It All in Order

"You must gain control over your money or the lack of it will forever control you."

—Dave Ramsey

Legal and financial preparations are not usually the first thing that comes to mind when evaluating survival plans. While they are not mentioned in the rule of threes, they are both just as critical to everyday provident living and survival as they are to disaster mitigation. We offer a quick review of important points for your consideration.

ORGANIZATION

The first step is to organize all of your important documents into one place. This may be a simple task or highly complex, depending on your stage of life and assets. The goal is to have all important information quickly accessible in an emergency or in the event of serious illness or death.

Create a binder with copies of all vital records which could be grabbed on the way out the door in an emergency. A binder that zips all the way around or small briefcase might do a great job of securely organizing the documents. Place copies in plastic sheet protectors to help with organization.

Keep this information in a safe place to prevent it from falling into the wrong hands. Label the binder something boring, like "Grandma's recipes" or "report cards." Store the originals in a safe and keep one copy in your home and another copy in a secure location away from home in case your home is destroyed. Copies of documents you may want to consider include:

- Personal documentation—degrees, professional licenses, driver's license, passport, birth certificate, marriage certificate, medical records, immunization records, concealed carry permit, social security card, military documents

- Insurance policies—life, health, property, auto, homeowners

- Property—deeds, car titles

- Legal—contracts, adoption, custody, or divorce papers, will, living trust or family trust, power of attorney, rent or lease agreement

- Financial—savings bonds, stocks and bonds, statements from investment firms, banking information, credit cards, retirement/ pension

- Contact information for all companies with which you do any business (banks, creditors, attorney, physician, pharmacy, and so on)

- Family and friend emergency contact information

- Electronic copy of family photos, critical computer files, and insurance video documentation

- Keys to safety deposit box, safe, bug out location, vehicles, and so on

- Recent photo of each family member and pet

- List of firearms, including serial numbers

- List of critical passwords or lock combinations (coded if necessary)

You may find other documents that would be helpful to have in this collection, or you may only need to include some of these. The purpose is to enable you to have all important documents in the event your house is completely destroyed. Having these documents readily available will make it much easier to put the pieces back together again quickly and completely.

Make a video inventory of all of your possessions for insurance purposes. Do a video walk-through, capturing brand names and serial numbers, and describe possessions. Record anything of value including art, jewelry, collections, firearms, and so forth. Remember to document inside cupboards, closets, and drawers. Make a copy of this recording and keep it in a secure location away from your home. You might also want to include still pictures in your documentation. If you are unable to prove what you have, the insurance company may not pay.

FINANCES

Take control of your finances by developing a realistic budget and learning to live within your means. It is tempting to take advantage of easy credit and instant gratification, but it is highly dangerous. Get-rich-quick recommendations flood the financial world with differing opinions. We believe that the safest way to ensure prosperity is to live on less than you earn, get out of debt, and stay out of debt.

One danger the economy presents is the risk of rapid out-of-control inflation referred to as hyperinflation. It can send a wealthy nation into the depths of poverty in a relative short time. When governments print massive amounts of money to cover government spending, rapid devaluation of the dollar occurs. The historical ability to juggle variable rate loans, credit card debt, and other unsecured debt suddenly disappears and can be devastating to the unprepared. The price of goods and services increase at the same time, making it impossible to pay on the loans. Consult an expert for professional advice for your unique circumstances.

Our family has been working on becoming financially ready for economic challenges. Our situation is unique to us. We have listed some of the goals we are working toward with the hope that it might provide you with ideas to improve your financial readiness.

- Our first goal was to establish a small emergency fund.

- We are working to systematically pay off all debt, including our home mortgage.

- Transportation costs take a large chunk of our budget so we are working to decrease them. Volatile gas prices motivate us to be less dependent. We walk and bike to school and around the neighborhood whenever possible. Jonathan uses public transportation to commute to work. We only shop once a week and combine that trip with any other needs, such as doctor's appointments and meetings.

• We buy used vehicles, shop classified ads, thrift stores, and garage sales.

• We want to decrease our dependence on public utilities by conserving wherever possible. We have purchased energy efficient appliances, plumbing fixtures, and light bulbs. When possible we heat with a wood stove and cook on it during the winter. We use a solar oven, thermal cooker, or other methods to conserve energy whenever possible.

• Producing our own food has been a rewarding family activity. We have chickens, fruit trees, berry bushes, grape vines, and plant a vegetable garden every year. The children each have their own gardens and they sell the produce they grow. Bottling, dehydrating, and storing our bounty is a family project. Growing our own food is a great way to protect against economic swings and helps us to be self-sufficient.

• We stock up on food and toiletries only when they are on sale. If it is not on sale, we do without it. This keeps our family storehouse well stocked and saves on our food budget.

• We eat breakfast and dinner as a family almost every day. This increases nutrition, builds relationships, and saves money as compared to eating out.

• We are trying to build streams of income so that if one source of income is lost, we will have other sources to fall back on. We embrace opportunities to improve our professional skills and value in the workplace. Survival trade skills are increased as we develop talents in car repair, communications, carpentry, food production and preservation, and other skills which may be valuable in a low-tech society.

BUILDING FINANCIAL SECURITY

Everyone is unique. Our goals may be quite different from yours. Consider what you can do to increase your resiliency during times of economic challenge. Come up with a plan that is tailored to your individual needs. Consider the following ideas:

- Keep enough cash (in small bills) at home to cover expenses for at least a couple of weeks. Credit and debit cards may not be accepted during a power outage.

- Build an emergency fund.

- Be prepared for periods of unemployment. Stash money to cover three to six months of expenses in savings to protect against periods of illness or unemployment.

- Budget. Learn to spend less than you earn. According to Robert D. Hales, "The three most loving words are 'I love you,' and the four most caring words for those we love are 'We can't afford it.'"

- Get out of debt. Visit www.daveramsey.com for some great ideas.

- Study the benefits of gold and silver. Decide if that is something you should invest in. Remember precious metals are not edible. Build your food stores before other investments.

- Review current insurance policies. Maintain adequate insurance policies appropriate for your personal situation.

- Increase earning potential through education and taking advantage of on-the-job learning opportunities.

- Diversify income. Develop streams of income so when one source dries up there are others to fill your bank account.

- Share your bounty. Be charitable with both your time and resources.

How is your financial standing? Plan to take steps to improve your financial security everyday as well as to prepare for times of economic challenge by completing the action plan at the end of this chapter. Small steady steps can make a huge difference over time.

LEGAL

What would happen if you were killed in a disaster today? Who would be responsible to take care of your assets and obligations? Does that person know details of your estate and have the legal right to act? What would happen to your family? Where would your children go? None of these questions are fun to think about or easy to address. Life is dynamic and complicated.

The size and scope of your estate, state laws, and family dynamics will dictate if you can realistically use online DIY software or if you require the services of an attorney. It is easy to put off getting your affairs in order until it is too late. A relative of ours was setting up a family trust and detailing how he wanted his assets distributed. Upon his death, the family discovered he had never finalized the paperwork. He had no voice in the distribution° of his life's work. If you want a voice, take the time now to legally prepare important documents.

A will is beneficial in giving you a voice in what happens after you are gone. You may include details of memorial service and burial wishes. Gifts of personal property, real estate, and other items can be outlined in the will. This document allows you to name an executor or a personal representative who will take charge of distributing personal property after you die as well as naming a guardian for minor children.

There are several reasons you may want to establish a trust that will take affect at your death. Trusts can be established as revocable or not. The most common reason for setting up a trust is for educational purposes for children of the deceased. They tend to be more difficult to contest than wills, can be flexible, impose discipline on the beneficiary to ensure wise spending, and can be helpful in making major charitable gifts.

Naming a guardian for your children and providing for their support should be a top priority if you have minor children at home. Take the time to legally implement the plan as well as to talk to all parties involved. If the children are old enough, allow them to have input in the decision making. Do not leave it to a judge to decide the fate of your little ones.

Health care directives may include a living will and a durable power of attorney for health care. The living will is a written statement expressing your wishes regarding medical care in the event you are unable to communicate. The durable power of attorney for health care appoints someone to make decisions regarding your health care and allows information about your medical condition to be shared with that person. Copies of these documents should be kept on file with your health care provider.

Once all of the paperwork is in order, it is a matter of simply taking time to review and update it annually.

FINANCIAL AND LEGAL ACTION PLAN

Take a few minutes to seriously review your financial and legal status. What changes do you need to make? We have created a worksheet at http://theprovidentprepper.org/the-practical-prepper/action-plan-financial-and-legal/ with a checklist for organizing your documents as well as a financial and legal action plan worksheet.

23

So Now What?

"What saves a man is to take a step. Then another step."

—C. S. Lewis

We congratulate you for finishing this book. Our hope is that you have taken the time to complete each action plan and have made significant steps toward accomplishing your goals and mitigating many of the risk factors that are within your control. Printable copies of each action plan and worksheet can be found at www.theprovidentprepper.org. The journey to preparedness is a dynamic process without a precise destination. It requires regular attention. Supplies should be rotated and checked, skills must be practiced and improved, relationships strengthened, plans updated, and confidence built. Allow these tasks to enrich your life along the way.

Balance is crucial in this journey. We challenge you to practice provident living, or the art of providing for the future while enjoying the present. Do not allow fear to motivate you. We live in a dangerous world, and it is easy to become frightened and discouraged. Make reasonable preparations which will enable you to live well when bad stuff happens. Challenges will come. Your level of preparedness and charity will dictate whether you thrive or just survive.

Your progress is commendable. Please make an effort to spread the word and encourage others. Remember, there is power and strength in communities. Be prepared use your talents and resources to assist others. One can make a difference. Imagine the power when many talented, well-prepared people come together to take care of each other? Everyone will thrive.

Your final action plan is to love life. Live every day and make the world a better place because you are in it. We wish you the best in your journey to self-reliance and preparedness. Thank you for becoming part of the solution.

Notes

Chapter 2: What Are the Odds?

1. "Health Effects," Centers for Disease Control and Prevention, http://www.cdc.gov/climateandhealth/effects/default.htm.

2. Rupa Basu and Jonathan M. Samet, "Relation between Elevated Ambient Temperature and Mortality: A Review of the Epidemiologic Evidence," *Epidemiologic Reviews* 24, no. 2 (Johns Hopkins Bloomberg School of Public Health, 2000): 190–202, doi:10.1093/epirev/mxf007.

3. Jean-Marie Robine, Siu Lan K. Cheung, Sophie Le Roy, Herman Van Oyen, Clare Griffiths, Jean-Pierre Michel, and François Richard Herrmann, "Death toll exceeded 70,000 in Europe during the summer of 2003," *Comptes Rendus Biologies* 331, no. 2 (2008): 171–178, doi:10.1016/j.crvi.2007.12.001.

4. UN Atlas of the Oceans, "Human Settlements on the Coast," *UN Atlas of the Oceans*, accessed January 13, 2014, http://www.oceansatlas.org/servlet/CDSServlet?status=ND0xODc3JjY9ZW4mMzM9KiYzNz1rb3M~.

5. "Tornado and Hail Risk Beyond Tornado Alley" (CoreLogic, 2012), accessed June 21, 2013, http://www.corelogic.com/about-us/researchtrends/tornado-hail-research-report.aspx.

6. "Tsunami," (NOAA National Weather Service), accessed July 19, 2013, http://wcatwc.arh.noaa.gov/pdf/deadlywaters.pdf.

7. Doyle Rice, "U.S. endures near-record wildfire season," *USA Today*, published November 12, 2012, accessed January 13, 2014, http://www.usatoday.com/story/weather/2012/11/11/wildfire-season-destruction/1695465/.

8. Alex Santoso, "5 Deadliest Pandemics in History." *Neatorama*, published April 27, 2009, accessed July 19, 2013, http://www.nea-torama.com/2009/04/27/5-deadliest-pandemics-in-history/.

9. Tamsin Carlisle, "Solar Storm Threat Returning," *The National*, March 14, 2011, accessed May 21, 2014, http://www.thenational.ae/business/industry-insights/energy/solar-storm-threat-returning.

10. Natural Resources Defense Council (NRDC), "What if the Fukushima nuclear fallout crisis happened here?" accessed July 12, 2013, http://www.nrdc.org/nuclear/fallout/.

11. Marty Ahrens, "Home Structure Fires" (National Fire Protection Association, April 2013): i–ii, accessed June 19, 2013, http://www.nfpa.org/assets/files/pdf/os.homes.pdf.

12. John Greenleaf Whittier, "Maud Muller," *Yale Book of American Verse,* ed. Thomas R. Lounsbury (New Haven: Yale University Press, 1912), http://www.bartleby.com/102/76.html.

Chapter 3: Survive or Thrive

1. Victor E. Frankl, *Man's Search for Meaning*.

2. *Oxford Dictionaries*, s.v. "survive," 1st definition, last modified 2014, accessed March 4, 2014, http://www.oxforddictionaries.com/us/definition/american_english/survive.

3. Amanda Ripley, *The Unthinkable: Who Survives When Disaster Strikes—and Why* (New York: Crown Publishers, 2008).

4. Franklin D. Roosevelt, "Inaugural Address" (March 4, 1933).

5. Melinda Smith and Jeanne Segal, "Traumatic Stress," (Helpguide.org) last updated December 2013, accessed February 11, 2014, http://www.helpguide.org/mental/disaster_recovery_trauma_stress_coping.htm.

Chapter 4: Family Emergency Plan

1. "Tsunamis" (FEMA, February 12, 2013), accessed January 18, 2014, http://www.ready.gov/tsunamis.

Chapter 5: Survival Kits

1. Chris Bradford, *The Ring of Earth* (London: Puffin Books, 2010).

Chapter 7: Water Storage

1. W.H. Auden, "First Things First," *Selected Poems,* ed. Edward Mendelson, exp ed. 1979 (New York: Vintage Books, 2007), 246.

Chapter 8: Water Disinfection and Purification

1. Samuel Taylor Coleridge, "The Rime of the Ancient Mariner."

2. Robert Metcalf, "Recent Advances in Solar Water Pasteurization" (Solar Cookers International), accessed November 12, 2013, http://solarcooking.org/pasteurization/metcalf.htm.

3. "Water Treatment" (American Red Cross), accessed January 13, 2014, www.redcross.org/prepare/disaster/water-safety/water-treatment.

4. "Calcium Hypochlorite" (World Health Organization), accessed August 10, 2013, http://www.who.int/water_sanitation_health/hygiene/emergencies/fs2_19.pdf.

5. "Drinking Water Contaminants, (United States Environmental Protection Agency, 2013) water.epa.gov. June 3. Accessed July 23, 2013. www.water.epa.gov/drink/contaminants/index.cfm#Inorganic.

6. "Technical Bulletin Sanitary Control and Surveillance of Field Water Supplies" (Departments of the Army, Navy and Air Force, May 1, 2010), accessed October 3, 2013, http://armypubs.army.mil/med/DR_pubs/dr_a/pdf/tbmed577.pdf.

7. Ibid., 22.

8. Ibid.

9. Ibid.

10. http://www.potableaqua.com/faq.php#7.

11. "Emergency Drinking Water Disinfection Procedures" (U.S. Army Center for Health Promotion and Preventive Medicine, May 2003), accessed August 10, 2013, http://phc.amedd.army. mil/phc%20resource%20library/31-008-1004.pdf.

Chapter 9: Sanitation

1. http://www.mspp.gouv.ht/site/downloads/Rapport%20%20 Web%2012.08_Avec_Courbes_Departementales.pdf, Originally "2010–13 Haiti Cholera Outbreak." *Wikipedia*. August 21. Accessed August 26, 2013. http://en.wikipedia.org/ wiki/2010%E2%80%9313_Haiti_cholera_outbreak.

Chapter 11: Food Storage

1. "Food Storage—Wheat" (Extension Utah State University), accessed March 4, 2014, https://extension.usu.edu/foodstorage/ htm/wheat.

2. Dale Blumenthal, "The Canning Process: Old Preservation Technique Goes Modern" (FDA), accessed September 10, 2013, http://www.fda.gov/bbs/topics/CONSUMER/CON00043.html (accessed through Way Back Machine).

3. "Diatomaceous Earth," accessed may 21, 2014, https://www.usae-mergencysupply.com/information_center/food_storage_faq/dia-tomaceous_earth.htm#.UwPazkJdW8W.

Chapter 12: Fuel Safety and Storage

1. "Unintentional Non-fire-related Carbon Monoxide Exposures— United States, 2001–2003," *Morbidity and Mortality Weekly Report* 54(02); 36–39, (Centers for Disease Control and Prevention, January 21, 2005), accessed May 21, 2014, http://www.cdc. gov/mmwr/preview/mmwrhtml/mm5402a2.htm.

2. "Material Safety Data Sheet Denatured Alcohol" (W.M. Barr & Co., April 15, 2013), accessed May 25, 2013, http://www.wmbarr. com/ProductFiles/1625%206%20Denatured%20Alcohol%20 MSDS%204%2015%202013.pdf.

3. See also "Material Safety Data Sheet Isopropyl Alcohol, 70%" (May 21, 2013), accessed May 24, 2013, http://www.sciencelab.com/msds.php?msdsId=9924413.

4. See also "Material Safety Data Sheet Isopropyl Alcohol 90% v/v Solution" (Science Stuff, Inc., September 1, 2006), accessed February 18, 2014, http://louisville.edu/micronano/files/documents/material-safety-data-sheets-msds/ap-140-adhesion-promoter.

5. See also "Material Safety Data Heat Safe Heat" (Candle Lamp Company, February 2, 2006), accessed May 24, 2013, www.biritefoodservice.com/pdf/811320.pdf.

6. "Material Safety Data Sheet Coleman Camp Fuel" (HOC Industries, Inc., June 19, 2007), accessed May 24, 2013, http://www.coleman.com/uploadedFiles/Content/Customer_Support/Safety/lantern.pdf.

7. See also "Material Safety Data Sheet Diesel Fuel" (Hess Corporation, August 30, 2012), accessed February 19, 2014, http://www.hess.com/docs/us-safety-data-sheets/dieselfuel_alltypes_includingultralowsulfur_diesel(ulsd).pdf?sfvrsn=2.

8. See also "Material Safety Data Sheet Klean Heat" (W.M. Barr & Co., March 19, 2012), accessed May 23, 2013, http://www.wmbarr.com/ProductFiles/GKKH99991KS%20Klean%20Heat%20MSDS%201%2030%2008.pdf.

9. See also Material Safety Data Sheet Kerosene" (W.M. Barr & Co., March 9, 2010), accessed May 25, 2013, http://www.wmbarr.com/ProductFiles/Kerosene%20(1210.2)%203-9-10.pdf.

10. See also "Lamplight Original Lamp Oil Material Safety Data Sheet" (Lamplight Farms, Inc., April 14, 2010), accessed September 20, 2013, http://images.tikibrand.com/lamplight/llfwholesale/knowledge/msds%20original%20lamp%20oil.pdf.

11. "Material Safety Data Sheet Kingsford Odorless Charcoal Lighter" (The Clorox Company), accessed May 23, 2013, http://callico.chemtel.net/msds/CP-71175.pdf.

12. See also "Material Data Safety Sheet Liquid Paraffin" (Fisher Scientific UK, February 8, 2005), accessed May 23, 2013, www.clayton.edu/portals/690/chemistry/inventory/MSDS%20paraffin%20liquid.pdf.

13. Ralph E Lewis, "Protecting Critical Emergency Fuel Supplies," *Survivalist Magazine,* no. 10: 30–33.

14. See also "Material Safety Data Sheet Butane" (Blazer Products, January 5, 2013), accessed May 23, 2013, http://www.blazerproducts.com/tools/MSDS.pdf.

15. See also "Material Safety Data Sheet Natural Gas" (Piedmont Natural Gas, September 8, 2009), accessed May 28, 2013, www.piedmontng.com/files/pdfs/safety/materialsafetydatasheet_090809.pdf.

16. "Material Safety Data Sheet Propane" (Suburban Propane, December 2012), accessed May 23, 2013, www.suburbanpropane.com/safety/pdf/propane/SAF%205152%20MATERIAL%20SAFETY%20DATA%20SHEET.pdf.

17. See also "Material Safety Data Sheet Black Solid Briquets" (The Kingsford Products Company, July 1998), accessed May 25, 2013, http://www.thecloroxcompany.com/downloads/msds/charcoal/kingsfordcharcoalbriquets.pdf.

18. See also "Material Safety Data Sheet Paraffin Wax" (Pro Chemical and Dye, January 24, 2010), accessed May 24, 2013, http://www.prochemical.com/MaterialSafety/Waxes/Paraffin%20Wax.pdf.

19. See also "Material Safety Data Sheet Beeswax" (Pro Chemical and Dye, November 24, 2010), accessed May 24, 2013, http://www.prochemical.com/MaterialSafety/Waxes/Beeswax.pdf.

20. See also "Material Safety Data Sheet Esbit" (Chemical Check GmbH Gefahrstoffberatung, July 26, 2004), accessed May 25, 2013, http://zenstoves.net/MSDS/MSDSEsbit.pdf.

Chapter 14: Emergency Heating

1. Sammy Cahn, "Let It Snow" (CA, 1945).

2. Judy Hedding, "Phoenix Average Monthly Temperature" (About. com), accessed November 13, 2013, http://phoenix.about.com/ od/weather/a/averagetemps.htm.

3. "Out in the Cold," *Harvard Health Letter* (Harvard Medical School, January 2010), accessed May 21, 2014, http://www.health. harvard.edu/newsletters/Harvard_Health_Letter/2010/January/ out-in-the-cold.

4. See "Hypothermia" (Mayo Clinic, June 8, 2011), accessed September 13, 2013, http://www.mayoclinic.com/health/hypothermia/ DS00333/DSECTION=symptoms.

5. See "Frostbite" (Mayo Clinic, October 7, 2011), accessed September 13, 2013, http://www.mayoclinic.com/health/frostbite/ DS01164.

6. "Landscaping for Energy Efficiency" (Energy Efficiency and Renewable Energy Clearinghouse, April 1995): 2, accessed June 18, 2013, http://www.nrel.gov/docs/legosti/old/16632.pdf.

Chapter 16: Shelter

1. U.S. Environmental Protection Agency. 2013. "Radiation Protection Basics." U.S. Enviornmental Protection Agency. July 6. Accessed March 4, 2014. http://www.epa.gov/rpdweb00/understand/protection_basics.html.

Chapter 17: Keeping Cool

1. "Extreme Heat: A Prevention Guide to Promote Your Personal Health and Safety" (Centers for Disease Control and Prevention, May 31, 2012), accessed October 28, 2013, http://www.bt.cdc. gov/disasters/extremeheat/heat_guide.asp.

2. "Heat Exhaustion" (WebMD, September 30, 2012), accessed October 28, 2013, http://www.webmd.com/fitness-exercise/ heat-exhaustion.

3. "Emergency First Aid for Heatstroke" (WebMD. September 1,

2011), accessed October 28, 2013, http://firstaid.webmd.com/tc/emergency-first-aid-for-heatstroke-topic-overview.

4. L. Bellows and R. Moore, "Potassium and the Diet" (Colorado State University Extension, March 2013), accessed October 28, 2013, http://www.ext.colostate.edu/pubs/foodnut/09355.html.

Chapter 18: Home Protection and Security

1. "FBI Releases 2012 Crime Statistics" (FBI National Press Office, September 16, 2013), accessed October 9, 2013, http://www.fbi.gov/news/pressrel/press-releases/fbi-releases-2012-crime-statistics.

Chapter 19: Personal Safety

1. "Pepper Spray Antidote and First Aid" (Pepper Spray Store, 2013), accessed August 23, 2013, http://www.pepper-spray-store.com/pages/antitdote.

Chapter 20: Medical

1. "Community Emergency Response Teams" (FEMA. June 27, 2012), accessed March 4, 2014, http://www.fema.gov/community-emergency-response-teams/frequently-asked-questions.

2. Cynthia J. Koelker, "Seven Antibiotics to Stockpile and Why-SurvivalBlog post," *Armageddon Medicine—Survival Medicine* (February 18, 2011), accessed September 16, 2013, http://armageddonmedicine.net/?p=2486.

3. Omudhome Oqbru and Jay W Marks, "amoxicillin, Amoxil, Dispermox (Discontinued), Trimox, Moxatag, Larotid" (MedicineNet.com, March 18, 2013), accessed September 17, 2013, http://www.medicinenet.com/amoxicillin/article.htm.

4. "Ciprofloxacin, Cipro, Cipro XR, Proquin XR" (MedicineNet.com, July 12, 2008), accessed September 17, 2013, http://www.medicinenet.com/ciprofloxacin/article.htm.

5. Omudhome Oqbru and Jay W. Marks, "doxycycline, Vibramycin, Oracea, Adoxa, Atridox and Others" (MedicineNet.com. January 7, 2008), accessed September 17, 2013, http://www.medicinenet.com/doxycycline/article.htm.

6. Annette (Gbemudu) Oqbru and Jay W. Marks, "erythromycin, E-Mycin, Eryc, Ery-Tab, Pce, Pediazole, Ilosone" (MedicineNet.com, 2013), accessed September 17, 2013, http://www.medicinenet.com/erythromycin/article.htm.

7. "Metronidazole, Flagyl" (MedicineNet.com), accessed September 16, 2013, http://www.medicinenet.com/metronidazole/article.htm.

8. "Using Expired Medications-Antibiotics and Antiviral Medication Part 1" (SurvivalBlog.com, October 15, 2010), accessed September 17, 2013, http://www.survivalblog.com/2010/10/guest_article_using_expired_me.html.

9. Laurie P. Cohen, "Drugs Frequently Potent Past Expiration" (Mercola.com, April 2, 2000), accessed May 21, 2014, http://articles.mercola.com/sites/articles/archive/2000/04/02/drug-expiration-part-one.aspx.

10. Lee Cantrell, Jeffrey Suchard, Alan Wu, and Roy R. Gerona, "Stability of Active Ingredients in Long-Expired Prescription Medications" (JAMA Internal Medicine. November 26, 2012), accessed October 16, 2013, http://archinte.jamanetwork.com/article.aspx?articleid=1377417.

11. "Diarrhoea Supporting Information," *Facts for Life*, 4th ed (World Health Organization), accessed September 17, 2013, http://factsforlifeglobal.org/07/5.html.

Chapter 21: Community

1. Amanda Ripley, *The Unthinkable: Who Survives When Disaster Strikes and Why* (New York: Crown Publishers, 2008).

2. Ibid.

About the Authors

Jonathan is a licensed civil engineer and an avid enthusiast of alternative energy sources, especially solar and wind power. He has served as vice president and advisory board member of The American Civil Defense Association (TACDA), as secretary/treasurer for a local chapter of Civil Defense Volunteers, and as an emergency preparedness and communications specialist. As a city councilperson, he has been tasked with developing the city emergency plan in his own community. He has coauthored numerous articles with his wife on emergency preparedness topics and published them in the *Journal of Civil Defense*.

Kylene has an educational background in business management and family studies. She has also served on the advisory board and on the board of directors for TACDA and is currently the editor for the *Journal of Civil Defense*. She has a passion for researching and experimenting, which adds a sense of real life to her writing and teaching. A firm believer in hands-on learning, she involves her family in emergency training for everything from fire drills to living off food storage and garden produce to turning off the power in the dead of winter just to see if they can survive it. She's learned many powerful lessons from these experiences, the best one being that people are tougher than any challenge. We will not only survive but will emerge as better, stronger people as a result of the adventure.

Jonathan and Kylene are the owners of Your Family Ark, LLC, an educational and consulting business designed to assist individuals and families in preparing for an uncertain future (www.yourfamilyark. org and www.theproidentprepper.org). They make a dynamic combination. Together, they have presented in a wide variety of events, including community education courses, educational seminars, preparedness fairs, employee education programs, and community classes. With Jonathan's extensive knowledge and Kylene's high-energy personality, they have a unique talent for taking a relatively boring topic and turning it into an exciting quest, motivating audiences to join the ranks of provident preppers.